LANGUAGE ACQUISITION IN
THE EARLY YEARS

ELS OKSAAR

Language Acquisition in the Early Years

an introduction to paedolinguistics

translated by Katherine Turfler

Batsford Academic and Educational Ltd
St. Martin's Press, Inc.

'*Emale, Abbele, Nennele*'

To mother, to Abbe, to Nenne

Translation from German
© Katherine Turfler 1983

First published in Great Britain in 1983 by
Batsford Academic and Educational Ltd
4 Fitzhardinge Street
London W1H 0AH

First published in the United States of America in 1982 by
St. Martin's Press, Inc.,
175 Fifth Avenue,
New York, NY 10010

Typeset by Deltatype, Ellesmere Port
and printed in Great Britain by
Billing & Son Ltd., Worcester

German edition
© 1977 Verlag W. Kohlhammer GmbH, Stuttgart

British Library Cataloguing in Publication Data

Oksaar, Els
  Language acquisition in the early years.
  1. Children—Language
  I. Title   II. Spracherwerb im Vorschulalter.
  English
  401'.9   LB1139.L3
  ISBN 0-7134-3694-8

Library of Congress Cataloging in Publication Data

Oksaar, Els.
  Language acquisition in the early years.
  Translation of: Spracherwerb im Vorschulalter.
  1. Language acquisition.   I. Title.
  P118.03713 1983   401'.9   82-42716
  ISBN 0-312-46597-1

Contents

Contents

1 Tasks and Development of Paedolinguistics

1.1 PAEDOLINGUISTICS AS AN INDEPENDENT INTERDISCIPLINARY FIELD OF RESEARCH

Let us begin by considering an observation by William Stern, who was epoch-making among psychologists and the pioneer of modern child language research. He emphasized that there are two ways in which man increases his knowledge. One of them leads out of the routine, the obvious, and the normal, and searches for the unknown and the mysterious, the pathological and the brilliant. The other, which follows the totally familiar and the universally known, presents this to us in a completely new form and leads to no less great discoveries – *since the obvious is no less than understandable* (1967:1).

The investigation of spoken language, especially primary language acquisition and the language of preschool children, belongs to an interdisciplinary field of research. The relatively late development of this field could have an explanation in the statement about it which Stern made as early as 1914 in *Psychologie der frühen Kindheit* (Psychology of Early Childhood). Many things in this area have been considered as much too self evident. And yet its questions on theoretical and practical problems are relevant not only for linguists, psychologists and educationalists, but also for physiologists and behaviorists and communication scientists.[1]

Clara and William Stern (1928:6) were surprised that linguists had until then almost ignored child language. Then, as now, the trend of child language research was connected, as we will see, with the development of linguistics and philosophy. In the nineteenth century, linguistics was historically oriented and had the literary language of culturally advanced European peoples as its research subject. Only gradually were pure spoken languages and dialects of main cultural languages discovered as fields of research. The prognosis of Stern & Stern (1928:7) that 'The next stage in this development will presumably be child language', is still applicable now. At the same time,

1

we can observe that, since the last war, there has been growing interest in the investigation of spoken language. The Czech phonetician Karel Ohnesorg (1955:95) has proposed the term 'paedolinguistics' for language acquisition and child language research; however, in many places, it is known as 'developmental psycholinguistics', following the example of the USA, which considers language acquisition and child language research to be part of psycholinguistics (see Leuninger, Miller & Müller 1972; Grimm 1973). The essential research spectrum has been without doubt limited by such a consideration, as the relatively new psycholinguistics[2] is mainly engaged with the processes of encoding and decoding as they relate states of messages to states of communicators (Osgood & Sebeok 1965:4; see also Slama-Cazacu 1966).

A psycholinguistic orientation is necessary for language acquisition and child language research, because psycholinguistics integrates the results of linguistics and the experimental approaches of psychology and reconsiders basic problems such as the relationship between cognitive and linguistic development. It cannot be considered, however, as the dominating or the only orientation, even when psycholinguistics is defined as the field dealing with the psychological processes which contribute to the acquisition, production and understanding of language (Fodor, Jenkins & Saporta 1967:161). Language acquisition, production and understanding are connected with other human sciences too, because language exists and develops within a biological and social context. It works as a primary means of human expression and communication. Social norms and ways of behavior and cultural traditions are acquired together with language. In order to understand the language acquisition and the language development of a person, it is necessary to consider that person as a biological, social and cultural-intellectual being.

Therefore, besides psychology and psycholinguistics there are many other sciences that child language research is connected with, including: sociology, cultural anthropology and medicine. In order to cope with its main task, the analysis of the origin and development of the child's communicative competence, paedolinguistics must take advantage of the critically analysed knowledge of other sciences which deal with the development of human beings. These sciences have to consider, for their part, that the definition of human beings already implies language, and that one deals with humans who speak and have the ability to speak. For this, paedolinguistics must have scientifically based knowledge of the development of speech structures, and of the functions of speech in the system of social relations. Moreover, the socio-cultural framework of the living conditions of the child must be taken into consideration as well as related questions such as nonverbal means of expression. Paedolinguistics is an interdisciplinary field of research. The term interdisciplinary is by no means used uniformly nowadays, and here is not to be considered as the simple coexistence of two or more sciences through which a problem is elucidated from different angles, but rather as a synthesis, as the incorporation of several techniques, theoretical and methodological approaches and basic paradigms in a way which I would like to refer to as creative integration focused on the object of research (see below 2.5.2). The interdisciplinary orientation in paedolinguistics should not however be taken to imply that there are no independent fields. On the contrary, since language is the primary material of the field, linguistics is obviously central to its study. This raises the point, however, as to whether there are subdisciplines of linguistics which would then come into question.

Language acquisition and child language research in the fields of linguistics and semiotics covers, besides pure linguistic problems, psycho-, socio-, and paralinguistic questions such as kinesics, in a constellation which shows itself to be an independent linguistic area. Therefore, it seems appropriate to regard the science which covers this area as an independent discipline of linguistics, namely, as paedolinguistics. Since the term paedolinguistics has no fixed meaning yet, it needs to be defined more closely for the purposes of discussion. Paedolinguistics deals only with children up to school age, unlike *paedology*, a term which is applied to both child and adolescent psychology.

This limit, to elementary school age, about six to seven years, is based first of all on the fact that, generally, until then one language mode – spoken language – is the child's only linguistic means of communication, and secondly by this time the most important phase of language development is completed.[3] The second language mode – written language – is added at school, and further phases of development follow. The first six years are considered as the first phase in the whole development of the child, where he learns, while playing and through play, to adapt to his environment and its language. The physical characteristics which indicate the end of this phase are the loss of baby teeth and the first metamorphosis between five and seven years (Stern 1967:2; Lewis 1963:101; Church 1961; see also Zeller 1952 on physical changes). The Swiss child psychologist Jean Piaget (1968) also determines a turning point at the age of 7 in his schema of cognitive development. He states that from two to seven years the child is in a stage in which his logical operations are characterized as pre-operational (see below 3.3.1).

The paedolinguistic field of research can be subdivided into two main areas which I would like to call *linguistic ontogeny* and *primary expansion stage*.

By linguistic ontogeny I mean the development of language in babies and infants. Because the development covers all components of the language system, from the first process of phonemization and symbolization to the formation of larger speech units, we can, without drawing a sharp line, consider the development of speech behavior patterns in the first four to five years as a part of this stage. It covers approximately the four periods of Stern (1967:142f). Both German and English speaking children have already mastered a number of important rules of language at the final stage of this period (see below 4.3.4). The boundary proposed above has its support in the results of modern and older paedolinguistics, psycholinguistics and biological research, as can be seen in Brown (1973:404ff), Menyuk (1971:147ff), Oksaar (1971:33ff), McCarthy (1954:551ff), Stern & Stern (1922:70) and Lenneberg (1967:179f).

The primary expansion stage extends from four to six or seven years of age. However, it should not be thought that the development of the linguistic repertoire first takes place here. The period of linguistic ontogeny is also characterized by a continuous dynamic. However, there are many factors which indicate such a turning point. This period is linguistically characterized by the use of more refined lexical and grammatical elements, original word constructions, and a growing use of hypotactic constructions (see below 4.3.4). Moreover, it is characterized by an expanding process of socialization and by an increase in environmental influences, since contact with people outside the family grows, with playmates and/or in nursery or primary school (see below 3.4.2.4). It is the period in which children's personal cognitive and orectic characteristics are finding more individual expression (Lewis 1963:108).

1.2 DEVELOPMENT OF PAEDOLINGUISTICS

1.2.1 THE FIRST BEGINNINGS
There have been some interdisciplinary shiftings in the investigation of

early childhood which are important for child language research. Child psychology, which is interested in child language and its development mainly as a medium for the investigation of mental development, was not established by psychologists, but by physicians and philosophers, and it originated in Germany. Tiedemann's *Beobachtungen über die Entwicklung der Seelenfähigkeiten bei Kindern* (Observations on the Development of Mental Abilities of Children) came out in 1787, but remained, however, an isolated approach until the middle of the nineteenth century. Interest in child language and its development first grew in the scientific climate of positivism and evolutionism in the second half of the nineteenth century, and was influenced by Darwin's evolution theory. The works of physiologists such as Löbish (1851), Sigismund (1856), Kussmaul (1859) and Vierordt (1879) should be mentioned, and above all that of Preyer (1882) which initiated a new era in child language research.

In fact, the initiators of child language investigation were not linguists, but philosophers, physicians, psychologists and educationalists. From the early phase we can mention the philosopher Schultze and the educationalist Lindner in Germany, and the philosopher and psychologist Taine and the educationalist Pérez in France.

In his basic study *Die Sprache des Kindes* (The Language of the Child), first published in 1880, Schultze developed a hypothesis for sound acquisition based on the principle of the line of least resistance, which, at the time, was intensely discussed. Schultze's phonetic rules are based on his own data and have been confirmed by Sigismund's observations. According to Schultze, the acquisition of sounds begins with the articulation of sounds which require the least physiological effort. The acquisition of German vowels begins, for example, with Ä, A, U, O, and then moves gradually to sounds which require greater effort: E, I, Ö and Ü.[4] This principle remains, up to the present time, a guide for a great number of works, but is also controversial.[5]

Taine (1876), through close observation of his daughter from the day she was born until the end of her sixteenth month, came to the conclusion that, at the beginning, the child moves his vocal organs just as spontaneously as he moves his arms and legs, and that he achieves full mastery through the principle of trial and error. Taine found correspondences between ontogeny and phylogeny, and emphasized that the mental characteristics of a child in the transition stage can be found in primitive cultures in a more stabilized form, just as the human embryo in a transition stage presents physical characteristics which are to be found in a more stabilized form in the classes of inferior animals.[6] Research in child language carried out by educationalists starts with Pérez's major systematic research into the development of the first three years (1878) and Lindner's representation of child language development (1882). Franke (1899) deserves special mention, not only because of his phonetic approach, but also because of the parallels he draws between child language learning and the language development of mankind (see Leopold 1948a:2; Stern & Stern 1928:5).

The Indo-European scholars Schleicher and Jan Baudouin de Courtenay belong to the first linguists who published, in this early phase of investigation, observations on child language development. Schleicher's sketch is outstanding, mainly because his phonetic observations were made at a time when phonetic science had not yet developed. Baudouin de Courtenay (1870) offered observations on Polish child language.[7] Subsequently there were the French linguists Egger (1879) and Deville (1890–1891) and the phonetician Grammont (1902).

However, the first to subject the child's entire development and his language to several years of systematic research was the physiologist Wilhelm Preyer from Jena, Germany. In the daily observation of his son, from birth to the end of his third year, a lot of attention was given to motor development as well as to psychological development, mainly to the development of the senses, memory, language and will. His work *Die Seele des Kindes* (The Mind of the Child) (1882), in spite of a large number of interpretations not based on data, has the merit of having considered the field as a whole and with scientific precision. At first this type of work, along with the diary method, found its adherents not in Germany, but abroad, as can be seen in the research of the American Shinn (1905), the Frenchman Compayré (1900), the Pole Oltuscewski (1897) and the Bulgarian Gheorgov (1905), to mention a few. The research on the language of a boy done by the English psychologist Sully (1896) was one of the most important surveys of that time.

Most of the observations made at that time were based on records of the observer's own children during the first three or four years of life, during which a lot of attention was given to the development of sounds. The methodological and theoretical discussion included, within the predominantly genetic oriented scientific climate of the time, the parallelism of ontogeny and phylogeny.[8] The frequently unsystematic handling of data in which individual occurrences served as evidence could not however lead to any convincing results. It is very interesting to see that the inquiry into certain genetic parallels on the side of linguistics arose again with Roman Jakobson many decades later (see below 4.3.2).

One can, through the activities of psychologists and educationalists, divide the child language research of the late nineteenth century into two separate trends which diverge from one another. Preyer and his followers such as Oltuscewski, Shinn, Lindner, and Ament belong to the so-called intellectualistic trend which, according to Stern & Stern 'overestimates the intellectual meaning of the child's first language phase and also the child's independence in language production' (1922:6). The intellectualistic era ended with Ament's detailed monograph *Die Entwicklung von Sprechen und Denken beim Kinde* (The Development of Speech and Thought in Children) (1889) and his study *Begriff und Begriffe der Kindersprache* (Concept and Concepts of Child Language) (1902).[9]

The teachings of the founder of experimental psychology, Wilhelm Wundt, started a new era. Among its supporters were his disciples Meumann (1902) and Idelberger (1903). They considered language acquisition mostly as a product of imitation and the first attempts at language as manifestations of emotion. Meumann, in his work *Die Entstehung der ersten Wortbedeutungen beim Kinde* (The Origin of First Word Meanings in Children), differentiated between the emotional-volitional stage and the intellectualization of emotional language which takes place in two stages (a) associative-reproductive and (b) logical-conceptual. Wundt, who closely observed, among other things, the sound development of his own children in his *Völkerpsychologie* (1900), considered child language as a product of the child's environment in which the child participates almost entirely passively. According to Wundt, this participation can be seen in the fact that the child imitates most easily those sounds which he perceives most clearly (1911:313).

The lively discussion which took place at the turn of the century between the intellectualists and the voluntarists, as the latter school was called, shows that the well-known opposing opinions on the origin of language from Greek philosophy – the nature-nurture debate – had also been carried over to child language research. The Platonic interpretation that language is *phýsei*, i.e. originated from nature, and the Aristotelian that it is *thései*, i.e. occurs because of man's determination, present two extreme points of view which, according to Stern & Stern (1928:127), lead to a distortion of the facts. The dispute as to whether imitation or spontaneity is most relevant in the process of

7

language acquisition is considered by Stern & Stern in their convergence theory (1907) to be futile: the real issue is not, therefore, imitation or spontaneity, but to what extent the inner tendencies and forces take an active part in the adoption, choice and processing of forms which are offered from the outside (1928:128).

As will be shown, these extreme viewpoints were posed again more than fifty years later by Chomsky and his followers who demonstrated a lack of consideration for research results previously obtained (see below 3.6.2).

It is very important to realize the problematic nature and results of child language research of that time as well as its empirical-theoretical basis, not only for historical reasons, but to estimate current research properly. The literature of the first decade of the century and in many cases all of the literature prior to the second World War has generally been neglected, most of all by those linguists who have, in the post-war period, worked on child language research. Consideration of this literature would have shown that most of what is nowadays presented as methodical enquiries or results, had already been anticipated at that time. First of all, they often included important methodological advice which could be useful for modern research, e.g. Preyer (1882) and Wundt (1900) on the role of imitation and gestures, and Stern & Stern 1907 (1928:11ff) on data acquisition and construction, to mention just a few. Secondly, we find in the works before the second World War data collections and analyses which offer modern research an important basis of comparison – but only, however, if the different background variables are taken into consideration.

Leopold (1948a) presents a survey of the research in the nineteenth century and the first decade of the twentieth century; in Bar-Adon & Leopold (1971) there are text extracts with commentaries from the early beginnings. The problems and results of this period are also discussed by Stern & Stern (1922:5f, 418ff), Stern (1967:3ff), Bühler (1930:51ff) and Richter (1927) whose dissertation deals with the development of psychological child language research from Aristotle to Stern. McCarthy (1954:494ff) presents a detailed critical analysis of works dealing with child language research from the end of the nineteenth century until approximately 1950.

1.2.2 CLARA AND WILLIAM STERN

Child language research done by psychologists reached its climax with the work of Stern & Stern (1907). It initiated modern paedolinguistics. Its pioneering importance lay, among other things, in the synthesis of the two theoretical positions mentioned before and in the method-ological questions which have resulted from it. They consider the realization of child language as the result of a convergence: only in the continuous cooperation of the inner, compelling aptitudes for speak-ing and the external factors of environmental language which offer these aptitudes contact points and material for their realization, can the child's language acquisition take place (1928:129; see also 3.6.3). Their research was based upon detailed observation of two of their children until after the first four years and it was supplemented with data from a third child and from relevant German and international literature. This work, in which linguistic problems were systematized in a way which had not been previously documented, is still a classic today. It deliberately dispenses with detailed representations of the physiologically based phonetic aspect of the initial stages and tries, instead, and for the first time, to define language development according to the psychological and the theoretical-linguistic (gram-matical, syntatic) aspects of language, which had been neglected up to that time, with a completeness not achieved before, and which included a previously neglected developmental stage (1928:11). Their methodological innovation was that the chronological approach, in which each new language element was registered, was accompanied by a synchronic one, so that the child's complete linguistic ability could be described at any given time. The work is among the first to strongly emphasize the systematic investigation of child language for the explanation of linguistic questions. The results of this work were included in William Stern's *Psychologie der frühen Kindheit* (The Psychology of Early Childhood) which was first published in 1914 and whose ninth edition came out in 1967. Stern & Stern (1928:149f) divide the general trend of child language development into a preliminary stage and four further stages. According to them, the main tasks in the acquisition of spoken language can be regarded as fulfilled by the fourth or fifth year of life.

A. Preliminary stage; covers the first year of life. The preliminaries to the actual performance of speech take place in four forms in this stage: crying and babbling as spontaneous ways of acting and sound imitation and language understanding as reactions to what is heard (1928:151).

B. First stage; covers the age of 1;0 to 1;6. According to Stern & Stern actual speech begins when the isolated functions of the preliminary stage, babbling, meaningless imitation and speechless comprehen-sion, build a unit. As soon as there is a connection between one's own utterances and understanding, and understanding is connected to one's own utterances, language exists. The utterances are to be perceived as one word sentences,[10] though they lack a certain grammatical and conceptual character. The objective and emotional aspects are still not differentiated in their meaning; articulation still has, in many cases, a similarity with babbling. An example of a one word sentence is: *änte* (hands). Curiously, the word was used for a long time to mean only 'take me in your arms'. If we said to the child sitting in his carriage: *nun komm doch* [come on], as a reply the child would lean over and say *änte*; which was certainly meant as an appeal to our hands (Stern & Stern 1928:22, Hilde 1;5).

C. Second stage; covers the age of about 1;6 to 2;0. This stage is characterized by an awakening consciousness of language meaning (that each thing has its name) and by a rapid increase in vocabulary (Stern & Stern 1928:150). Questions concerning the names of things come up. Sentences of two and more non-inflectional words which are classified as exclamative, interrogative and affirmative sentences follow the one-word stage (1922:43f). The different viewpoints under which the child classifies the world around him occur successively and become apparent in differentiation of his vocabulary. Stern & Stern differentiate substance, action, relation and attribute stages: first, nouns are developed, then verbs are added in larger numbers, and finally adjectives and prepositions appear (1928:150, 239).

D. Third stage; covers the age of about 2;0 to 2;6. Typical character-istics of this stage are inflexion and differentiated sentence con-struction within parataxis. Conjugation, declension and comparison begin developing at about the same time. Questions include the names of things, the what and where type of question and confirmation. Examples *Apfel wo?* [where apple?] (Hilde 1;9); confirmation question: *die essen darf ich?* [can I eat it?] (Stern 1967:138). In this period, the most important syntactic developments are 'intense use of series of sentences, whose parts are still grammatically in paratactic relation to one another, although they should logically express manifold relations and even subordination' (1928:58). For example: *mama weggelauft, papa läft tatei* [Mummy runs, daddy runs too] (a compound of sentences); *Äst anzie dann bä gähn* [first get dressed then go] (enumerative sentence compound) (1928:58, Hilde).

E. Fourth stage; covers the age from about 2;6 years. In this stage the child learns how to express the coordination and subordination of ideas by means of hypotaxis, and to develop different types of subordinate clause, even if the differentiation of the particles and the command of more difficult verb forms (e.g. the subjunctive) still take a longer time. This stage also includes temporal and causal relations. New formation of words is noticeable. It occurs partly by combination, partly by derivation. For example: *Milchapfelmus* [=milk+apple-sauce – a fantasy meal], *Kinderzeugkasten* [a box of toys], *Naseputzschnupfen* [nose blow sniffles], *die Lese* [printed text], *kaffrig* [coffee spotted] (1967:141).

Examples of compound sentences (1967:139, Hilde 3;0):

> *Indirect interrogative clause: ich wer se in de Küche mal fragen, ob se hierher kommt*
> [I am going to ask her in the kitchen, if she will come over here]
> *Temporal clause: will de puppe durchhaun, bis ihr weh tut*
> [I am going to spank the doll, till it hurts her]
> *Causal clause: das bewegt sich heut so, weil's kaputt ist*
> [it moves like that today, because it's broken]
> *Conditional clause: kriegst keine Schnitte wenn du so unatig bist*
> [you won't get any bread if you are so naughty]
> *Final clause: musst de Betten wegnehmen, dass ich rausgehen kann*
> [you must take the bed away, so that I can go by]
> *Consecutive clause: Puppe hat mich estört, dass ich nich schlafen konnte*
> [the doll disturbed me, so I couldn't sleep]

Stern & Stern (1928:234f) consider, at the same time, actual language improvement as a process of progressive intellectualization. It is manifested in the sharpening and stabilization of lexical meanings, in progressive objectiveness – from affective volitional to objective establishing behavior, and more obviously, in the transition from concrete to abstract (see Brown (1973:53f) for a more differentiated classification of the stages).

1.2.3 THE PERIOD UNTIL 1941. ROMAN JAKOBSON

As a point of reference for the classification of this period one has Roman Jakobson's contribution to child language research from the year 1941.

Research into primary language acquisition was first undertaken through systematic approaches from the linguistic side and asking linguistic questions, during and after the Second World War, although before that Stern, and Grammont (1902) had already emphasized its importance for linguistics, and after Stern there were other linguists such as Pavlovitch and Jespersen in the twentieth century. Pavlovitch (1920:2) saw in child language research the key to the study of language development and language change. Jespersen (1922:8) pointed out that linguists through research in this field come across questions which have been ignored as uninteresting by the most attentive observers amongst psychologists, but which have, nevertheless, some importance for life and the development of language.

Special attention should be drawn to the following linguists who were, in the first decade of the twentieth century, concerned with child language research: the French phonetician Grammont (1902); the Bulgarian Gheorgov (1905; 1908) who observed the language acquisition of his sons and who first analyzed morphological development in detail. Sound acquisition and syntax come to the fore in the research of the French linguist Bloch, among others (1913; 1924), who, however, gave less attention to the first year of life. Various grammatical questions concerning child language are treated in the articles of the French linguist Cohen (1925; 1933). Most of the works of linguists are in general, however, too fragmentary and unsystematic particularly for the first beginnings,[11] although they make reference to a number of important points. Thus, today's central problem of emphasis and the development of dialogue was anticipated by the well-known Dutch linguist van Ginneken (1917; 1924).

The research of the French linguist Ronjat (1913) also belongs to the basic works of this period. This work is the first extensive analysis of the language development of a bilingual child; the languages are German and French (see p..161). The work of Pavlovitch (1920) on Serbian–French language acquisition also treats aspects of bilingualism which are very important for language theory, but which have been neglected until today.

The work of the Belgian Grégoire (1937) is classified by Leopold (1952:11) as being the first detailed research on child language by a linguist; it has been characterized by Jakobson (1972:18) as being strongly systematic and microscopically accurate. Grégoire's precise analysis of the language behavior of his two children in their first two years of life gave a new direction to the research. For the first time the phonetic side of child language research was fully described, systematically analyzed and the functions of the utterances were established. The children here had also grown up using French and German. Grégoire (1937:31f) suggests a global comparison: one should observe in different parts of the world if the children's first vowels or sound groups are everywhere the same as those which he determined [a:, ÷:, ÷r÷].[12] The problems which are posed by such a question are enormous, because one cannot know how exact Grégoire's metalanguage is: he uses the international phonetic alphabet for his transcription, but only gives short descriptions. Since there are a great number of modern works in which the phonetic aspect is still problematical, it must still be emphasized today that one cannot record the whole scope of children's sounds with an alphabet oriented to adult language. A comparison such as that of Grégoire's has not been carried out on a larger scale, even though the problems of recording and analyzing sound production have, after the development of the spectograph and sonograph, been considerably diminished, if not eliminated.[13]

Just as Grégoire's research, which was followed by a second volume published in 1947, pointed out specific linguistic problems in the field of sound development, and, based on accurate data, illustrated the gradual development of language structure, so the basis for linguistic analysis in language acquisition research was laid by Roman Jakobson. In his programmatic explanation of 1941 he recommends: 'The structural analysis of language acquisition is from now on on the agenda: its general rules must be discovered, or if one prefers a less pretentious term, rules which strive for universal validity.' (1972:19)

Jakobson's work *Kindersprache, Aphasie und allgemeine Lautgesetze* (Child Language, Aphasia and Phonological Universals), which was published in Uppsala in 1941, like his contribution to the Fifth International Congress of Linguists in Brussels in 1939, brought a fundamental change to child language research which, however, only took effect long after the Second World War. What is new in Jakobson, who was one of the founders of the Prague School, is his methodology, which is characterized by the combination of structural and functional analysis. This characteristic, typical of Prague structuralism, leads him to inquire into system conditioned development; he searched for rules which explain the successive command of phonemes, and worked with phonetic oppositions. His monograph, the most important publication on the acquisition of the phonological system to date, develops not only phonetic rules for different stages of child language, and phonological lines of development, but also discusses its structural conditions. The acquisition of the phonemic system follows '*the principle of maximum contrast* and advances from *simple* and *unstructured* to *refined* and *differentiated*' (1972:93). Jakobson goes still further, however – he puts the sound acquisition rule which he presents into a larger framework: the synchronic comparison of the languages of the world. His goal was to work out universal rules of sound acquisition and, thereby, to explain the phonetic development of the languages of the world much more systematically than had been done before. He also referred to the observation that various languages could, in their development, be linked to some mutations of child language, and he refers to Grammont who had already in 1902 emphasized : 'If the grammatical peculiarities of a great number of children were gathered, one could construct a type of grammar of all changes which have taken place somewhere in human language, or which could take place' (cited by Jakobson 1972:16). Jakobson's innovation is manifested, however, in the subsequent development of these principles at a phonetic–phonological level. He emphasizes that there are important and constant correspondences between the two fields, besides all these occasional possible points of contact, and that exactly this basic problem has hardly been mentioned so far (1972:17). Jakobson used data from earlier works and also made use of Grégoire's investigation. He was not only concerned with the construction of sound systems but also with its destruction and he established a connection between the process of language acquisition and aphasia. In the same order that a normal child learns sounds, an aphasic 'unlearns' them.

Jakobson's theory of the construction of the phonological system (see 4.3.2 below) shows how indispensable phonetic knowledge is for the revelation of universally valid constructional principles of child language (1972:17); in general, that is exactly what psychologists and educationalists were lacking. But also, in the field of linguistics before the thirties, interest in the study of language systems and their structural rules was not in the foreground; that came first with the integrative approach of the Prague School which paid a lot of attention to the interrelations between the parts and the whole.

Whereas on the one hand child language research was activated by the problems of developmental psychology, on the other hand there was a field, which is still very active today, which was motivated by a practical interest in speech disorders, the rehabilitation of deaf mute children and aphasia. Gutzmann is considered as the pioneer of this field. The second edition of his work *Des Kindes Sprache und Sprachfehler* (Speech and Speech Disorders of Children) (1894) came out in 1931.[14]

Jakobson's appeal for the discovery of rules for language acquisition which strive for universal validity has so far only had a hearing in phonology. Before the Second World War psychologists still dominated the development of international child language research.[15] In the twenties and thirties child language was examined mainly with the goal of determining, through the study of language behavior, the child's personality and his intellectual life.[16] Relevant works for this aspect are the research of Karl Bühler in 1918 (1930) on *Die geistige Entwicklung des Kindes* (The Mental Development of the Child) in which there is a chapter dedicated to language development, as well as the research of Charlotte Bühler (1928) on *Kindheit und Jugend* (Childhood and Adolescence). We can add the works of Piaget (1923; 1924), Luria (1928; 1930) and Vygotsky (1962). As these and other works, e.g. the analysis of child imitation by the French psychologist Guillaume (1925), or the analysis of language and thought of Delacroix (1924) show, systematic language analysis was not central to their analysis. This can also be seen in the work of the English educationalist Lewis (1951) on early child language, which was published in 1936. Extensive primary and secondary material is analyzed here from the psychological point of view and the semantic system is also thoroughly treated.

In this period, Karl Bühler (1935:410), an outstanding figure in Prague structuralism, emphasized the importance of child language research focusing on linguistic aspects. He drew attention to the fact that the child is the only one who offers us the opportunity of observing language *in statu nascendi*. In general, psychologists and linguists, whose number was considerably smaller, worked separately. The psychologists Piaget and Vygotsky stimulated active discussion in both schools of child language research (see 3.3.1 below for details).

Piaget's books, published in 1923 and 1924, present a developmental theory of the child's systems of logic, language and thought. Language acquisition is considered as a means of the development of intelligence and personality. Here the linguist finds little material with which he can work; what is important, however, are the questions concerning the development of cognitive structures. Important for this aspect is Piaget's concept of egocentric thought and speech. According to Piaget (1923) infant language is egocentric, it develops out of pre-logical thought. This type of speech is not social, it does not refer to the hearer, but rather is used in order to give expression to ideas and emotions. Piaget's coefficient of egocentrism, which is a little below 50 per cent in children of five to six years, has not been free from criticism. We will consider the egocentrism controversy later on (see page 78). Only two important critics will be mentioned here: the Russian psychologist Vygotsky and Luria. According to Vygotsky (1962), whose work on language and thought was published in Russian in 1934, child language is social from the very beginning. He emphasized that the relationship between thought and speech during the whole period of development is not constant (1962:33). He differentiated between a pre-intellectual stage of child speech and a pre-linguistic stage of mental development, which develop independently up to a certain point. The two lines ultimately intersect and as a consequence of this, thought becomes speech and language intellectual (1962:41). However, according to him, thought and speech must not be considered as two forces which are independent of each other (1962:119f).

Vygotsky, together with Luria and others, carried out a constructive examination of egocentric language on an experimental basis in 1929 and showed that this language has a very specific function for the child's activities: it organizes the activity of the child. It was most often used in situations in which the child had a certain behavioral problem to solve. They also maintained that egocentric language changes gradually into the inner language of adults (Vygotsky & Luria 1930: Vygotsky 1962:16ff). The Russian psychologist and physiologist Luria, Vygotsky's disciple, became known in this period, with his first publications on the relationship between language and intellectual development (1928; 1930, see also 3.3.1 below).

These statements are important for linguists as they direct attention to the different functions of speech. This is a field which, till the present time, has not been fully treated for adult language, even though different aspects of the problem were addressed by Bühler's three basic functions of the sign, and Jakobson's amplification of Bühler's concept and speech act theory (see below 3.5.1.1).

This short survey of the development of paedolinguistics shows that until the Second World War the linguists' contribution was relatively small. The demand for linguistic methodology and a structuralist way of working was clearly determined, and, therefore, in the post-war period those in the field were faced with an increasing number of linguistic questions. The number of quantitative studies, mainly vocabulary studies, has considerably increased since the twenties (McCarthy 1954:496f). Teamwork was encouraged by the development of better experimental and testing techniques. The most important themes of that period, and subsequently up to 1952, can be seen in McCarthy's (1954) Index: besides quantitative studies such as vocabulary tests, there are mainly sound studies, imitation, language of gestures, the first word, increase of vocabulary, parts of speech, sentence structure and grammatical form, egocentric language, national and race differences, sex differences, bilingualism, language and intellectual development, language and social development, late language beginning, and speech disorders (see also the bibliographies of Leopold 1952; 1959; Slobin 1972; McCarthy 1954). Brenstiern

Pfanhauser (1930:329–55) provides guidance for Slavic works.

1.2.4 THE POST-WAR PERIOD

Since the fifties the number of publications has run into thousands, mainly in the form of papers and essays, so that in the present chapter we can only determine general tendencies and point out the most important basic works.

One could, from this large number of publications, conclude that child language, the basis of language acquisition and its different stages have been thoroughly investigated in the last decade, so that one could use its results for practical purposes – from the language of instruction in the first school years to questions about the complexity of semantic structure in books for preschool children, even more so since linguists regard a better understanding of language as a means of human communication, through examination of the structures and functions of isolated languages, as one of their most important tasks. Linguistics has, since the fifties, become a widespread interdisciplinary field of research in which branches such as psycholinguistics, socio-linguistics, pragmalinguistics, philosophic linguistics, mathematical linguistics and paralinguistics have been formed, to mention only a few. Their independence is maintained by different points of emphasis, although the boundaries between the individual fields are not distinct.

The connection between corresponding valid linguistic and psychological theories can be observed in the development of paedolinguistics. Whereas Jakobson's theory of the construction of the phonological system was focused on the Prague School, which he helped to found, and on gestalt psychology, the paedolinguistics research of the sixties and seventies received its impetus from discussion of the different theories of grammar, mainly transformational grammar, case grammar and dependency grammar. Also the demand, contrary to classical structuralism, that semantics should be incorporated into scientific language analysis has influenced paedolinguistic research, especially since the end of the sixties. On the other hand, it also happens that criticism of linguistic theories proceeds from paedolinguistic research, such as for example the premises of transformational grammar which are incompatible with natural language communities. On the basis of empirical observations of language acquisition in longitudinal studies, it has been shown that the approach through which Chomsky and his pupils' concept of linguistic competence is applied, is restricted and does not correspond to linguistic reality (Raffler-Engel 1968; Oksaar 1971; 1973; 1975a; Bielefeld 1972; Bowerman 1973; see also 3.5.2 below).

The increasing interest in paedolinguistics is evident in the growing number and diversity of publications – questions of language acquisition and child language are not only discussed in handbooks of psychology, but are also frequently discussed in linguistic reference books – among others in symposiums and conferences, and in exercises, seminars and lectures concerning this scientific theme in German universities and abroad; and further, in many research projects (see the bibliography in Slobin 1972).[17] The first international child language symposium took place in Brno in 1970, the second in Florence in 1972[18] and the third in London in 1975; the First International Congress for the Study of Child Language was organized in Tokyo in 1978, the Second in Vancouver in 1981. The theme 'Language Acquisition and Child Language' is discussed in numerous articles from the Tenth International Congress of Linguists in Bucharest in 1967, the Eleventh in Bologna in 1972, the Twelfth in Vienna 1977, the Thirteenth in Tokyo 1982, as well as the Ninth International Congress of Anthropological and Ethnological Sciences in Chicago in 1973 and the International Nato Conference on Language Psychology in Stirling in 1976.

Even with this encouraging activity it must be said that most of the research, from the fifties to the present time, has been methodologically so carried out that it hardly offers a stable basis for comparison and generalization. It does not offer any reliable information about all the factors which influence language acquisition and language development. The reason for this lies mainly in the fact that the methods of data collecting are different (see also 2.2.3 below).

Further, the researcher's subjectivity, which is also not completely unavoidable in the analysis of adult speech, can be a particularly important factor here, especially in the semantic field. Frequently, far too much is read into the first utterances of the child. When a child of 16 months says *Mama* as he points at his mother's dress or gloves, no clue is given for a definite interpretation of this information, such as is found in Bloom (1973:98). According to her the child wants to name the object, but does not have the words to do so, and therefore he uses the person's name in such a context.

An analysis of Slobin's Cross-Index (1972:187–200), which counts 970 publications for the period from 1945–1967, proves that the dominating field of research is phonology, with 211 works (20 per cent). Out of the 211 works, 150 (71 per cent) concern the English language. Next comes syntax with 132 works (14 per cent) from which 74 (56 per cent) deal with the English language. Vocabulary studies include 80 works (8 per cent) from which 52 (65 per cent) concern the English language. Semantics appears as a subject of research in 57 publications (6 per cent) and English dominates here, too, with 25 titles (45 per cent). The result of these elementary statistics of a relatively complete bibliography belongs to the factors which universally confirm the validity of the statement by Leopold (1956/57:117) who was one of the pioneers of research in bilingualism in children: the time has not yet come for valid generalizations in the present status quo of research and must be attempted only with caution and reservation (see also Murai 1963). This statement is also valid for our knowledge of speech ontogeny, as well as for language in the period of the elementary school which has not been so intensively studied, especially in the German language. It hardly reduces, however, the value of isolated information from the case studies nor from group studies, but implies that one is still far from a perfect language acquisition theory.

Child language acquisition studies at the preschool age which are based on primary material can, in the post-war period, be divided into two groups:
1) Works based on the *observation of one or several children* who live close to the researcher. It happens very often that the observation is of the researcher's own child.

The data covers different lengths of time, from some months to several years. Longitudinal studies over three years are rare. The two volumes of the Russian Gvozdev (1947), which are based on eight years' records (1921–1929) of his son's language, analyze in detail the development of grammatical structures. The second volume of Grégoire (1947) focusing on phonetic analysis with regard to vocabulary is relevant here, as well as the studies of Ohnesorg (1948; 1959), who observed the development of his son's phonetic system for the five years from his birth. Oksaar's Hamburg Project focusing on the Estonian, Swedish and German syntax, semantics and pragmatics of her multilingual son (with control group) covers the whole preschool age from 0.2 to school age.

As for the beginning of the period we can mention Leopold's detailed studies (1939–1949) in the fields of sound acquisition, vocabulary, and morphological and syntactic structures of his daughter. It concentrated on her first two years of life in a German and English speaking environment. From the fifties we can mention the methodologically independent work of the Dutchman Kaper (1959). His work on the language awareness of the child takes the situation and spoken context into consideration. The material of this work covers six years' observation of his two sons. The child's discrimination of word choice, sound form and grammatical form; the need for appellatives and names; self-correction and mature appreciation of word meanings, constitute the main fields of his work. The pioneer work of Weir (1962) should be pointed out among the works of the early sixties. She analyzes the monologues of her two-and-a-half-year old English speaking son. She also considered the conative, meta-linguistic and poetic functions of language which we can also find in Jakobson (1960:355f; see below 3.5.1.1).

Further, we can make reference, outside this group, to the American works from the Harvard Project, which stimulated research in language acquisition in the USA in the first half of the sixties, characteristically the psychologists: Brown & Fraser (1964), Brown & Bellugi (1964), and McNeill (1966) among others, who investigated the development of syntax in three children, aged 18, 27 and 27 months (on this project see Brown 1973; Ferguson & Slobin 1973: 295f). It is notable that in these studies, as well as in other American works such as those of Braine (1963), Menyuk (1964), and Bowerman (1973), the data collection has been carried out in too great a linguistic isolation, without due respect for the situation, text-context and socio-cultural framework in which language is used and heard by the child, and also without taking account of paralinguistic and kinesic means which reinforce or complete verbal communication (see also 2.4 below). Even if new research such as that of Menyuk (1969) and Bloom (1970; 1973) describes the situations in the raw data, they are not system-atically handled. Of course this has considerable implications for the results. However, the methods of data collection and analysis have, both for studies in this group and in group 2 below, been changed through the development and expansion of technical aids, for example electronic aids, and video recorders, as well as, since Leopold's statement, through the improvement of linguistic and socio-psycho-logical approaches.

A great many American works of the early sixties focused mainly on the methods of classical structuralism, in which distributional regu-larities were found through segmentation and classification. Later on, the two models from Chomsky – the 1957 model and the aspects model of 1965 – provided a methodological structure; which meant, among other things, that syntactic categorization could not be made by means of surface structure data and that semantic interpretation would be carried out by syntactic deep structures (see for example Bloom 1970, and 2.1 below).

A Russian study published in 1956 should be mentioned here. Luria & Yudovich (1956) studied a pair of linguistically retarded five-year-old twins, with the purpose of gaining insight into the role of language in the organization of more complex mental performance. They demonstrated that improvement in language development can cause changes in mental structure (see also 3.3.1 below).

2) Works based on the *study of a larger group of children* have been carried out mostly by psychologists. It is relevant to mention here, above all, a great number of Soviet works influenced by the Pavlovian school in determining distinct learning processes which depend on motivation (see 3.6 below); as well as studies carried out by the Piagetian school, such as Sinclair (1967; 1973). Further, the work of McCarthy (1954), Luria (1959), the studies of Slama-Cazacu (1962) and the Berkeley project of Miller & Ervin (1964) and Slobin's Cross-Cultural Project should be mentioned. Slama-Cazacu's data was collected from 200 Rumanian children aged from two to seven years. Their goal was to determine the relationship between language and thought. Miller & Ervin, whose longitudinal study took into consideration tests with 25 children from two years on and an intensive study of five children, centre their attention on grammatical development. The studies of Irwin and his co-workers, published in more than 30 articles, belong to the most extensive experimental approaches in the field of articulatory development of English hearing children; see, for example, Erwin (1947; 1960) and McCarthy's analysis of his results (1954:507ff) and the discussion in 4.3.2 below.

We will discuss the present state of research in the next chapter (2.1). In general, it can be stated that the seventies were characterized by an increasing interest in semantic and pragmatic questions and the related methodological approaches, as can be seen in Campbell & Wales (1970), Oksaar (1971; 1973; 1975), Bielefeld (1972), Bloom (1970; 1973), Clark (1973; 1975), Schaerlaekens (1973) and Bowerman (1973).[19] The main areas of emphasis of this period are reflected in the survey by Lewis (1963) which is based on his own observations and on secondary literature. It fills a gap, as innumerable studies of different aspects of language and its place in human behavior are integrated in a systematic account of the growth of language in relation to general development in infancy and childhood (1963:7). The central theme of Church (1961) is language as a means of communication, as a means of discovery and command of reality; see also Francescato (1970) and Kegel (1974).

These necessarily short references should give insight at least in a bibliographical sense, into the manifold approaches adopted in paedolinguistics in the post-war period. For more detailed information see the surveys and discussions by McCarthy (1959), Ervin-Tripp (1966), Slobin (1966b; 1972) and McNeill (1970); also Hayes (1970) and Braine (1971), Slama-Cazacu (1972b), Ferguson & Slobin (1973) and Oksaar (1975a). Afendras & Pianarosa (1975) offer the best source of information on child bilingualism.

1.3 SUMMARY

In order to understand language acquisition and language development, one must remember that man is a biological, social, cultural and intellectual being. Questions about language acquisition at the preschool age should not therefore be handled from an isolated psychological or sociological point of view, but from that of paedolinguistics, which is an interdisciplinary field of research, which considers the results of linguistics and semiotics, the experimental approaches of psychology and basic questions such as the relation between speech and cognitive development, as well as the socio-cultural aspects of the child's living conditions and the problems of language acquisition which are related to them. The investigation of speech ontogeny (0 to 4;0) and the primary expansion stage (4;0 to 7;0) are part of its functions.

A general view of the development of paedolinguistics, its analysis and methodology has been given in the course of this chapter. It introduced the approaches to child language research adopted by physicians, philosophers, psychologists and educationalists, by Clara and William Stern and in the period up to Roman Jakobson's structural–functional analysis after the war.

We only know of extensive studies of child language development in the major languages. Their value and reliability vary, because most of the studies, even the ones done by linguists, are based on data which has often been collected without technical aids and without considering the different situational contexts. Even though, in the fifties and sixties, interest in syntax increased, there are still relatively few works, most of them American and Russian, which systematically treat syntactic problems.

Several of the works cited in the above will continue to be referred to in the following chapters, and a number of the issues and approaches touched on here, will be examined in more detail.

QUESTIONS

1.1 How does the author define paedolinguistics?
Why does she limit it to that age group?
What major division is made in this group?

1.2.1 Which scientific fields first began to consider child language?
What sort of studies were made? (i.e. what did they concentrate on, how were they carried out, etc.)

1.2.2 What major contributions to child language research did Clara and William Stern make?
What were their four stages of language development?

1.2.3 Which school did Roman Jakobson help found, and what was his approach to language acquisition?
Name two other leading linguists of that time.
What was the central disagreement between Piaget and Vygotsky?

1.2.4 What characterizes the development of paedolinguistics after the Second World War, particularly what weaknesses are evident in the studies of that time?

1.3 Into what major groups can the studies of the post-war period be divided?

2 Theoretical and Methodological Foundations of Paedolinguistics

2.1 PRESENT RESEARCH SITUATION

It can generally be said that in the seventies the trend which was observed in many places at the beginning of the decade grew steadily. It led from approaches focusing on form, to semantics and then to the investigation of, amongst other things, still more complex performance oriented contexts. One can characterize this field as functional communicative and cognitive. In the following, we will discuss some important research trends in the development of current theory and method.

In the sixties and the early seventies in the USA and Western Europe, attention was chiefly concentrated on *what* the child learns. This goal is found mainly in those works which have their theoretical background in one of the various models of transformational generative grammar.[1] Attention to what the child learns was confined to a 'search for the grammar' of the child's language production which has often been compared with the search for syntactical rules and genesis of rules.[2] It is clear however, that no further results can be achieved in language acquisition research if a series of further questions, beginning with *how* language is acquired, are not taken into consideration in the field of investigation. The solution to the problem of how language is acquired is closely connected with the answer to the central question: What are the strategies that are employed by children to use their linguistic resources as an effective means of communication, i.e. to use an appropriate means of communication according to the particular requirements of the situation? (Oksaar 1975a)

The research on syntax mentioned above did not consider the ways in which the grammatical structures, which have been thoroughly analyzed (see below 2.2), represent the child's intentions. The complex problem which needs to be answered here, can best be stated as *Under what conditions?* and *What for?* and leads into the necessary pragmatic aspects of language acquisition research. A new trend was signalled several years ago when the inadequacies of an exclusively syntactic description based on the model of so-called pivot grammar were determined, for example by Bloom (1970) in her observations of a number of semantic distinctions which had the same syntactic structure in a child's early utterances. Today, however, it should be noted that such a method is inadequate to cover important pragmatic aspects of language acquisition and related social aspects.

It can be established that children under two years of age[3] already use syntactic structures with distinctive grammatical and semantic relations to express something which a simple syntactic analysis would not show. It can, however, be clearly interpreted through the situational context. For example, the Estonian sentence of 1; 10-year-old Sven (=Nenne): *Ema, ema . . . Nene uki* (=ukse) *taga!* [Mommy, mommy . . . Nenne behind the door.] (from Oksaar 1971:348) was uttered in a situation with the following characteristics: the child was standing behind a closed door and could not open it; the paralinguistic elements, such as voice tone, signal dissatisfaction. An exclamation[4] is used here in the sense of Bühler's appelative and expressive functions (see below 3.5.1.1) and it is interpreted as something like [open the door, I want to get in]. With adults in such a situation one can establish a clear variant of the implicature in the sense of Grice (1975) i.e. a proposition is then implicated if one expresses it without saying it. With a child, however, this type of example illustrates how he tries to cope with the requirements of reality. He learns how to control situations and in this case he interacts with his mother, to whom the first two words were directed as an attempt to establish contact, and achieved the following: the mother answered *ma tulen kohe* [I'm coming] and opened the door (see also 3.4.3.1 below).

This type of communicative experience, the social speech action of the child, which the infant makes in interaction with other people, must be systematically considered in the field of investigation if further results about the semantic and communicative aspects of language acquisition are to be achieved – a field which has gained increasing interest (see Halliday 1975; Oksaar 1975a).

The present time, without any doubt, has found its way back to the important questions of semantics, cognitive development and language change of early child language research (see Ferguson & Slobin 1973:170). However, it should not be overlooked that questions based on the social aspects of language acquisition had been considered earlier.

Stern & Stern (1928:126) referred to 'moments of social drive', which, in part or chiefly, employ phonic means and are, therefore, a powerful driving force for language development. They emphasized that in the first few weeks mental contact between the child and other people readily develops and is manifested in different activities, including, amongst others, the exchange of primitive sounds and efforts to attract people's attention. The feeling of being involved with the same type of sounds as the rest of the community (crying, yelling, singing, etc) leads to the reinforcement of the feeling of being part of it (1928:125). It is also important to point out that the child's expressive and social actions are merged with one another (1928:126). The studies of Bühler et al. (1927) on child social behavior patterns demonstrate the social functions of laughing, babbling and a rich development of social means of contact during the first year of life.

✳   It should be mentioned that Soviet research had for some time considered language development in connection with the whole dynamic of the child, i.e. with the active communication of the child with his environment, with his cognitive development and with the feedback of his actions. This is evident in the works of Luria (1930) and Vygotsky (1962) among others. Nowadays, this tradition is carried on mainly with practical psycho-pedagogical goals (see Luria & Yudovich 1959; Leont'ev Russ. 1968; Slama-Cazacu 1972b:546ff; Slobin 1966b; 1972).

Already, these facts make it apparent that many case studies in different languages are still necessary if the factors regarding communicative and social functions are to be taken into account. The same is also true of questions concerning the cognitive aspects of language acquisition, which, as we have mentioned above, are being regarded with increasing interest because of, among other things, Piaget's growing influence on international research.[5] Subsequently, different attempts have been made to integrate the two central models of the development of perception and the development of language into a theoretical setting. This involves the biological and logico-mathematical model of Piaget, who was originally a biologist, and Vygotsky's primarily social and cultural frame of reference (see also Schmidt 1973; Bain 1973; Riegel 1973).

There have already been several important approaches to this question (see e.g. Merleau-Ponty 1945; Church 1961). Nowadays, however, more emphasis is directed to the necessity of treating the whole cognitive scope of a child's relations for the purpose of, among other things, observing his cognitive behavior from the beginning on with regard to his social contacts and communicative possibilities (see

Shields 1975 and below 3.2). In the post-war period, Piaget's thesis of the egocentric thought and speech of the child has, beyond any doubt, slowed the systematic investigation of these other aspects. In the demands of today's developmental psychology for a 'comprehensive theory of human development', the role of language in cognitive development is made clear in the following:

> Language is not a *deus ex machina* that solves all the problems of getting to know or rubricating and categorizing what the individual child ought to know in the opinion of the adults involved or according to the prescriptions of the culture. Language is not a substitute for direct experience; it is itself a mode of expressing and an activity of apprehending and transforming direct experience as well as symbolically mediated experience. (Schmidt 1973:119)

There is, moreover, a further important aspect for paedolinguistics. The development of child language sets up a basis for an investigation of the components which distinguish human language from other code systems, e.g. from those of animals. It illustrates, however, not only a general process of humanization, but shows, above all, how biological human beings become social human beings. This is recognizable in social interaction: one of the most important functions of language is as a means of expression and communication in a group. Moreover, group affiliation is also determined by its language. It is exactly these sociological and socio-psycholinguistic aspects which, in the investigation of the preschool child in many countries, have lagged behind others, e.g. the psychological and pedagogical aspects. The role of several environmental variables such as group affiliation, family structure, socio-economic status, parents' education, etc., in the development of speech ability, has however been documented by a number of earlier studies. McCarthy (1954:584–8) summarizes the most important studies. Children from higher status groups have a larger vocabulary, and use not only longer sentences but also develop functional categories, such as questions, faster than children from underprivileged groups (see below 3.4.2.2). Although the connection between social structure and the language behaviour of schoolchildren has been discussed in several countries as the result of the reception and criticism of Bernstein's language barrier theory, until recently the speech development of the preschool child has hardly been investigated according to group specific criteria.[6] In order to avoid further misunderstandings of the linguistic realities and Bernstein's viewpoints, his theses and arguments should now be read in the collection (1972) which he authorized, together with the editor's critical preface. The critical reader can find suggestions here for corresponding research into the preschool stage, as well as in Brandis & Henderson (1970) and other works from Bernstein's school (see also Schlee 1973).

What has been stated above shows that it is also important to observe differences in the development of language and the reasons for them, and to develop methods of establishing them. This statement is only apparently superfluous. Most works on the early language development of children are based on the premise that there are universal aspects in this development (see Slobin 1971a). Therefore, they concentrate their attention almost exclusively on invariant research in the process of development. The close connection between transformational generative grammar and psycholinguistics in the USA has contributed considerably to the fact that this approach has dominated the last twenty years. Slobin emphasizes that 'The underlying semantic-cognitive structure of human experience is universal, and these universals of structured experience seem to be expressed in strikingly similar fashion in child speech around the world.' (1971a:175). As supposed universals in the acquisition of grammar in the field of word order Slobin lists the following:

Universal C1: The standard order of functor morphemes in the input language is preserved in child speech.

Universal C2: Word order in child speech reflects word order in the input language.

Universal C3: Sentences deviating from standard word order will be interpreted at early stages of development as if they were examples of standard word order. (1973:197f)

Methodological objection can be made to this and many other similar propositions in today's research, in that the results of the universals investigation can still by no means be verified. Furthermore, we only know very little about language acquisition and language development in non-European languages. It is not correct to compare general tendencies in a very small number of languages with universals, particularly when using data based on an extremely small sample. It is also more than questionable to make statements of the type: 'Universal C3' (Slobin 1973:198) about the interpretative activity of the infant. Moreover, the size of the sample must be observed. Data from one or two children do not constitute substantial evidence for the whole language.

It is necessary to establish a secure methodological-theoretical basis, based on empirical research in different languages, which makes it possible to compare factors in the language acquisition process, before regularities in development are even mentioned, or generalizations attempted. This includes, among other things, a clear definition of concepts such as 'developmental universals', 'linguistic universals' and the like. If universals research was advanced enough to describe the elements that are common to all languages and which belong, consequently, to the basic elements of human language, that description would apply only to adult language, as has been shown in the most important works of universals research (see Greenberg 1966 and compare Coseriu 1974; Seiler 1975).

Slobin's studies (1971a), which are based on the hypothesis of linguistic and cognitive universals, do however refer to the differences, e.g. between a Finnish and a Russian child in the acquisition of word order. The differences cannot be explained using such an approach. Slobin (1971a:182) admits the difficulties and states that an examination of the basic elements of such individual differences is lacking and that such differences have methodological consequences. They call attention to the important problem, which has by no means been solved, of an appropriate sample size.

The general tendencies of language development will be discussed in Chapter 4. We have touched on the problem of universals here, because it has had a strong methodological and theoretical influence on subsequent research and has almost blocked other research trends.[7] The methodology had been developed with the purpose of investigating the universal nature of language. Contrary to these goals of developmental psycholinguistics, other psychological trends emphasize individual differences in child development. Individual styles in the development of thought are outlined by Wallach & Kogan (1965) and Lee et al. (1963). Methodological interest in the problem of the systematic differences in language development has, however, hardly been shown until recently; for instance an approach in the field of syntax can be found in Ramer (1976).

Based on what has been mentioned above, it can be concluded that a complete language acquisition research program including both goals is necessary. And so we have arrived at further basic problems.

As we have already stated, child language research has always been guided by the linguistic, psychological and philosophical theories which were dominant at the time. In the past few years, a paradigm change has gained more and more ground in the discussion of theory and method in linguistics: from sentences to texts, from the exclusive research of the system – langue – to the analysis of speech behavior – parole. This is reflected, of course, in the questions mentioned above; however, the research position in paedolinguistics can, to a large extent, still be defined, with Slama-Cazacu's (1972a:30) statement that one can often see, especially among the younger scientists, that theories and methodological procedures tend not to be creatively adopted from transformational or generative linguistics.

As we have already mentioned, theoretical linguistics had long ago realized the limitation of Chomsky's transformational generative grammar and had proposed further different developmental models and new approaches.[8] Language acquisition research in many places still retained the postulates and metalanguage of Chomsky's school, which has not infrequently resulted in the same theoretical settings being supplied with corresponding examples from different languages. The deficiency of methodological awareness is also reflected in the procedure in which hypotheses, which cannot be empirically con-trolled, are set up and then considered not as hypotheses, but as positive information. A few examples may illustrate this.

Chomsky's school operates with the supposition of a universal language acquisition mechanism, an innate linguistic theory, as the basis for the acquisition of language. Chomsky (1965:25) explains it in a dogmatic way: 'As a precondition for language learning he [the child] must possess, first a linguistic theory that specifies the form of the grammar of a possible human language, and, second, a strategy for selecting a grammar of the appropriate form that is compatible with the primary linguistic data.' Apart from the fact that central terms such as *linguistic theory* are not explained, one can also criticize this process in that it is connected with a further hypothetical component – the linguistic universals. This intuitive knowledge of universals is ascribed to the child (Chomsky 1965:27).

Such statements are considered as true preconditions, and this has hindered the productive development of language acquisition theory and the theoretical arguments of its methodology (see Oksaar 1975a:723). It can be observed that certain unproven hypotheses – e.g. also Chomsky's LAD (Language Acquisition Device) the universal innate language acquisition mechanism – are overvalued by psycho-logists and psycholinguists, such as McNeill (1966). In a field such as language acquisition in which empirical research cannot be ignored in theory formation, this overvaluing leads to the precipitate formation of invariants, and this can have serious consequences for further research. Starting from Chomsky's concept that speech universals can be considered as a product of the innate ability of all children, McNeill himself (1966:46f) emphasized that certain basic grammatical relations e.g. *subject of*, must be considered as innate knowledge. The consequences of such an approach would be that one could set up hypotheses about universals in language acquisition based on the accomplishments of universals research, again without empirical language acquisition studies (see Bowerman 1973:5). It is with good reason that Chomsky's starting point (1965:32), which ascribes to the child 'an innate theory of potential structural descriptions', is criticized by various groups.[9] It avoids the problem of gaining a basic understanding of how the child learns the basic grammatical relations, since they are explained as innate. It also gives a false picture of the child's situation:

> The child seems to be viewed as if he were a computer judging the grammaticalness of sentences, instead of an immature, dependent human trying to survive. If we must attribute motives to the infant, we are on biologically firmer ground in attributing to him a motivation to survive than we are if we attribute to him a motivation to make grammatical analysis. (Olmsted 1971:20)

The dilemma of this theoretical starting point is appropriately characterized by Schlesinger's (1967:400) statement: 'The linguist makes a model of language competence, and it remains for the psychologists to explain how this linguistic model works.' He emphasizes that it would be just as judicious or injudicious if one argued that a theory which explains *how* language is learned could be used for the evaluation of theories which describe *what* is learned.

We will return to this problem in 3.6 below, when we discuss the problem of *how* language is acquired. The minuteness of detail in the present methodological context has been necessary because paedolinguistics, as an interdisciplinary field of research, is still working on its methodological principles. These must be guided by the demands of any empirical science, if we are to consider the determination of universally valid statements about the acquisition and development of preschool child language as one of the most important goals of paedolinguistics. Because the term 'empirical' has brought about a lot of misunderstanding within linguistics, a theoretical explanation must still be given. According to Seiffert (1970:219), in the social sciences empirical research can mean both 'the exact *ascertainment of individual details*' and 'the inductive *deduction of universal statements* out of such empirically determined facts'. For paedolinguistics too, 'empirical' is by no means limited to the first interpretation. Research in this field should not be seen from a perspective which separates the 'empirical' from the 'theoretical', but as a complementary unity.

Two types of procedures are generally distinguished in any discussion of method: the analytical methods which originated in the natural sciences, and the non-analytical methods, which have been applied primarily in the human sciences. Linguists, mathematicians, and formal logicians proceed *analytically* when they analyze their subject matter in isolated parts and investigate their relations. The phenomenologists and hermeneuticists work according to *non-analytical* procedures. The subject matter of research is seen and interpreted as a unity; (see Seiffert 1970:3 and the discussion in 3.6 below). The researcher must consider the principles of *induction* and *deduction* in order to find the procedures which are appropriate for him. The inductive method leads from individual to general cases and includes the following steps: observation – statements about things which have been observed (the so-called protocol approach) – hypotheses – rules – theory. The deductive method proceeds in the reverse order: the rules are derived from a theory and they lead to further specific findings.

For paedolinguistics it is obvious that the investigation has to start from real life, i.e. from the observed facts of the communicative language behavior of the child. The proceedings which have to be observed, can be induced by experiments, interviews and tests according to the child's age. These empirical research techniques do, however, raise different methodological problems, which have to be studied in a special methodology (see Seiffert 1970:161).

The choice of the method or combination of methods must fit the questions, not the other way around. This statement is by no means superfluous. The tendency and practice which Blumer (1968) determined for social sciences and psychology can also be observed in the linguistic sciences: one allows research to be dominated by theory, model, conception, technique and scientific program, and so forces the analytical description of the empirical world into their form.

A combination of analytical and non-analytical procedures in a problem-oriented synthesis determined by specific questions seems to be a productive procedure for paedolinguistics. Stern & Stern (1928:121) mentioned the importance of such a methodological procedure. A complete analysis of methodological questions and research techniques within paedolinguistics is a pressing task which this science has still to start. Yet it is not sufficient to be content with theoretical arguments for different methods; one must also use the methods as instruments and clearly describe the possibilities of their application for research work. Neurophysiologically oriented research requires other procedures from those of syntactic research, and phonetic research different procedures from semantics research. 'Every dogmatic definition of methodology reduces the possibilities of cognition, due to the fact that it impedes or even prevents inquiries about explanations, which are not possible with the available methods.'[10]

2.2 LANGUAGE ACQUISITION AND LINGUISTIC MODELS

We mentioned in 1.2.4 and 2.1 that paedolinguistic research has been guided by prevailing grammatical models and linguistic theories and that the present trend in linguistics to performance oriented and pragmatic questions is also present in the change of focus in the analysis in language acquisition research. In the present chapter we will discuss some linguistic models from the standpoint of their application to paedolinguistics.

2.2.1 PIVOT GRAMMAR

The so-called pivot grammar received its name from the results of the distributional analysis which Braine (1963) carried out at the two-word stage based on data of three children at the age of 19–24 months. This grammar, whose principles have also been confirmed by Brown & Fraser (1963) and Miller & Ervin (1964) in the speech of children between 18 and 28 months, belongs to the generative type of grammar models, i.e. its purpose is to present the mechanism of sentence production and thereby, the linguistic competence of the child at this stage. The method operates according to the classic principles of structuralism: distributional analysis determining frequency, determining the combination of the elements. First, according to the principle of 'privilege of occurrence', it was determined in which combinations the words occurred, and based on the combinations the lexical classes were determined. The principle of 'privilege of occurrence' considers both the position of a word in a sentence and the range of possible combination with other words.

Braine (1963) considered two classes. One class contained fewer elements (words), they appeared frequently and always in certain positions and were combined with a great many other words. He called words from this class *pivot words*, e.g. *all* in *all broke, all fix*. The other class had a considerably larger range, though the frequency of the individual words was considerably smaller than in the pivot class. Braine designated these *X- words*. The term pivot in Braine (1963) corresponds to *modifier* in Brown & Fraser (1963) and *operator* in Miller & Ervin (1964). Nowadays, one generally refers to *pivot class* and *open class*. The pivot words always appear in certain positions and only appear with words of the open class. The words of the open class can, on the other hand, appear alone, or together with another word of the open class.

In the pivot class, one can, according to position, distinguish two sub classes: P_1 and P_2. Brown (1973:92) gives examples for three construction types in Gregory's and Andrew's two-word sentences:

Child	P_1+O	$O+P_2$	$O+O$
Gregory	*See boy*	*Push it*	*Mommy sleep*
	See sock	*Move it*	*Milk cup*
Andrew	*All broke*	*Boot off*	*Papa away*
	All fix	*Water off*	*Pants change*
	I see	*Airplane by*	*Dry pants*
	I sit	*Siren by*	

A sample from this two-word grammar includes, according to Slobin (1971:6), the following rules of sentence production:

$$S \rightarrow \left\{ \begin{array}{c} P_1 + O \\ O + P_2 \\ O + O \end{array} \right\}$$

$P_1 \rightarrow$ *allgone, byebye, big, more*
$P_2 \rightarrow$ *off, in*
$O \rightarrow$ *boy, sock, Mommy*

The symbol $S \rightarrow P_1+O$ implies that, for sentence generation one must combine a word from the first position of the pivot class with a word from the open class.

Such an analysis of the two-word stage suggests a sort of system for the utterances, which is manifested in two word classes with two sub-classes and three sentence types.

However, what do these statements explain? Are they representative of the linguistic competence of the child in the two-word stage? Is it legitimate to claim, as McNeill (1970) does, that pivot grammar is a generic basis for a universal hierachy of lexical categories?

Nowadays after a great number of studies which have not only analyzed new data, but also questioned the underlying material of the pivot principles, the standpoint has been reached that pivot grammar is inadequate to determine the competence of English speaking children, not to mention fulfilling demands for universality. Bloom (1970), Bowerman (1973), van der Geest (1974), Brown (1973) who also refers to his earlier essays in this book, and Park (1974) to mention just a few, have empirically demonstrated that pivot grammar is not capable of covering perceptible characteristics of the child's two-word sentences, which are much more complex than has been suggested by this model. It is not true that the pivots cannot appear alone and never in combination with other pivots. Bowerman (1973:28–38) also points to instances of this in the underlying pivot grammar works by Braine, Brown & Fraser and Miller & Ervin. For example pivots like *more* occur alone, and combinations like *that off*, *want more* demonstrate that pivots can be combined with each other. My own analysis of two Finnish children and further literature on American and Samoan children show that their two-word sentences do not correspond to the rules of pivot grammar. The most frequent words did not have any fixed position, and also occurred as one-word utterances and combined with each other.

Park (1974:61) also found in his German material a great number of utterances of the type P+P: *oben hier* [over here], *da ein* [there one], *das auch* [that too]. Further, he determined that the P+O constructions are very rare (12 out of 108 two-word sentences by a child of 24 months), and that the pivots do not have a fixed position and can also occur alone. The two-word stage of five Dutch children also speak against the model (see van der Geest 1974).

Besides distributional factors, there are, however, more important arguments against this model, namely, its inadequacy in considering semantics and distinguishing between grammatical and semantic functions. Different syntactic and semantic relations which the pivot model does not include are found in two formally identical but semantically different utterances: *Mama da* [Mama ist da = Mommy is there] and *Mama da* in which *Mama* is a vocative (the child points at another child). They can be quite unmistakably interpreted according to the situation (see Park 1974:65; Bloom 1970:5f).

My Estonian and Swedish data on the two-word stage also presents a great number of instances which show that although the child uses similar forms he expresses quite different intentions and therefore also different relations between the two words. Sven (16 months) called, in Estonian, all light-colored cars *pappa auto* (possessive construction). When he wanted to take a ride in the car, he would go to his father and would say *pappa auto* too (vocative construction). Christina (21 months) used the Swedish sentence *där lego* [there Lego] in two different contexts: 1) when she wanted to call one's attention that she was playing with the 'Lego'; at the same time she pointed at the brick; and 2) when she wanted to have the Lego, which she could not take from the shelf herself. Here, the intention was explained by extra-linguistic information, too.

Alone these examples show, however, that it is important to consider the entire behaviour of the child and his kinesics (see 2.5 below). Criticism of pivot grammar has not included these components; it has, however, furnished enough arguments against the pretentions of this model in explaining the linguistic competence of the child at the two word stage.

2.2.2 TRANSFORMATIONAL GRAMMARS

The range of transformational grammar and its criticism has already been referred to in 2.1 above. In the beginning, the transformational grammar was well received by psychologically oriented scientists, due to the fact that it claimed not only to be descriptive but also explanatory, in particular for the 'creative processes of language'. It was supposed to describe and explain the innate language competence of the ideal speaker/hearer. Competence is regarded as the ability to produce and understand sentences which have never been heard before (see Chomsky 1965:3–10). So it is not surprising that language acquisition research has been concerned with this goal (see for example Bloom 1970:23). Chomsky (1965) claimed to explain mental processes and to specify the real linguistic knowledge of the speaker with his Aspects model of 1965.

Before this model was applied to the analysis of language acquisition, however, a number of basic questions should have been answered. Besides the question of universals, which has been mentioned earlier and the 'Language Acquisition Device' (LAD), the artificial division of performance and competence and the exclusion of performance from analysis should be considered here. This is even more surprising because the only way to examine competence is through performance, and' performance is the primary given. Also relevant to this is the concept of the ideal speaker/hearer in a homogeneous language community (Chomsky 1965:3). In reality there are only real speakers and listeners in a heterogeneous language community. A language theory which from the very beginning is not able to consider linguistic reality should not pretend to give an explicit formulation of the 'creative' processes of language (Chomsky 1965:8). How does a very individual child become the ideal speaker/hearer in the Chomskyan sense, for whom the model is formed? In the rest of this chapter we will consider carefully some model types.

2.2.2.1 SYNTAX ORIENTED MODELS

Chomsky's Aspects model will be outlined briefly here. In the Aspects model, the primary emphasis was placed more on syntax than on semantics. Although it presents a three-tier grammar with syntax, semantics and phonology, in opposition to the two-tier syntax and phonology in the 'pre-Aspects era', the semantic and phonological components are only interpretative. The generative part is the syntactic component. It consists of a base component and a trans-formational component. The base generates abstract syntactic structures – the deep structures; the transformational component conveys this to a concrete syntactic surface structure. The basic rules appear in the base: phrase structure rules and sub-categorization rules. It also includes the lexicon. The deep structures are relevant as input for the semantic interpretation of the sentences. The syntactic surface structure serves as input for the phonological component.

Obviously, this model is syntax oriented. In the transformational school, this results in the fact that 'grammar' often means simply 'syntax'. However, this goes so far that scientists such as McNeill (1970) consider the concept of sentence as part of the innate mental capacity of human beings.

Bloom's monograph (1970) can be mentioned as an example of the use of the Aspects model; it is based on data from three children aged 19–23 months. Proceeding from the inadequacy of pivot grammar – only the earliest examples of her material show any of its features – her goal is to use explanations of child language which not only consider the surface constituents of the sentence, but also explain its semantic interpretation. In order to understand the child's statement it is necessary to consider the extra-linguistic information of the context and his behaviour in relation to performance.

Since Bloom uses surface structure and deep structure, according to the Aspects model, she is able to trace identical surface structures, such as *Mommy sock* to two different deep structures. Here, theoretical and practical problems arise, mostly because of constraints in the model. The contexts of the utterances are: 1) Kathryn picked up her mother's sock; and 2) Mommy putting Kathryn's sock on her (Bloom 1970:5). Let's have a look at the second sentence. Here, there is a relation between agent and object, i.e. the relational meaning of *Mommy* is, in this case, 'agent', of *sock* 'object'. In transformational grammar the phrase structure rules for this sentence generate the following deep structure (cited by Brown 1973:234):

'With this deep structure the noun *sock* is derived out of *VP* along with an unspecified verb. As a consequence the grammatical relation "object of the predicate" has its proper configurational definition; it is a *NP* directly dominated by *VP* and generated with *V* out of *VP*.'

Now the question arises, why with such a deep structure, is there no verb, e.g. *put*, in the surface structure? For the elimination of the constituent, Bloom develops a reductional transformation, represented here by the symbol △, for the constituent *V* (verb). Bloom follows Chomsky's opinion that 'there is surely no doubt that the child's achievements in systemizing linguistic data, at every stage go well beyond what he actually produces in normal speech' and that there is without doubt 'an underlying, fuller conception of sentence structure [which may be] unrealized in his speech' (cited by Bloom 1970).

More than one empirical work has criticized this approach of explaining the construction of two-word sentences by means of reductional transformations (see Schaerlaekens 1973:43f; Bowerman 1973:129f). This method could only be applied when the basic grammatical relations – subject-verb-object – are available in the child's grammar. As Bloom (1970:227) admits, that is not the case. Park (1974:125) observes in German material that it is not possible to apply such a reductional transformation as a component of the child's linguistic competence. In the German child, Kathryn, all three categories of subject-verb-object were established, but she nonetheless used substantive + substantive utterances in the third phase of the research. For example *Fernseh Bum* [television bang] (she heard noise), although she knew the word *machen* [make].

Child behavior, as Park (1974:126) says, can be better explained by the principle of non-production. This means that two-word statements must still be considered as less complex structures; the approach with reductional transformation on the other hand, pre-supposes a linguistic competence coinciding with the three-word phase, otherwise a reductional transformation would not be applied. How-ever, Park also sees a theoretical difficulty in this approach. The two-word chain occurs earlier in the development of the child's speech than the three-word chain with, for example, Subject + Verb + Object, because this is syntactically more complex. When, however, the chain Subject + Object is conceived as a result of a reductional transformation, through which the category *V* is represented by the place marker △, then the chain Subject + Object would be connected with more syntactic complexity than the chain Subject + Verb + Object. This would mean, as Park (1974:125) states, that the language development of a more complex structure develops towards a less complex structure, which would speak against generally accepted opinion about the development of the cognitive functions of the child.

Moreover, it is necessary to say that this model does not consider the fact that, in many communication situations, not everything needs to be verbalized and, as a rule, it is not. As Bühler (1934:155f) stated in the discussion of the range of language signs, there are 'empractical namings and indications with the help of isolated language signs'. According to Bühler (1934:158), long before he utters a clause with several words the child uses the empractical naming and gestures which are entirely meaningful and intelligible to us. But in the spoken language of many adults, too, many constituents may be omit-ted when they can be clearly supplied by the context or when they have less significance. Sentences such as *Schulaufgaben fertig!* [homework finished], or *etwas Zucker?* [some sugar?] are reminders that the thesis of the well-formedness of sentences was established on the basis of written language. The spoken language of the environ-ment with its deviations from the normative models, can influence the child's speech. This question will be discussed in 3.4.3 below. From what has been said, it can be seen that, using the syntax oriented Aspects model, no statements can be made which would explain the development of sentence structure at the two-word stage (see Bowerman 1973: 217–223; Schaerlaekens 1973:192f; and, on Bloom's work, see also van der Geest 1974:72–9).

For the ages three to seven years most of all, transformational developments – relations between the deep structures and surface structures of sentences – have been studied according to transformational grammar. Pioneering work has been carried out by Menyuk with cross-sectional studies of 48 English speaking children. The results of the analysis are discussed together with the results of other works, in her monographs (1969 and 1971), which also include semantic and phonological questions. Menyuk's goal is to test if the syntax model of transformational grammar can be used to describe the child's syntax at different stages of life as a self-contained system, and if developmental trends can be derived from possible structural changes. Further, it was asked to what extent the child's syntax differed from the adult's.

It appears that with increasing maturity an increasing use of transformational rules can be determined. They are more often used by older than by younger children. The age groups differ as to the use of phrase structure rules and morpho-phonemic rules. The older children – in their first school year – use passive constructions and *have*-constructions, as well as nominalization and parataxis, more frequently than younger children. According to Menyuk, the child has, by the age of four, already acquired the essential syntactic rules of the grown-up's grammar and has command of the rules of addition, deletion, substitution and permutation transformation. By this Menyuk does not mean (1969:151) that the whole syntactic development is completed even after seven years. Other studies such as Carol Chomsky's (1969), which is based on an experiment with five to ten-year-old children, state that a child hardly has command of the structures of his mother tongue before nine years or even later.

The works of Menyuk clearly show the weaknesses of studies based on Chomsky's competence model. It lacks the essential steps from spontaneous speech to competence; it emphasizes that the child acquires rules, although it does not consider *how* that happens. For this reason Menyuk's hypotheses (1969:154f) about the process of first language acquisition, which she summarizes, also have less practical and theoretical value:

1) The child acquires some rules in order to understand and produce clauses.

2) When he applies the rules of his grammar he determines the structural description of the utterance.

3) When he applies the rules of his grammar, he generates an utterance, but sometimes does not complete the sequence of rules which would generate a complete well-formed structure.

4) He learns the rules of his grammar according to the capacity for

learning which is available to him.

5) His grammar can be enlarged when his capacity for learning increases i.e, the number of rules increases when the capacity for learning is reorganized.

The works based on the transformational model, and modifications of it, concentrate mainly on the *formal* structure of the successive grammars of children (for a general view see Menyuk 1969, 1971; McNeill 1970; Brown 1973; for criticism see Bielefeld 1972; Grimm 1973; Oksaar 1971; 1975a). There are no reference points which would make it possible to explain psychological processes using such a model.[11]

What can be explained through this model? When one knows that the child hears and uses ordinary language in concrete interactional situations – therefore in context – and one knows that the transformational model analyzes single sentences, it can be stated that the results of an analysis using this model, which considers neither the linguistic text, context, nor the pragmatic situational context, are not very meaningful. Chomsky's competence model has, as Campbell & Wales state, left out the most important aspect of competence – 'the ability to produce and understand utterances which are not so much grammatical but more appropriate to the context in which they are made' (1970:247).

The critics mention further that the child's knowledge of the rules of transformational grammar cannot be established (see Kaper 1968). There is still no agreement, as Ervin-Tripp (1966:78) states, as to what criteria are relevant for the evaluation of the productive use of the transformations. How can we know if the child, with his sentence, actually has command of the mechanism of sentence formation? Compare to this the discussion on the question of imitation in 3.6.4 below.

2.2.2.2 SEMANTICS ORIENTED MODELS

Since a semantic component was introduced in the Aspects model, there has been a lively discussion in the relevant literature concerning the relation between syntax and semantics. The more developed models of transformational grammar have in common that the priority of syntax over semantics has been abandoned. This has also had implications for language acquisition research.

The most far-reaching change is the development of generative semantics, as the counterpart of interpretive semantics. Generative semantics considers the assumption of a deep structure as unnecessary, and considers the 'labelled trees', which are generated from the base and to which the transformational rules are applied, as semantic representations. The transformations here have the function of supplying the surface structure with meaning (see McCawley 1968; Lakoff 1971). Several questions such as that of focus, presupposition and pronominalization make it clear that the relation between syntax and semantics is much more complicated than the above mentioned models demonstrate.

The semantic orientation of this development causes the so-called deep structure[12] to become increasingly abstract. After many earlier categories were ascribed to the surface structure, the supporters of generative semantics incorporated into deep structure the categories of logical predicates. In other theories, for example case grammar, new elements appear in the deep structure – cases – which specify the particular relations of the verb to other parts of the sentence (nominal phrases). A clause consists of a modality and a proposition. S → M + P. P is 'a tenseless set of relationships involving verbs and nouns'. The proposition is enlarged to a verb and one or more case categories (Fillmore 1968). The categories of the deep structure, which Fillmore regarded as universal – agent, dative, factitive, instrumental, local, objective, and in an enlarged model (1971) agent, experiencer, instrument, object, source, local, time, causal – obtain their case frame through the verb. The verb *kommen* [come] appears, for example, in the frame [—— A], *machen* [make] in [—— O, A] (see Oksaar 1976b:46f for an enlarged model with an interpretation structure consisting of 14 elements of reference).

The model of generative semantics has been used for the analysis of the two-word stage by Antinucci & Parisi (1973), while Brown (1973:214–26), using material from three children, has discussed the model of case grammar. Bowerman (1973:197–211) gives a detailed description of the approach of case grammar, and demonstrates, through her Finnish material and through a comparison with data from American English, Luo and Samoan, that this approach is preferable to that of transformational grammar.

The following points are considered to be the advantages of case grammar in comparison with transformational grammar:

1) the deep structure differentiation between subject and predicate can be eliminated. The child's speech behaviour does not give any clue indicating that this abstract linguistic knowledge is existent.

2) The approach allows the same formal explanation, not only for the absence of the locative ending in the language of the Finnish child,

but also for the missing preposition in the utterances of the American child Kendall, such as *Kendall water*, and is more suitable for comparisons.

3) Unlike transformational grammar, case grammar allows a description of deep structure in unordered sets. Therefore, it is possible to set up a sort of 'universal grammar' for the first stage , in which the common knowledge of different children can be demonstrated.

Bowerman (1973:211f) regards as a disadvantage of case grammar the fact that certain deep cases, such as dative – 'the animate being affected by the state or action identified by the verb' – or the objective case – 'anything representable by a noun whose role in the state or action named by the verb depends on the meaning of the verb itself' – are too abstract or semantically empty to be useful for the description of the child's language. Fillmore's dative in the substantive + substantive combination functions almost exclusively as possessor in the genitive, also in my Estonian material: for example *Papa auto* [papa's auto]. Difficulties also arise in the description of the modality components, which include (taking intonation into consideration) negation, question and tense, and concern the whole clause, because in this early stage and also in three- and four-word sentences, it is not clauses which are negated, but rather single substantives or verbs. The basic differentiation between modality and proposition, as well as between subject and predicate in transformational grammar, seems to be inappropriate for the language of the child in the early stages.

It also becomes clear with this model that – because it is a model for adult language – in spite of, or because of its relative differentiation, it cannot explain the child's competence. The semantic function of a substantive in the two- or three-word sentence stage in sentences such as *Auto fahren* [drive car] and *Papa Flugzeug fliegen* [Daddy fly aeroplane] can be determined if at all, only through extra-linguistic information: are *auto*, [car] and *Flugzeug* [aeroplane], I (instrumental) or O (objective)? Park (1974:146f) discusses this question in detail in his case study and emphasizes that, in practice, it is not clear if the child makes a distinction between instrumental and objective and if he can in this developmental stage (circa 26 months) distinguish between the two semantic functions of the verb *fliegen* [fly] – *etwas fliegen steurn* [fly something, pilot] and *sich im Flugzeug fortbewegen* [to fly by aeroplane].

When the child says *Auto fahren* [drive car] and points at a picture in which there is a child in a car, or uses *Auto fahren* [drive car] for the situation in which he is pushing his toy car and there is a doll in it, according to the adult grammar, it can only mean that *Auto* [car] occurs with the verb *fahren* [drive] in the frame [—— A (I) (O)], and is either I or O. However, one must know whether the child is the driver, in which case *car* is objective, or if he is a passenger, in which case it is instrumental. The most difficult question is whether the child makes these distinctions in the same way as case grammar, or if he makes them at all.

Among the semantics oriented models, Schlesinger's (1971a; 1971b), which has become famous as a production model, should be mentioned. He starts from the assumption that the intention of the speaker is to express semantic relations. The aspects of the speaker's intention, which are represented in the linguistic output, are represented as Input-Markers (I-markers). The I-markers represent all of the semantic information; they include both the ideas and the relations between them. The ideas are realized through words; the relations through grammatical means, such as word order and inflexion. The I-marker is hierarchically arranged. The sentence *John catches the red ball* has the following relations in the I-marker (Schlesinger 1971:88):

a	relates to	b	Notation
red	is attribute of	*ball*	Att (a, b)
the	determines	[*red ball*]	Det (a, b)
[*the* [*red ball*]]	is object of	*catches*	Ob (a, b)
John	is agent of	[*catches* [*the* [*red ball*]]]	Ag (a, b)

Formally, the I-marker can be represented as Ag (John [Ob([Det (the [Att (red, ball)])], catches)]), whereby, Ag, Ob, Det and Att characterize the relations. The parentheses distinguish the ideas between which a relation exists.

The realization rules, i.e. position rules and categorical rules, give every element a position in the I-marker and determine its grammatical category. There are four rules for the clause *John catches the red ball*: attribution, determination, object and agent. It is important to mention that in this model the prelinguistic semantic relations are carried directly into the surface structure of clauses, without a deep structure.

How then does the child acquire the realization rules? For Schlesinger (1971a:85) position has a very important role, due to the specific characteristics of his English data. He emphasizes that when A is the object of B, the English speaking child must learn that the corresponding words, *a* and *b* must come in the sequence *a + b*. Before the child learns the realization rules, he is familiar with concepts such as 'agent' and 'object' and learns that the word which represents the agent is in the first position in the clause.

Based on his data from English speakers at the two-word stage, Schlesinger (1971b:73–81) sets up eight semantic relations. The following table gives a view of these relations according to the position rules, with examples of two-word clauses:

Semantic relation	Position rules	Examples
agent, action	agent + action	*Bambi go*
action, object	action + object	*see sock*
agent, object	agent + object	*Eve lunch* [Eve is having lunch]
modifier, head	modifier + head	*big boat*
negation, x	negation + x	*no water*
x, dative	x + dative	*throw Daddy* [throw it to Daddy]
introducer, x	introducer + x	*it ball*
x, locative	x + locative	*baby highchair* [baby is in the highchair]

Word order has a central position in the designation of semantic relations in this model, whose task according to Schlesinger (1971a:84) consists of deriving from the pair meaning–utterance a set of rules which show how meaning and utterance are connected. It makes it possible to determine semantic differences in identical surface structures. Because it is based on data from the two-word stage, its range is of course limited (for a type with 12 relations see Brown 1973:214).

The model has only limited application in other languages, for example German, at the two-word stage. Park (1974:68f) discusses some cases which cannot be explained by it. For example:
1) *auch Mama*, *auch Papa* [Mommy too, Daddy too] which do not fit because *auch* [too] is not a modifier
2) the negation in *Nein Häschen* [no Bunny] can be explained by the model, but not that in *Nein Auto* [no car] because *nein* [no] here negates a preceding utterance: *Nein. Das ist nicht ein Auto.* [No. That is not a car.]
Park (1974:71) does not find any fixed position rules in his German data – all semantic relations are uttered in two different ways: *ab* and

ba (for a discussion of Schlesinger's model see also Brown 1973: 212–17, and Schaerlaekens 1973:186f, in whose model the semantic relations have a certain correspondence with the realization rules of Schlesinger).

Our discussions of these models have shown that none of those discussed here are sufficient to describe the child's early speech development. This can be traced to the fact that, among other things, they have their origin in adult language and that they are sentence, and not text oriented. Text linguistic approaches,[13] which include communication with the child in their analysis, could be productive here. However, the sentence models are worth developing, especially the semantically oriented ones. Chafe's (1970) semantic model regards surface structures as a product of post-semantic processes, which operate on semantic configurations. This model, which has not been discussed here, could also be tested for language acquisition questions (see also Olson's 1970 cognitive semantic model).

2.2.3 FUNCTIONAL APPROACH
Models in which the function of language, rather than its structure, is in the foreground promise to be useful for language acquisition research. In the second chapter of his book Halliday (1975:19f) develops a functional model for language development in the period 6–18 months, using data collected from the observation of his son. He regards the following functions as primary:
1) the instrumental function, which serves to satisfy the material needs of the child, and is the 'I want' function of language
2) the regulatory function, which serves to control the behaviour of others, the 'Do as I tell you' function
3) the interactional function, the 'Me and you' function of language, in which the child also articulates proper names, such as *Mummy* and *Daddy*, in order to interact with the reference person
4) the personal function, which is the 'Here I come' function of language, expressing the child's personality
5) the heuristic function; in this 'Tell me why' function of language the child manifests at an early stage the need for names, this allows him to categorize the objects of the physical world
6) the imaginative function; through this 'Let's pretend' function of language the child creates his own environment.

In a later stage, from 22 months onwards, Halliday establishes the informative function, the 'I've got something to tell you' function of language. All the functions develop through generalization and abstraction in the larger components of the adult semiotic. 'All those utterances which we identify as language can be interpreted in the light of some such set of functions as these.' (Halliday 1975:21)

Even though one can question whether the early utterances of the child serve only a single function and if one should not, instead, proceed hypothetically from a functional hierarchy in the sense of Jakobson (1960), the functional approach promises to offer better possibilities for the interpretation of the infant's language than any other model. Using empirical material, Weir (1962) established several functions of language at a later stage of language development (see above 1.2.4). The six functions of Halliday have a lot in common with those of Jakobson (1960:355f).

2.2.4 HOLISTIC MODELS

Among the linguistic models which should be studied for their usefulness for language acquisition research, if necessary after modification and further development, tagmemics and stratificational grammar should be mentioned.

Tagmemics, which has its origins, above all in Pike (1967), is the most detailed attempt so far to describe language as a part of the whole behavior of human beings. Among modern grammatical theories, except for stratificational grammar, it is the only one which can be applied to units larger than a sentence. The name *tagmemic* comes from one of its basic principles: the *tagmeme*, which is a functional grammatical unit, that is, it should link function to structure. It is a slot–class correlative, which can appear on all grammatical levels, from morpheme to levels beyond the sentence, e.g. paragraph and discourse. The tagmeme gets its form, as the morphemic sequence, at the level in which its function is fixed. For example, a tagmeme can be manifested in a simple sentence by the symbols S:N, i.e. here, function and form are combined in a *slot–filler* unit, which means the noun has the function of subject.

Tagmemics is characterized by the *etic* (concerning external criteria), and *emic* (concerning functional data) aspects, under which all linguistic phenomena are examined, and furthermore, by three modes, which concern all the emic units: *Feature mode*, including distinctive characteristica; *Manifestation mode*, including the concrete realization of observed facts; and *Distribution mode*, including the relation within structures larger than functional language components. In this way the important unit of *syntagmeme* (=emic construction of tagmemes) is distinguished from other structuralistic concepts. The hierarchical arrangement of tagmeme and syntagmeme produces a matrix, which describes language as structure. The distinction between feature mode and manifestation mode corresponds more or less to the distinction between deep structure and surface structure.

In the tagmemic model, which works with an interdependent syntagmatic–paradigmatic system, syntax and semantic are separated. This theory, which is constantly being developed, can be interpreted in a narrow sense as a theory of morpho-syntax; in a broader sense however, it is a theory which purports to describe human behaviour patterns (the largest unit is 'the composite verbal–nonverbal behavioreme'), whereby, the three hierarchies phonology, grammar and lexicon are adopted for the language system. Pike emphasizes that:

> . . . language is behavior, i.e. a phase of human activity, which must not be treated in essence as structurally divorced from the structure of nonverbal activity. The activity of man constitutes a structural whole, in such a way that it cannot be subdivided into neat 'parts' or 'levels' or 'compartments' with language in a behavioral compartment insulated in character, content, and organization from other behavior. Vocal and nonverbal activity is a unified whole. (1967:26)

Hence, the correlation slot–filler is also used as a descriptional element for nonverbal behavior patterns. This model is meant for synchronic description, it is strictly based on the observation of external data and has been tested in the description of numerous unwritten languages.

It is of great interest to note that the tagmeme matrix of Pike (1964), which operates with situational and grammatical roles – subject as actor, subject as goal etc. – already includes the deep structure cases described by Fillmore (1968). There is also considerable correspondence of terminology: the terms *actor*, *place*, *goal* in Pike correspond in Fillmore to *agentive*, *locative*, *goal*. However in Pike, these concepts are systematically incorporated in a larger context. Also, because this model considers both situational and grammatical roles, it can give a direction for the description of the many stages of children's language (see Oksaar 1972b on tagmemics, and for further references).

Lamb's stratificational grammar which in its basic concepts shows a development of Hjelmslev's and Uldall's ideas belongs to the newer holistic linguistic theories of the mid 1960s. The most important distinctions are adopted from Hjelmslev, e.g. utterance–content and form–substance, and an enlarged strata-conception is developed. A language has at least four strata (=subsystems): sememic, lexemic, morphemic and phonemic. Meaning forms the starting point.

Lamb's goal is to explain the individual's encoding and decoding competence, language's mode of operation. He considers the system on which the characteristics of natural languages are based as a network of relations. The main task of linguists, as Lamb says, is to uncover and describe the network of relations between the strata and the subcomponents on the one hand, and between the strata on the other hand. While conventional grammar states, for example, that morphemes consist of phonemes, according to stratificational grammar, the morpheme does not consist of phonemes, but is connected with them in a relation, which is called realization. Semantics is considered the highest level and phonetics the lowest.

Stratificational grammar has paid particular attention to working out a system of representation for linguistic relations. Every relation can be described in two ways: through graphs and through algebraic formulas. It is possible to begin at any point of the system (the relation does not have a direction) and the representation can go upward to the content level or downward to the expressive level.

This model, which has been developing continuously since Lamb's *Outline of Stratificational Grammar* appeared in 1966, has the following four strata in the 1971 version: the sememic, lexemic, morphemic and phonemic. In addition to this, however, there is still a conceptual or gnostemic system, which includes the whole nonverbal and verbal knowledge of the individual. The characteristic elements of every stratum are the emic units, e.g. lexemes in the lexemic stratum, which corresponds approximately to traditional syntax. Every stratum also has a tactic, a rule complex, which specifies how the emic units are connected to one another in the stratum. The different strata are joined by realization rules.

However, this is not the place to go into details of the model; a general view of the state of research can be found in Makkai & Lockwood (1973). I have referred to this model and tagmemics not only because they are still relatively unknown in European linguistic reasearch, but also in order to draw attention to them as a basis for discussion – not as perfect patterns – for models describing the language of preschool children. Lamb has, in the 1971 version, described his stratificational theory as cognitive linguistics and has tried to expand it with the object of recording cognitive structures. The same network procedure which is used for linguistic structure, could also be applied to cognitive structures (see Lamb's 'Linguistic and Cognitive Networks' in Makkai & Lockwood 1973). The model is not restricted to the sentence as the unit of analysis, but will also describe larger texts. To what extent this goal of describing the verbal processes is achieved will depend on further developments. Halliday (1975:7) emphasizes that the terminology can be applied to the description of early language development.

As discussed in 2.1 above, it is necessary to include pragmatic and socio-cultural aspects in the field of research in order to understand the language acquisition process. This cannot be observed in isolation from the whole actional and communicative behavior of the child, of which verbalization is only a part. But, even when language is seen from a perspective which incorporates it into communicative be-haviour, it is still necessary to establish pertinent models for linguistic description and analysis. Language is acquired in a social environment and in social interaction. The sciences which are active in these areas – above all, sociology and psychology – must, as we have already emphasized, be encouraged into interdisciplinary cooperation. By interdisciplinary is meant here, with Piaget (1972c:136), research which leads to a real interaction among different disciplines or the heterogeneous sections of one science, and to a certain reciprocity, which contributes to a mutual enrichment. This implies, however, that formation of paedolinguistic theory must incorporate components which language acquisition research has, until now, overlooked (see below 2.4 and 2.5).

Experience has, as Schlesinger (1972) states, shown that it is of no use to write individual grammars for individual children: 'There is no way of evaluating a grammar constructed for an individual child on the basis of the corpus obtained from him: for one and the same corpus different grammars might be appropriate.'

As we have seen above, the reach of linguistic models was tested with the aid of evidence from different stages of the child's develop-ment, for example from Bloom (1970), Bowerman (1973) and Park (1974). For an explanation of language acquisition which includes the *how*, these schematic explanations are not sufficient. For that purpose one needs an analysis which shows how one stage develops from another. This presupposes a language acquisition theory which is still not available, although attempts have been made to create one (see Schlesinger 1972). However, for such a theory, it is important to differentiate clearly between adult language, which always represents a whole community, and child language. Data from a two- or three-year-old child cannot be traced to a language system as can data from adults. Since the goal of language acquisition is to learn adult language, the data from children must be designed in such a way that it can help determine the dynamics of development and allow for the formation of hypotheses about the process of the changes. This leads us to the question of the autonomy of child language. These questions, together with nonverbal behaviour, are problem areas which have been neglected until now.

2.2.5 AUTONOMY OF CHILD LANGUAGE

In answering some of the central questions of paedolinguistics such as: what means and strategies are used by the child in order to use language as an effective means of communication?, more arguments can be found in addition to those mentioned in 2.2.2.2 above, to contradict the methods of constructing grammars of child language used up to now.

They are almost always based upon categories of adult language with the result that, at the metalevel of description, units must be used which are not suitable to the object level.

It is self-evident that the language system used by adults is taken as the measure and goal of child language acquisition. However it is not at all a matter of course that in almost all of the major studies, the child's utterances are judged according to the grammar of the adult written language.

Methodologically it is not correct to judge the inventory and the competence of the child against adult models. An analysis of the child's *spoken* language with the apparatus of the *written* adult language runs the risk of disguising the proper relations, rather than elucidating them (see Oksaar 1971:336f; 1975a:726). Since there is still neither a grammar of spoken language nor a performance grammar for any larger language community, the discrepancy is even greater, and this must be considered by the scientist. The features which child language has in common with the spoken language of adults cannot be clearly distinguished by such a procedure, no more than the peculiarities of child language.

As is well known, the spoken language in many communities deviates from the written language – ellipses, discontinuities and anacolutha are frequently found. It is also known that in the spoken language of many communities words which are important in the situation can be placed at the beginning of a sentence. Until we have a systematic investigation of the spoken language in most languages we must be very careful in making normative comparisons between adult and child language. The deviations from the norm of written language

51

made by older children cannot all be seen as errors, nor those by children in a multi-lingual environment as interference from another language.

That does not mean, however, that one could use a grammar of the spoken language of adults as a basis for child language, although there is no doubt that the child is influenced by the spoken language of the adults in his environment. One should rather ask how the system of the child's language at a certain point is formed and how it changes. At every stage in its development, we must proceed from the independence of child language, without losing sight of the goal of the development. Since, unlike the spoken and written language of adults, the language of preschool children, as already mentioned above (page 4), is characterized by a continuous dynamic, not only in the period of linguistic ontogeny, but also in the period of the primary expansion stage.

From these facts it can be seen that communicative situations must be included in the description of this language and that one must, on a larger scale than for adults, connect this with the study of the child's whole behavior.

2.3 DATA COLLECTION

Since the result of any investigation depends not only upon the linguistic model and its underlying premises, but, above all, upon the reliability of the data, the procedure of collecting the data – visual, acoustic or other – is considered from the start as one of the most important and complicated methodical steps. It is surprising, that there is no basic discussion of this matter in language acquisition research, much less of the problem of which of nonverbal behavior observations should be procured. Undoubtedly, a synthesis between data collecting in natural or spontaneous situations and the use of experimental method in spontaneous and elicited situations, e.g. in a research room is important, even necessary, for some questions, but this synthesis is often sacrificed in favour of one direction or another.

Although the data, as in every empirical scientific study, depends on the problem, its constant examination is necessary in order to determine if a revision or a rejection of the problem is required (Blumer 1968). Special emphasis must be put, therefore, on the proposition of the problem, the choice of the total quantity, the method of observation and the collecting of the data.

If one wants to investigate language acquisition, for example, the development of language in one child or in a group of children, then, continuous systematic observation is the ideal way to determine the sequence of development. Although continuous systematic observation covering a certain time is very difficult to carry out, the corpus must if possible be collected continuously, and also different aspects in various situations and at different times of the day must be covered for several successive hours.

Half-hour tape recordings once a week such as Bowerman (1973:16) made, or even more seldom, two hours every 14 days, as in works from the group of Brown (1973:51f), raise the question of how much weight this material can actually have in the development of child language research, particularly since they are not longitudinal studies covering several years. Also, one can hardly regard it as representative, when there is such a large space of time between the recording sessions such as the six weeks in Bloom's study (1970:15), with about eight hours of tape made in the course of three or four days; moreover, the total time of her data collection covers only six months. We should also ask what can be achieved through seven hours of recording every 28 days within a 16 month period, particularly when the material is not collected for a statistical survey on certain points, but for a grammar of language development, as Schaerlaekens did (1973:25).

Longitudinal studies are necessary; they must, however, be made at the shortest possible intervals in order to be valid for a larger group. Since in the language acquisition process it is a matter of a dynamic with (+) and (−) features, a form, a lexeme, can be correctly applied in condition A, but not the day after when condition B appears. After a few days, condition A can return, as is shown in my Estonian, Swedish and German material. Observations of a child in natural situations, which are made only once a week, either do not record these dynamic synchronic phenomena at all, or record the same situation as before and can lead to the wrong conclusion about the stability of the acquisitions. The structure of the periodicity of development, which was emphasized by Stern (1967:115), cannot be covered in all its details by such a procedure (see below 4.3.1).

It has been shown that the greatest possible density of observations, made by tape recordings, and in situations where it is possible, by video tapes or film, as well as sketches of the situational context, should be combined with a breadth of situations. Apart from several play situations and picture book activities, the collection of data is, above all, productive in two types of situations:

53

1) dialogue situations, in which it is necessary to distinguish whether the interactive partners are adults or children at different stages of life, and how they are related to each other.
2) in monologue situations when the child is alone, while playing (role playing yields dialogue situations) and before going to sleep.

In these situations the poetic and metalinguistic functions (Jakobson 1960:357) of language may come to light more clearly than in situations where other people are present. In such situations, the referential, expressive and appelative functions in the sense of Bühler dominate (see below 3.5.1.1). In these two types of situation the planning of the observation should also be adapted to the problem in question, not just to the medium. Interactions between children younger than 2:6 years show that children should be observed without their being aware of it, because the presence of an adult, even after a period of adjustment, leads to attempts to establish contact (Schloon 1976:6). Also in monologue situations the child must not notice that he is being observed.

If tape recordings, for various reasons, are not possible, perhaps because they have an inhibiting or distracting effect and could, consequently, influence the behavior of the child, notes should be taken by several observers. Even so it must be considered that the data is only useful for a limited range of problems and, for example, not for phonetic questions. The quality of notes taken directly in phonetic writing even by a skilful phonetician, must also be questioned especially from younger children (see Truby 1976:94). Moreover, many difficulties arise in the reproduction of dialogues and various interactions (which are also numerous in tape recording). Besides, there is no possibility of verifying the interpretation of the data by returning to the original situation. Also for other linguistic levels, recordings which cannot be verified are disadvantageous: the adult receives what he hears through his linguistic competence and he is frequently unsure of what form he has heard: a form which corresponds or one which deviates from his language system. Languages rich in inflexions such as Finnish and Estonian cause many problems here.

With video and film recordings, a reduction of the visual field must be taken into account, and therefore the superiority of human eyes cannot be dispensed with in many situations (Costello 1973). On the other hand, a film cutting projector, coupled with a tape recorder, permits the isolation of micro-behavior to 1/40 sec.

The data collection should also be combined with a lot of background information about the child's experience and knowledge.

More than 70 years ago Stern & Stern (1907) in their introduction to the observation of language development, pointed out methodological questions which could be of interest to modern observers of child language, among other things, concerning continual observation, environmental influences, and spot-check experiments. They mentioned that 'the optical fixation of the child's expressional gestures and sign-language' are very important factors in communication. Now, we will turn our attention to the question of this nonverbal behavior.

2.4   NONVERBAL AND PARALINGUISTIC BEHAVIOR

Since the beginning of child language research, it has been stated again and again that the child understands gestures and other types of contacts earlier than words. When a mother approaches a child lying in a pram with her arms open and with little lifting gestures, the child sits up expectantly and reaches out to her – completely regardless as to whether the mother says: *come on* or *go away* or *viens* or *non bébé*, or if she does not say anything (Stern & Stern 1928:167).

The child himself uses gestures as a way of expression and communication and connects them with arbitrary vocalizations. A baby at the age of six months stretches his arms to his parents – and is picked up. When the child wants something he stretches out his arms for it, etc. (see Wundt 1911:309f; Stern & Stern 1928:166f; McCarthy 1954:523f; Church 1961; Bruner 1975:8f).

The child also reacts to vocal behavior, to voice quality, such as loudness and pitch and, as we saw on page 25, gives information through these means. Escalona (1973) states that the child, in his first month of life, already reacts to the presence of others by looking at them, smiling or vocalizing.

Human communication develops not only through verbal forms, but also through nonverbal ones, of which gestures and facial expressions may be independent vehicles of information, but may frequently occur together with verbal ones and form a functional whole, which is known as speaker synchrony. The paralinguistic components such as voice quality, intonation, tempo and rhythm are always directly connected with the verbal signs.

As Malinowski stated:

> . . . the integral role of gesture in speech is quite important for our understanding of an utterance as the one or two significant movements or indications which actually replace an uttered word. (1935:26)

In communicative acts the speaker and listener may adapt mutually in their body movements, which forms an interactional synchrony. Kendon (1970) also demonstrated this with interactants who could not see each other; the listener also adapts his movements to the speech of the speaker. Trevarthen et al. (1975) mentioned that a three-week-old baby could already adapt to the rhythm of the environmental language. Condon & Sander (1974) found that there is already an adaptation of the body motions to adult language in babies who are one or two days old, in the same way as adults.

Therefore, it is also methodologically important to observe children's nonverbal expressions, which belong to communication in the same way as verbal expressions. The investigation of child language in the post-war period has almost completely neglected these aspects; only four of the 79 (=5%) registered lectures at the Third International Child Language Symposium in London, 1975, deal with nonverbal themes. Each direct observation of the child's verbal behavior must be selected from the whole communicative behavior, in which, for semantic interpretation, paralinguistic and kinesic utterances are among the most important. Communication is conducted simultaneously on several channels, which are allocated to each of the qualities of the five senses.

Verbal language together with prosody and paralanguage which interprets the *how* of the articulatory behavior, belong to the *auditory* field: voice quality and diction ('patterned tone-of-voice aspects of human communication'). In paralanguage, Trager (1958) differentiates between:

1) Voice quality (pitch, type of control of the lips and glottis, articulatory control, etc.)
2) Uses of voice, which are subdivided into (2.1) Voice characteristics (laughing, whining, crying, sobbing, yelling, belching, wailing, etc.) (2.2) Voice qualifiers (tone intensity, tone pitch) (2.3) Voice segregators (noise made by the tongue and lips accompanying interjections, nasalizations, breathing, grunting, etc.).[14]

The *visual* field includes facial expressions and gestures which have been summed up, after Birdwhistell (1952), as *kinesics*. The visual communicational channel allows the perception of facial expressions, eye movements, body motions, interpersonal distance, etc. Primary emotions such as pleasure, surprise, fear, sadness, anger, disgust, and interest are perceived through the facial channel (see Ekman & Friesen 1969). Darwin (1872) pointed out that some primary emotional states are expressed in the face, due to the action of certain muscle groups. Wegener (1885:16f) differentiates between the 'tone or the nature of the performance' and the 'language of the eyes, the face and gesture'. The eye movements signalize to interaction partners, for example, their willingness or refusal to establish contact.

Among the other channels of communication, the tactile system has been investigated, above all, from the standpoint of communication with the visually, orally, or aurally handicapped. The importance of observations of the olfactory channel (sense of smell) for communication has hardly been investigated; the gustatory channel allows the sense of tasting.

It was already well known in classical rhetoric that body motions have an important communicative function.[15] However, the increasing interest in semiotics and communication research on one hand, and the socially conditioned variation of speech behavior on the other hand, have first activated interest in this range of the problem again, and led to the systematization of paralanguage and kinesics; first by Trager (1958) and then by Birdwhistell (1952). A detailed survey of the problems and methods of this field of research can be found in the reports and discussions of the conference on paralinguistics and kinesics in Indiana (1962, ed. by Sebeok et al. 1972), (see also for both fields Argyle 1973:92–126 and Scherer 1970; see also Crystal 1974 for paralinguistics and Birdwhistell 1970 for kinesics. Ducan jr. 1975 investigates language, paralanguage and body motions; and in Poyatos 1976 one can find a good survey of actual theoretical and methodological problems).

Kinesics, a discipline which is very important for language acquisition research as well as for spoken language, is systematized according to linguistic technique. A *kine*, the smallest element of perceptible action, is parallel to a *phone*, the smallest concrete distinctive element of sound; a *kineme*, which is a class of kines, corresponds to the *phoneme*, which is a class of phones.

From present research, it can be seen that, in children, the kinesic system of their communicative behavior can develop simultaneously with the verbalization system. Long term observations have proved that the child does not consider the kinesic elements and verbalization as redundant factors, but rather as obligatory supplements (see Raffler-Engel 1973). In interaction, kinesic elements can alternate with verbal elements mostly when those are missing. An example: Sven (1:9) sees the tape recorder moving, and asks, in Estonian, *mis see on*? [what's that?]. His mother asks a counter-question: *mis asi*? [literally: what sort of a thing is that?] The child makes two circular motions with his right forefinger (see Oksaar 1971:336; 1973:321f).

Branningan & Humphries (1972:39) state that the investigation of nonverbal behavior offers the best results up to the age of four because after this time language becomes the dominate means of communication. This statement is, above all, true for child–child interactions. Their four year research program in a kindergarten in Birmingham has shown that the verbal language of three- to four-year-old children is used a good deal in communication with adults. While playing in a group with other children, however, they only used verbal language occasionally, and they generally confined themselves to imperatives. Instead, they used gestures, facial expressions and body movements in order to integrate their activities. De Long found the most kinesic activity at the end of the utterances in kindergarten children, but only 'in the case of other directed speech. Self-directed utterances did not display this characteristic' (1974:65).

Micro-analysis of the behavior of infants and their mothers, with the aid of film and recorded data, makes possible the observation of very early interaction sequences between mother and child. They result from visual contact and gestures, as has been shown in the studies of Jaffe et al. (1973) and Bullowa (1974) among others. These questions, which are also connected with the first social reactions of the child, will be discussed in detail in 3.4.3 below. They are, however, also connected with the methodological approach resulting from the questions treated in 2.3 and 2.4, which we will turn to now.

2.5 AN INTEGRATIVE APPROACH

Based on empirical data, I would now like to summarize how important it is, in order to judge and interpret the child's linguistic behavior, to proceed from an approach that I would like to call an integrative approach (see Oksaar 1975a:737f). Such an approach should consider, aside from verbal elements, not only the perceptive, cognitive and social behavior system, but also the nonverbal factors, above all, the paralinguistic and kinesic ones such as intonation and gesture. It is of special interest to determine which type of relations could exist between the paralinguistic and kinesic behavioral units and the verbal contents. We still need many case studies which would examine this aspect of the problem and explain its causal factors. *Communicative acts* are chosen as the starting point of the integrative approach.

2.5.1 COMMUNICATIVE ACTS

I consider a *communicative act* to be the *whole frame of action* in which speech activity takes place. Communicative acts include interactions using both verbal and nonverbal means. Therefore, it is methodically important to record not only the verbal and nonverbal expressions of the child, but also those of the interactive partner. The communicative act is embedded in the situation. Among the most important elements of communicative acts are:

1) Partner/Audience; Theme/Themes. Here, of course, distinctions must be made according to the age and social variables of the partner – mother, father, other child, etc.
2) Verbal elements.
3) Paralinguistic elements.
4) Kinesic elements.
5) All affective behavior characteristics.

These characteristics belong to (3) and (4) – e.g. loud voice, raised hand – and they do not necessarily express an emotion in and of themselves. Only together with certain body movements and facial expressions do they signal anger, for example. Also proxemic elements, i.e. elements of space-related behavior, as distance – near or far – between interactive partners, are part of this; as well as the characteristics of the 'channel' (concerning proxemics see Hall 1966; Eco 1968; for other models of verbal behavior see Hymes 1962; Ervin-Tripp 1964).

Before we refer to empirical observations of the communicative act, it is necessary to offer some explanation of its basic concepts. Contrary to the speech acts of Austin (1962) and Searle (1969), it has the advantage of retaining both sender and receiver relatedness in communication, and this is also implied in the terminology; whereas the speech act is too one-sidedly sender-related. According to Searle (1969:16), the speech act is 'the production or issuance of the symbol or word or sentence', understanding and interpretation are not taken into consideration. Also the speech act is not appropriate for the analysis of language acquisition due to the fact that nonverbal units of communication have not been taken into consideration.[16] The communicative act happens first and through this the child starts producing and understanding speech acts in the sense of Searle.

Due to the fact that communicative acts do not occur in a vacuum, but in a situational context, it is important to explain in detail the term *situation* in this connection. In his situational theory Wegener (1885) had already created the basis for understanding the role of situation in the communication process. In our century, it has been developed further in the ethnographic language theory of Malinowski (1935) and in the contextual theory of meaning of Firth (1957). Wegener emphasized:

> The situation is the ground, the environment in which a fact, a thing and so forth, appears, but also, the previous time in which an action originates, i.e. the action, which we call the predicate; in the same way, the person to whom the information is addressed belongs to the situation. In the case of an oral message, the situation is not only conditioned by the words, but more normally and, on a larger scale alone through the surrounding circumstances, through the immediate preceding facts and the presence of the person with whom we speak. The situation formed by the surrounding circumstances and the presence of the person to whom we speak becomes clear to us through perception; we call it therefore, perceptional situation. (1885:21)[17]

The concept of situation of William I. Thomas, a classic in American empiric social research, whose major work was published shortly after the First World War, is of interest for paedolinguists. He considers the situation as the real unit of human experience. The concept places particular emphasis on the fact that human behavior takes place only under certain conditions and that explanatory principles must be found in the analysis of situations (Volkart 1965:47). Further, it should be emphasized that the situation is the existing values and attitudes which the individual or the group have to deal with in an interactive process, and which represents its relation for the planning of this action and the evaluation of its results (Volkart 1965:84).

We have intentionally mentioned only the most important elements of communicative acts. Of course, one can proceed with greater differentiation, although, with these variables it can already be shown that in face-to-face interaction – which is typical of preschool children – the elements in (3–5) especially belong to the primary factors which help us to understand what the child wants to say. In adult language, a stylistic norm-correct interpretation of what has been said depends on them. We will discuss a few empirical examples now:

1) The child, Kirsten (1:11) is visiting her uncle A in Hamburg. While playing, she gets her hands dirty. Uncle A, noticing this, says: *Komm, waschen wir Deine Hände!* [Come, let's wash your hands!]. Kirsten accepts without further ado: she follows him, without saying anything; once in the bathroom she reaches out her hands and says in an interjectional intonation: *Mami sauber!* [Mommy clean!]. From this

situation it can be concluded that the child develops an associational system where the new situation (her hands are dirty and are washed by somebody) is related to similar situations, which have been experienced earlier. Uncle A has not washed her hands before. The statement of the child can be interpreted as an agreement to the actor in the situation of hand washing: *Früher Mami, jetzt Onkel!* [before Mommy, now Uncle!].

If only the verbal elements in this interaction between uncle A and Kirsten are analyzed, one could interpret *Mami sauber!* [Mommy clean] as an appeal, let us say: *Ich will, dass Mami meine Hände sauber macht!* [I want Mommy to clean my hands!]. An interview shows that such an interpretation can even be considered customary. Of ten adult women, eight interpreted the present data in this way. The consideration of all essential data, therefore also (3), (4) and (5), shows that we do not have an appeal in the sense of Bühler (see in addition 3.5.1.1 below), but of his three functions of linguistic signs – reference, expression, appeal – a combination of the first two. A differentiated functional study shows, however, that in this communicative act, it can be established that the child used *Mami sauber!* [Mommy clean] in the informative function mentioned in 2.2.3 above.

2) Sven (1:6) comes to his mother and says in Estonian: *ema Nenne!* [Mommy, Nenne!] or [Mommy's Nenne!], in which he particularly emphasizes his nickname, Nenne. This utterance is an appeal and can only be interpreted as such through paralinguistic units such as intonation, voice quality and kinesic units. He wanted to sit on his mother's lap and accompanied his words, which do not express anything about his wishes, with the corresponding gestures – lifting both arms towards his mother. The meaning of the verbal elements used by infants can, as seen in this example, only be deduced within the whole scope of the behavior in a certain situation. His mother also answered using both kinesic and verbal means.

3) A further type of example might illustrate the relation between verbal and nonverbal elements in a communicative act. It also makes it possible for us to understand how the child develops certain proxemic relations in a concrete situation.

Kirsten (1:9) says *Tante malt das* (small pause) [Aunt draws that] *Onkel malt das* (all the words were spoken with the same intensity) [Uncle draws that] and while she is speaking, she points at two different pencils. Aunt *Ja* [Yes]. Sometime later, when the aunt has the pencil with which the uncle has written before in her hand, Kirsten says: *Tante haben* [Aunt has] (small pause) *Onkel malen das* [Uncle draw that] again, however, pointing to that particular pencil. Here we have a case in which the verbal and kinesic elements were applied in the same sentence sequence. The semantic relation – comitative – is expressed here with the help of *that + a kineme*. Such a case forms the pragmatic basis for the acquisition of grammatical rules: The aunt replies, indicating the pencil, *damit!* [with it!].

We have seen why it is so important to present intervening variables in the descriptive model of child language behavior, through the analysis of paralinguistic and nonverbal ways of acting in the scope of communicative acts. Other communication models, such as the one of Hymes (1962; 1967), mention the paralinguistic elements and the kinesic elements only as components of the key. The function of this linguistic component is 'to distinguish the tone, manner or spirit in which an act is done . . . The signalling of key may sometimes be a part of the message-form itself, but may be nonverbal, as a wink, gesture, attire, musical accompaniment.' (Hymes 1967:24) Wunderlich's (1970:20) model, which recalls the main factors of Hymes's representation, includes the phonetic characteristics of accompanying paralinguisitic phenomena, the structural characteristics of the non-verbal utterance forms, and the structural characteristics of the accompanying actions of speakers as elements of the utterances. However, it remains purely a list.

Let us recapitulate: Through the integrative approach with the communicative act as foundation, conditions could be provided for analyzing the utterances of the child in a context of variables which are important. Since the child learns language through interaction with reference persons, the object of investigation must not be isolated communicative acts, but should be as many continuous act sequences as possible.

2.5.2 METHODOLOGICAL OUTLOOK

Connected with the interdisciplinary perspective outlined above in 1.1 and the methodological postulates presented in this chapter, we are confronted with the following question concerning the above mentioned integrative approach. Because the field work of the paedolinguist involves everyday communicative situations, the functionalistic anthropologically oriented sociolinguistic approach in 'The Ethnography of Speaking' by Hymes (1962; 1967) (and 'The ethnography of communication' in Gumperz & Hymes 1964; 1967; 1972), which rests on the culture theory of Malinowski (1935), and Pike's model (1967) (see 2.2.4 above), offer the paedolinguist a frame of reference, which is useful for many methodological questions. In which way should sociological approaches which also deal with social behavior, above all with interaction, be drawn on?

Two more theories belong here: Mead's (1935) symbolic inter-actionalism, which has been summarized by Blumer (1968), who originated the name of this school of thought, and the phenomeno-logically oriented ethnomethodology, which originated from this tradition, as it has been developed by Schegloff, Garfinkel, Sacks and Cicourel (see their papers in *Arbeitsgruppe Bielefelder Soziologen* 1973 and Sudnow 1972) and the conversational analysis of Schegloff and Sachs (see also Cicourel 1973). All of them attempt to analyze everyday interactions based on the general knowledge of the members of a community; Schegloff and Sacks concentrate mainly on the field of conversational analysis.

It must be emphasized, however, that there is no theory of social behavior which can explain the linguistic behavior of adults, much less that between children and adults. This is also true for the philo-sophically oriented speech act theory of Austin (1962) and Searle (1969), which considers speech as a rule governed form of social behavior. The different approaches could very well be included, however, in interdisciplinary considerations but only according to the principles of creative integration, which have been mentioned in 1.1 above.

A direct acceptance of the models of symbolic interactionalism does not suit language acquisition research, because they presuppose a common symbol system, which however, the child has first to learn. Also, Mead's concept of role-taking proves to be very problematic in infants, because mutual role-taking is considered as a prerequisite to an affective and symbolic interaction. We hardly know anything about such ability in children in natural speech situations, and also, in experiments, the role[18] has to be concretely determined each time (compare this to Flavell 1974:74, who shows the beginnings of role-taking in two- and three-year-old children). Further, we can state that the important aspect of creativity in interaction has been neglected by these approaches.

In my opinion, an important task for paedolinguisitics is to examine the impetus which socio-psychological theories could give to questions of language acquisition and the methodological treatment of child language and also to work out description according to the premises handled above in 2.5. In this way, one could observe areas of linguistic and interactional reality which one cannot identify using conceptional devices adequate for adult interaction; since the child begins to speak after he has already succeeded in communicating with reference persons by other means (see 3.4.3.1.1 below) and that occurs in an area, which, according to Bruner, can be interpreted as 'joint attention and joint activity within the context of mutuality between mother and infant' (1975:1).

Future techniques of description must consider the development of the child's abilities in social interaction in their dependency on sociocultural norms of the group, according to their age – an area which has hardly been studied up to now. In order to grasp the important dimensions of social and linguistic variations, a combination of the two major approaches of sociolinguistic research – the correlational approach, represented by Labov and Bernstein, and the interactional approach whose major representatives are Hymes and Gumperz – could, on the basis of the communicative act, form a far-reaching methodological framework (see Oksaar 1973).

The combination of models is more effective than each on its own, because, although the correlational model uses exact methods and correlates a number of specific linguistic and sociological variables, its reach is restricted, owing to the fact that many relations are left unnoticed. These must be presented in detail, of course, from the paedolinguistic field of observation.

The interactional model proceeds from the observation of natural communicative situations and, by means of its emic units, which are analyzed in components such as code, participant and situation, makes it possible to identify extra-linguistic factors of linguistic variation, which are not found by the other approach. Its reach is large, but the methods it works with are not as exact. However, the above mentioned communicative act forms the centre of analysis for paedolinguistics. The mutual process of comprehension takes place here, and also the mutual adaptation, the accommodation and assimilation of speech behavior, which may lead, depending on the interlocutor, to the formation of variants even for adults (see Oksaar 1977). This adaptation also affects kinesic elements (see 2.4 above). In these interactional fields, the interdisciplinary cooperation with psychologists must be intensified, too.

Besides the methodological difficulties and the hindering effect of the theory of egocentrism, two tendencies, as Shields states, have been obstructive to this:

> One is the identification of cognitive activity almost exclusively with the development of schemes about material objects in space rather than schemes about persons acting in time. The second is the tendency to treat the social

world as a kind of extension of primary social attachment, thus concealing its cognitive and rule following nature in a fog of affect. (1976:26)

2.6 SUMMARY

The purpose of this chapter on the theoretical and methodological basis of paedolinguistics was threefold: First; to explain the theoretical and methodological basis of the current research situation. The new trend of the seventies, which leads from points emphasizing semantic forms to the investigation of still more complex fields, and which can be summed up as functional, communicative and cognitive, requires some methodological rethinking. A method concentrating on the universal nature of language development cannot consider individual differences. A great number of basic questions were discussed, among others, in connection with the criticism of the acceptance of an innate universal language mechanism, which will be also considered in 3.6.2 below. Second; it was important to discuss a series of *linguistic models* from the point of view of their applicability to paedolinguistics:
1) pivot grammars, developed from distributional analysis
2) transformational grammars, in which a differentiation between syntax and semantic oriented models was made
3) the functional approach, which does not concentrate on the structure but rather on the function of language, and finally
4) holistic models such as tagmemics and stratificational grammar.
Following that, principles of interdisciplinary work were taken up, together with the question of the metalevel of description, the problem of child language autonomy, which has been widely neglected up to now. Third; it was necessary to direct attention to other fields that have been neglected, such as the problem of *data collection* and *nonverbal behavior*. Based on empirical data, an integrative approach to judging child speech behavior was developed. This approach should consider, in addition to verbal elements, not only the perceptive, cognitive and social systems of behavior, but also paralinguistic and kinesic factors, such as intonation and gesture. Communicative acts were chosen as the starting point of this approach. *Communicative act* includes the whole frame of action in which speech activity takes place. Its single elements were discussed, and finally a methodological overview was given of research questions which still need to be investigated. In addition, we have referred to the necessity of using suggestions from the theories of social psychology in looking at problems of language acquisition, and of developing description procedures, which take

individual variations into consideration. A combination of the correlational and interactional approaches of sociolinguistics could be productive for paedolinguistics, taking the communicative act as a basis.

QUESTIONS

2.1 What 'new' aspect of child language acquisition was taken up in more recent research?

2.2 What assumption had dominated child language research, and why had it blocked other ideas?

2.2.1 What are the main principles of pivot grammar?
What criticism has been made of pivot grammar?

2.2.2 What was Chomsky's basic assumption about language acquisition in children?

2.2.2.1 How did Bloom and Menyuk apply Chomsky's transformational grammar to child language?
What difficulties do their models present?

2.2.2.2 Which grammars attempted to incorporate semantics into Chomsky's transformational grammar?
What are some of their main features?

2.2.3 How does Halliday attempt to describe child language?
Where are the difficulties in his functional approach?

2.2.4 In what way do tagmemics and stratificational grammars change the focus of language research?
How is Pike able to explain language as a part of the larger framework of human behavior?

2.2.5 Should adult language be used as a basis for describing child language acquisition? Why or why not?

2.3 What are some of the difficulties of data collecting?
What points should be taken into consideraton?

2.4 What are paralinguistic and non-verbal communication forms?
What role do they play in communication with children?
What scientific discipline deals with these aspects of communication? How is it organized?

2.5 How does the author define a communicative act? How does this definition differ from the speech act as defined by Austin and Searle?
What importance does this concept, as she defines it, have for child language research?
Theories from what science could be used for child language research?
What caution does the author make, concerning these theories, and what does she suggest?

3 Framework of Conditions for Language Acquisition

3.1 NEUROPHYSIOLOGICAL FOUNDATIONS

In the last decade, biological aspects of language acquisition have been analyzed in detail by Lenneberg in his *Biological Foundations of Language* (1967). As an introduction, he states that the actual foundation of language acquisition is still unknown for the most part, and that he considers his extensive presentation as a basis for discussion. In an earlier discussion of the problems (1964b:65–9), he lists five reasons which support the idea that certain biological peculiarities are responsible for the human ability to acquire language:
1) Verbal behavior is related to a great number of morphological and functional specializations
2) The onset of speech is an extremely regular phenomenon;
3) The ability to learn language is so deeply rooted in man that children learn it even in the face of dramatic handicaps (congenital blindness or deafness)
4) No nonhuman form has the capacity to acquire even the most primitive stages of language development
5) Every language, without exception, is based on the same universal principles of semantics, syntax, and phonology.
According to Lenneberg, the assumption that a certain brain size is a necessary prerequisite for linguistic ability is unfounded. Language is a species – specific ability of human beings.

In the present state of research, it is not possible to locate linguistic ability clearly in the human brain. Penfield & Roberts (1959:207) state:

> It is proposed . . . as a speech hypothesis, that the function of all three cortical speech areas (that is, Broca's, Wernicke's, and the supplementary motor speech area) in man are coordinated by projections of each to parts of the thalamus, and that by means of these circuits the elaboration of speech is somehow carried out.
> (cited by Lenneberg 1967:62f)

The well known hypothesis, that the main speech centre is found in the left hemisphere of the brain, and perception of space in the right, has been supported by experiments with epileptic patients, whose brains were bisected to relieve their epileptic seizures. Gazzanigas's (1970) experiments and long term neurological studies on the effect of bisected brains promise even further insights into the biological foundation of language, and the control of language exercised by the brain. Experiments with visual perception based on English revealed that patients with bisected brains could recognize and understand such words as *pencil* and *clock* with the right hemisphere, but not verbs. With the left half they could only understand verbs and nouns which were derived from verbs, such as *teller*, from *tell*, *locker*, from *lock* (see Lehmann 1974:313f; see Sperry & Gazzaniga 1967 on various experiments; Wood et al. 1971; Krashen 1973).

However, it is important that, although for a right-handed person the left hemisphere is dominant for speech, reading and mathematics, and the right hemisphere for perception of space and various gnostic functions, this dominance is not present at birth, but is acquired in the course of the first decade of life (see Leischner 1973:290). Maruszewski (1975) gives a good survey of important research results.

However, there are differences of opinion concerning the length of time during which the lateralization of functions takes place, e.g. during which the dominance of the left hemisphere is developed, which is more directly connected to language than the right half. Whereas Lenneberg (1967:152f), using various studies, sets the time limit around puberty, Geschwind (1972) mentions functional asymmetry in the brain as being present much earlier. After analyzing Lenneberg's material Krashen (1973) found that lateralization was already complete around the age of five years, although functional transfer can take place up to puberty. Dennis & Whitaker (1976) state that 'the two hemispheres are not ontogenetically equal up to the close of the first decade of life.' Gardiner (1975) conducted an EEG experiment with an eight-month-old baby of bilingual (Japanese–English) parents, who heard Japanese, English and French texts, and three different types of music. He discovered that English and Japanese lateralized in the left half, English further left than Japanese, while French did not lateralize. All three types of music lateralized in the right half. This experiment shows that evidence of cerebral lateralization of language can be found very early, and that language is processed in the brain with great differentiation.

Interdisciplinary cooperation between neurophysiologists, psychologists and linguists is necessary for research on the neurophysiological foundation of language acquisition processes and above all, its relations to brain functions. For some time, they have devoted themselves to research into various effects on the brain cortex and the resulting aphasic disorders. Jakobson (1974:209) hopes that the development of interdisciplinary neurolinguistic research into aphasic and psychotic language will reveal new perspectives, not only for a more extensive study of the brain and its functions, but also for linguistics, and research on other semiotic systems.

Experiments and observations of functions and structures of the human nervous system have not yet been able to answer the question of *how* the linguistic abilities of a newborn child develop. Among the unanswered questions are several problems, which were pointed out by Jakobson (1974:209). He emphasizes that we know almost nothing about the inner processes of communication, especially nerve reactions in connection with the input and output of distinctive features.[1] It may be hoped that further studies of intraorganic communication, particularly communication in the nervous system as a natural link between human communication on one side and communication on the cellular level on the other, will bring us closer to answering these and other open questions.[2] It would seem particularly important to study the trophic, i.e. tissue nourishing mechanisms, as well as other factors which control neural connections; this field also includes questions concerning nerve regeneration, and the plasticity of the nervous system. It is not yet clear when the various parts of the nervous system reach their highest degree of plasticity; it is assumed that some parts can only be influenced during early childhood, others up to and including puberty. It is also assumed that information processing in the brain is conditioned in many aspects by childhood experiences (Ingvar 1975:18) (concerning the structure of the human nervous system see Leischner 1973:289; Lenneberg 1967:52–71; on the anatomical prerequisites of language see Campbell 1971; Lenneberg 1967:33ff).

Among the questions which have not lost their importance are:
1) Does the ability to acquire language depend on the diversity of the brain structures, or on the brain functions, or both?
2) Can the structures and functions connected with language acquisition be isolated from cognitive functions in general? (on this point see the discussion in Menyuk 1971:37, which also poses the question whether those structures and functions are inborn or formed and developed by experience; see above p. 30 and below 3.6.2.)

Numerous experiments and observations have shown that the

biological history of language cannot be explained by comparisons to animal communication; Lenneberg summarized the question of language in the light of evolution and genetics in the following way:

> Our present capacity for language may well go back to species-specific alterations in genetic material (intracellular changes) which, however, affected certain rates and directions of growth during ontogeny (temporo-spatial gradients), producing a peculiar ontogenetic phase of an optimal confluence of abilities. (1967:265)

Even when the details of the process cannot be verified, it is generally accepted that a child, in order to understand and produce language, must have achieved the necessary organic maturity or 'readiness' (Church 1961). It has also been established that this biological readiness is diminished and delayed in infants who do not receive enough social and emotional stimulation (see below 3.4.3.1.1). These questions lead us to the complex problem of socio-psychological and cultural foundations.

3.2 SOCIO-PSYCHOLOGICAL FOUNDATIONS

One of the characteristic features of human existence is the fact that a child is born into a group in which certain linguistic and cultural behaviour patterns are valid. There is no limit to language acquisition, every child can learn every language, it can even learn several languages at once.[3] As can be seen in multilingual language acquisition, this can only take place through the social contacts of the infant; it does not happen by itself.

The role of the human environment as a socio-psychological stimulant for the development of child language has been emphasized since the beginning of child language research. In contrast, instances of so-called wolf-children, who are supposed to have been raised by animals or without any human care, and who were not able to talk are pointed out. Panconcelli-Calzia (1955:274f) included 28 cases in his analysis; the most important known cases in the Middle Ages are reported in detail in Malson et al. (1972) (see also Brown 1973; Stern & Stern 1928:293). The reliability of the various reports, even in our time, can hardly be established. According to Lenneberg:

> The only safe conclusions to be drawn from the multitude of reports is that life in dark closets, wolves' dens, forests, or sadistic parents' backyards is not conducive to good health and normal development. (1967:142)

The course of the linguistic and social development of a completely isolated individual can be seen in the case of Genie, the wild child of modern times, which is described by Curtiss et al. (1974; 1975). Genie, whose parents had isolated her from her surroundings from birth and who had heard no language, was admitted to a hospital in Los Angeles in November 1970, at the age of 13;7 years. She could neither speak nor react to language; she could not stand or chew her food. From then on her development was cared for and watched by an interdisciplinary research team. After four and a half years of emotional and linguistic attention, she learned to express her emotions, she laughed and cried, and cared for her appearance and clothes. She could use a sewing machine, ride the bus to school and play sports; she could run, jump and play basketball. Her language made great progress. In three years she had reached a stage similar to Brown's (1973) late Stage I English, which is normal for a child of two to three years. At this stage, each noun next to the verb is identified as a subject.

Among Genie's first words were the colours; very early she could differentiate between various colours, forms, and shapes, and understood size relations. In test situations she could correctly point to a 'big red circle' a 'small red circle' a 'big yellow circle' etc. It is of particular interest to note that she learned English although she was older than the pre-puberty stage, which Lenneberg (1967:142) considered the most important for first language acquisition. The language which was used with Genie at first was, according to Curtiss et al. (1974), even slower, more repetitious, clearer and simpler than baby talk (see below 3.4.3.1.2).

The role of the human environment, and human attention and care, in the development of child language has been emphasized by Panconcelli-Calzia, for the following reasons:

> So, if the functions of central and peripheral vocal organs are sensori-motorically 'normal', then the person is able to produce a voice and sounds. The human goes further, however, voice and sounds are not an end in themselves, but rather a means to an end: They serve as acoustically perceivable expressions of inner psychic processes, the spoken exchange between humans, that is, language. If children are separated very early from other humans, all causal stimulation for the formation and development of language is removed. (1955:273)

This statement should not, however, according to Panconcelli-Calzia (1955:276), lend support to the view that language is a picture of the mental development of the child and that the so-called wild children are retarded as a result of neglect. Daily experience supports the assumption that in otherwise normal children who cannot talk in spite of their relatively advanced age – children who are deaf-mutes, or mentally deaf, and who for some reason have not been treated – it can be expected that when they are removed from their previous environment, a normalization of language expressions and understanding will take place (concerning slower and abrupt language development, see Stern & Stern 1928:288f).

While it is established that a child does not learn a language without human surroundings and contact, still this statement should also indicate the child's own activity in language acquisition. The order of his acquisition is generally known: in speaking, the child is first of all a passive, that is an understanding, not-yet-speaking, member of the linguistic interactive processes of his group, then an active one (see Stern & Stern 1928:137f; Lewis 1951:105ff; Oksaar 1975a:788).

Language acquisition is promoted in communication – in which the role of the dialogue is considered very important – first between mother and child (see below 3.4.3.1.1) and at the same time is connected with visual, auditory and kinetic components. Linguistic interaction always takes place in a situational context in which certain socio-culturally conditioned behavioral patterns are also valid. The acquisition of linguistic behavioral patterns usually implies more than the acquisition of pronunciation, grammar and lexis. At the same time it is the acquisition of new behavioral patterns which are dependent on the situation and which belong to communicative competence (see below 3.5.2). For someone who has learned the German syntagm *guten Tag*, it is not only important to know in which combination it is used in various situations, e.g. *guten Tag Frau Müller*. He must primarily learn in which situation the connection can be used at all – in coming or going or in both situations, etc. The usage rules are not the same in various areas, as is well known.

This example, which is one of the greeting rituals, illustrates that the child not only finds linguistic behavioral patterns in the group, but also cultural patterns, and what is true of language is true of these: every normal child can adjust to every culture. Here, we draw on Thomas's definition of culture. Thomas (1965:21) equates culture with a way of life, for him a culture consists of the definitions of the 'situation', which have been established in the course of time by the consensus of the adults. These definitions are, as products of human life, together embodied as rules, regulations, instructions, guidelines, traditions and standardized social relationships on culture (see Church 1961).

In order to learn to understand and use the form and function of signs, the child must experience them in their communicative context. This socio-cultural foundation is particularly clear in Sapir's presentation:

> Eliminate society and there is every reason to believe that the child will learn to walk, if indeed, he survives at all. But it is just as certain that he will never learn to talk, that is, to communicate ideas according to the traditional system of a particular society. (1921:2)

However, one should not overlook the fact that there are always various social groups with specific subcultures, and that we deal with social and cultural subsystems, which can not only influence the forms of thought of the group members but also their common colloquial language. Even the question of social classes, which we touched on on p. 27, and whose influence on child language development has been emphasized by Stern & Stern (1928:291), belongs to this complex of questions. We will discuss the question of the socio-cultural framework of the language acquisition process more thoroughly in 3.4 below, but let us first turn to the problem area of language and thought.

3.3 LANGUAGE AND THOUGHT

'As a man thinks, he speaks' – 'As a man speaks, he thinks' – these opposing views, the first of which goes back to Aristotle, the second of which has gained importance with the renaissance of Wilhelm von Humboldt and the Sapir-Whorf Hypothesis[4], mirror the basis on which the discussion of language and thought is still carried on today, since 'the reciprocal relationship between the two processes of thinking and speaking is still basically an enigma to the psycholinguist' (Rieber 1975). In the discussion of the present state of research above in 2.1 we pointed out some trends and demands, which are characteristic of research on the cognitive development of children. In this chapter we will analyze certain aspects of this discussion in more detail.

The great progress in neurophysiology and the methods of treatment of speech handicaps have no doubt contributed a new impetus to research on the relationships between language and thought. About 100 years ago, supporters of the opinion that thought is not possible without language – such as the Oxford linguist Max Müller – were countered with arguments based on the behavior of aphasics and deaf mutes, from prominent psychologists such as Sir Francis Galton and

George Romanes (Rieber 1975) among others. Today, it seems that most psychologists agree in general that there are forms of thought without language, but that thought without language is limited (Lawton 1969). The Harvard psychologist Miller (1963) considers the problem in his chapter 'Words, Sets and Thought' and states: 'Thinking is never more precise than the language it uses. Even if it is, the additional precision is lost as soon as we try to communicate the thought to someone else.'

In respect of the question which is still under debate today, whether and to what extent there is a causal relationship between language use and cognitive development (Lawton 1969), it is interesting to point out that the presentations have not progressed much beyond the level of the discussions between Max Müller and Sir Francis Galton. In the linguistic sessions on 'Language and Thought' at the Ninth International Congress of Anthropological and Ethnological Sciences in Chicago in 1973, the arguments against Plato's statement that one thinks in language were: the ability of deaf mutes to think; the intentionality of language; the function of reference; the nature of speech acts; and the phenomenon of translation (Vendler). Methodological difficulties can be seen in, among other things, the fact that a description of thought requires a description of language and vice versa (Rossi-Landi). Further when we talk about thought, we must make statements about something which is non-linear, and language can only be used linearly (See Oksaar 1973:324f).

3.3.1 IMPORTANT RESEARCH APPROACHES

Since its beginning, child language research, as has already been said in 1.2 above, has occupied itself with this question, with more or less enthusiasm. Since the appearance of William Stern's *Psychologie der frühen Kindheit* (Psychology of early Childhood) in 1914 the relationship between child language research and theoretical psychology has deepened. The various approaches have in common that they turn away from a sensualistic and associational psychological explanation of the mind (Stern 1967:7). The older theories had, as Stern states, regarded the beginnings of the child's mental life as the receiving of sensory perceptions and the connecting of these perceptions and their after-effects to imaginative complexes, which is possible because of association mechanisms. Stern himself is the founder of the personalism theory, which states that the independent meaningful unit of personal life forms the starting point and continuous carrier of all emotional mental development (Stern 1967:7; and see Vygotsky 1962:32 for a criticism of personalism).

In his book *Die geistige Entwicklung des Kindes* (The Mental Development of the Child) (1918), Bühler applied the psychological principles of thought of the Würzburg School to child language research. This school ascribed a certain independence to actual thought processes, and does not trace them to perception, imagination or association processes. Using empirical observations, he sees the first evident signs of intellect in the small discoveries and inventions which the child makes in his daily operations. This early 'tool thinking' is supposed to be independent of linguistic thinking and starts earlier (1930:365).

Bühler (1930:85) illustrates this by means of an experiment with his nine-to-ten-month-old child, which required problem solving: reaching for a piece of toast which was attached to a string. The toast was out of the child's reach, while the string lay within his reach, and the object was to see if the child would pull the toast to himself with the string. At the beginning of the experiment, at nine months, the child always reached directly for the toast and ignored the string, and even when he got the string in his hand, he let it go or pushed it away. Only in two trials did it seem that the connection had been grasped, and that logical solutions followed each other (the experiment was only carried out every few days.) However, by the next few times everything had been forgotten. The child first had a firm and continuous grasp of the situation toward the end of the tenth month. Then the string could be laid anywhere, for example, to the extreme left, while the toast lay to the right, or the other way around – the child always looked for the string, grabbed it and pulled the toast to himself; but only when the toast was too far away to reach directly. Bühler calls this stage, which is independent of language, 'tool thinking, that is the comprehension of mechanical connections, and the working out of mechanical means to mechanical ends, or . . . before language, the actions become *subjectively meaningful*, that is, consciously purposeful' (1930:88).

This and numerous other observations are evidence of the existence of prelinguistic thought. Stern (1967:60f), too, lists several examples of 'practical intelligence' at the age of seven to eleven months. These consist of 'meaningful new acts that are made possible by insights into the connections between means and ends'. This can also be observed in animals.[5] In animals, expressive and socially motivating forces can be established as the roots of sound expressions, emotional and mood sounds, mating calls, warning cries etc. In the same way speech is rooted in the basic expressive and social tendencies of infants. For an infant however, there is an additional motive during the period of the one-word sentence, that of *intention*, in which language is raised to something particularly human. According to Stern & Stern, all higher linguistic development first becomes possible with this step. These intentional acts, which include the signalling of what is meant, can be spoken of as intellectual achievement – sometimes primitive, sometimes more developed – and so, the advancing intellectualization and objectivization of language is introduced with the appearance of intention (1928:127;190f; 317f).

In mentioning Bühler and Stern, we wanted to point out two child psychologists who carried out pioneering work, but who are all too often overlooked in survey works. The progress of a child's speech is, for Stern, the clearest expression of the psychogenesis of the first years of life. When Vygotsky (1962) emphasizes that the most important thing which we know about the development of thought and language in children, is the fact that around the second year the development curves of thought and language coincide, and introduce a new form of behavior which is characteristic of humans, then he is right in stating that William Stern proved this earlier and better than others, in that he showed how the first consciousness of the meaning of language and the desire to conquer it awakens in the child. Stern & Stern (1928:190f) had also dealt with this question. During the period of one-word sentences (1;6–2;0) they established a transformation which has its explanation in the awakening of the consciousness of symbols and the demand for symbols. During this process, the child makes one of the most important discoveries of his life. He discovers that every object is accompanied by a sound complex which symbolizes it and which serves as a signal and message, in short, that *everything has a name*.

When a child asks for the name of various objects, according to Stern & Stern (1967:133) this should already be regarded as an intellectual achievement in a very real sense. In this he sees a growing understanding of the relationship between sign and meaning. This is something fundamentally different from simply dealing with sound forms, the visualization of objects and their associations; and the demand that every object, whatever it is, must have a name, can be regarded as a genuine, perhaps the first, general thought of the child. Language, to Bühler (1930:365), is 'the most useful tool of thought' as has already been mentioned (see Bühler 1928).

On page 15 in another context, we have already mentioned Piaget's theory of development and touched on his critics, Vygotsky and Luria, and on page 26 pointed out the efforts to integrate the models of Piaget and Vygotsky. Now, we will concern ourselves with the main tendencies of both lines of research.

Piaget, professor of psychology at the University of Geneva, occupied himself for 40 years with child research, during which in numerous publications he presented a new point of view of cognitive development, the processes of thought and memory. His earlier basic works *Le langage et la pensee chez l'enfant* (Language and Thought of the Child) (1923) and *Le Jugement et la raisonnement chez l'enfant* (Judgment and Reasoning in the Child) (1924) are, as already mentioned, concerned with the qualitative characteristics of child thought, with the basic features of child logic. Piaget (1924) traces the most characteristic features of child logic back to the egocentricism of child thought.

He considers egocentric thought to be a form of thought which stands between two fundamental forms of thought which psychoanalysis calls controlled, or intelligent thought, and uncontrolled thought, which Bleuler calls autistic thought.

Controlled thought is intelligent, conscious, and adapted to reality, and can be communicated in language. Autistic thought, on the other hand, is unconscious, not adjusted to reality and creates an imaginary reality for itself. These forms of thought, according to Piaget, differ in their origins. One is socialized, this thought is guided by the progressing adaptation of individuals to each other. The other form of thought, on the other hand, remains individual, and is not communicated.

According to Piaget, in order to understand child thought correctly it is very important that intelligence be socialized, step by step, and that it operate more and more with terms, thanks to language which connects thought to words. On the other hand, autistic thought, because it remains individual, always adheres to the pictorial imagination, bodily activity and movement itself (1924).

On the basis of empirical observations of children in preschool classes (in an institutional milieu, with ages from three to seven years) made while the children engaged in play, drawing, and other activities, Piaget differentiates between *egocentric* and *social* utterances. Egocentric sentences are not directed at anyone, the child does not care who he is talking to or even if anyone listens at all. It is not important to him to activate a listener, that is to communicate and be understood. There are three types of egocentric language: 1) repetition (echolalia) 2) monologue (thinking aloud) 3) two person monologue, or collective monologue. In the last group, the partner is considered only as a

77

'stimulus' for the child's own speech.

Socialized speech, in which the child adapts to his partner, is divided into five types: 1) adapted information 2) criticism and mockery 3) commands, demands and threats 4) questions 5) answers.

All of these categories together, except answers – all illustrated with numerous examples – make up spontaneous speech. The extent of egocentricity is established by the relation between egocentric utterances and spontaneous utterances; (see the egocentricity coefficient p. 15). It can be shown that, at the age of three to six years, about half of the spontaneous speech of children consists of egocentric utterances, at seven years about a quarter; the mean for three-year-olds was 0.51; for four-year-olds was 0.48; for five-year-olds was 0.46; for six-year-olds was 0.45; and for seven-year-olds was 0.28 (1924). These statistics are based on 12,000 utterances.

Up to a certain age, about seven, the language of a child is more egocentric than that of adults. The proportion of egocentric features in their linguistic behavior, as we have just seen, remains constant between three and six and decreases at seven years. Piaget (1924) concludes from this that children at this age think and act more egocentrically than adults, and communicate less of their intellectual thought processes than we do. Children talk much more than adults, but for themselves; adults are more silent, but their language is almost always socialized.

Even Piaget's critics do not argue that there is no egocentric language; that there is a large proportion of egocentric language has not been supported, however (see McCarthy 1954:564f; Ch. Bühler 1928; Katz & Katz 1928; Garvey & Holgan 1973; Keenan 1974; Shields 1976). Of course, this depends on the milieu in which the children are observed. Stern & Stern (1928:147f) emphasize that Piaget did not consider the social situation enough. Not only age, but also the conditions of the surroundings influence these values. They established that the findings should not be generalized outside the special milieu of the Geneva child care centre – for example in German kindergartens the egocentricity coefficient is lower, since closer social intercourse dominates play and group activities there. In a family setting the child has so much to ask for and to wish for to satisfy his practical and emotional needs that the desire to understand and to be understood, the desire for socialized conversation must play a much greater role in the very early years. Vygotsky (1962) too, belongs with the critics. As was mentioned on p. 15, in his opinion child language is social from the very beginning; in this he follows Stern & Stern. Since he, too, advocates a thesis which differs from Piaget's in respect to the relation of thought and language, we will examine his ideas in more detail later. But first let us ask how Piaget sees cognitive development. The outline of his model is based on summarizing articles (1968), from which his opinion on the question of thought and language can be derived.

This model describes intellectual development from the simplest sensori-motor activities of early childhood to the logical abstract thought of adults. For Piaget, intelligence is a special form of *adaptive* behavior, e.g. behavior which makes possible, and supports adjustment to the environment. This development takes place in four main stages, in which the transition from one stage to another is gradual, and should be regarded as a result of the coordination of internal factors (maturity) with the external (milieu) between which it is very difficult to differentiate.

All behavior is the result of two processes: *assimilation*, i.e. integration of the data from the environment in a given situation into earlier patterns; and *accommodation*, i.e. adaptation of these patterns to the present situation. Piaget (1964) emphasizes that a developmental theory must operate with the concept of balance, since all behavior is directed towards balance between internal and external factors or – more generally expressed – between assimilation and accommodation.

Assimilation and accommodation are parts of all intellectual activities, regardless of what level of development they occur at. Balance of the assimilation and accommodation processes results in new behavior patterns.

The four main stages of development are:
1) **The sensori-motor stage,** which includes the first one and a half to two years. The child develops abilities to coordinate motor and perceptual functions, and to establish causal connections between himself and his surroundings. A 10–12-month-old child only protests, for example, when his favorite object is taken from his hands; a few months later, he also protests when he is about to grasp it. A few months later, he protests when he sees that it is removed from his field of vision, etc. It is the beginning of symbolic actions which are expressed among other things, in fantasy games such as 'pretending'.
2) **The pre-operational stage** which extends approximately from the second to the sixth or seventh year of life, and is characterized by the development of organized symbolic behavior, and above all, lan-

guage. At this stage thought is egocentric, centric, static and irreversible. Egocentric thought is mirrored in the inability to take over different roles. The ability to accustom oneself to the role and situation of someone else develops as the child is more often confronted with situations in which he must consider the various standpoints of others. The importance of social interaction for cognitive development is particularly prominent here (Piaget 1964).

Concerning other characteristics of thought at this stage – centricity, stasis, irreversibility – the following is meant. The child concentrates his attention on only one striking feature of an object or action. When he sees two beakers with the same amount of water, he thinks that the taller one must contain more than the wider one, because it is so tall. He observes individual steps of a process (statically) and not the transformations included; when a pencil falls, he can only repeat the individual parts of what happened. His thought is irreversible when it cannot lead him back to the starting point: for example, he can string a series of colored balls according to a certain pattern, but can not complete the task when asked to string them in reverse order.

3) Stage of concrete operations which is reached around the age of seven and extends to 11 or 12 years. The child is not dependent on the direct situation, and operates with symbol usage directed at past, present and future situations and with reversibility.

4) Stage of formal or abstract operations which is first reached around the age of 11 or 12, and which develops into adulthood. It is characterized by the ability to think hypothetically. The various levels of reality, games, linguistic reality, and observations are finally all arranged in a hierarchy according to one single criterion: experience. This hierarchy is, in fact, possible because of the ideas of necessity and possibility which are now used in linguistic thought (Piaget 1924).

Concerning the function of language in this development Piaget considers it as accompanying thought; thought is primary to them both, 'the function of language is restricted to a deep reaching transformation of thought' (1964). Even though he in no way negates the important role language plays in the formal operations of the fourth stage, he does not regard it as decisive, nor as the only prerequisite.

Concerning the development of the last stage, newer approaches, such as those of Bever (1970) also follow Piaget's functional standpoint, according to which the child employs actions (movement) and perception as a means of interpreting and categorizing his environment.

Bruner (1966:12–32) presents the first stage as even more differentiated. He distinguishes between *enactive, iconic, symbolic* and *linguistic* systems. In the *enactive* system the child's world is represented by actions and perceptions, in the *iconic* system this already takes place by means of inactive perception. The *iconic* system is bound to visual perception, and starts around the end of the first year. Finally, the child reaches the stage at which the representation of his environment becomes *symbolic* (around two years of age). The new means, which make participation in the linguistic environment possible, are added gradually, step by step, to the concepts which were formed in the enactive and iconic processes.[6]

The exact function of language in the process of cognitive development is not quite clear in Piaget's model. This is the result of concentrating the study on behavior with material objects, instead of individuals. The model leads to a series of questions; we choose two from Lawton:

1) To what extent is it possible to achieve the higher forms of cognitive development without language, for example, in the case of deaf children?

2) Do languages or varieties of a language differ in their ability to facilitate cognitive development? (1969)

Both of these questions lead to areas in which there are not yet enough systematic studies available.

The problem of whether deaf children can develop normal cognitive achievements does not offer much hope of a final answer. In the studies of the 1950s which Lawton discusses, this ability is questioned. According to him there is no evidence to support the view that deaf children are not at a severe disadvantage in comparison to children with normal hearing in dealing with abstract propositional cognitive tasks (1969). However, this statement should be compared with the case of Helen Keller, a blind deaf mute, who even gained her Bachelor of Arts degree. The deaf could, however, achieve Piaget's stage of concrete operations. In his comprehensive study published in 1966, Furth demonstrates that there is a fundamental similarity between the thought of deaf people and that of people with normal hearing. At the same time, he establishes some effects of the missing linguistic competence, which are manifested in, for example, a certain deficiency of information about their surroundings, a smaller degree of curiosity, and less opportunity for exercising thought. However, we cannot exclude a certain connection between cognitive retardation and the particular socio-cultural situation of the deaf child.

In this connection, it is interesting to discover which operations of language can promote the cognitive development of higher stages; for example, the stage of concrete operations. In asking what part language plays in concrete thought, Piaget's third stage, Lewis (1963:178f) discovers a considerable lack of information, since it is only touched on very generally. He is justified in asking, why it should not be assumed that the monologue, which is helpful to the child in his activities at an earlier period, is not also helpful to him at the age of seven to twelve, when he thinks concretely and approaches formal thought (1963:181f).

Lewis (1963:176f) offers a series of examples of how language can promote the child's progress in concrete thought, for example in classifying objects, in multiplying – that is, according to Piaget, the ability to classify things using two or more features, for example, color and form – and further, in ranking things, and in remembering earlier situations. And he emphasizes that the cognitive force is awakened and developed by social influences, by living together and by communication with others. Language is the main factor by which these social influences are effective.

The second question mentioned above, whether language variation affects cognitive development, involves the complex problem of language and culture, and part of the socio-anthropological approach, which has been known as 'linguistic determinism' and 'the linguistic relativity principle' after Sapir and Whorf. Here, in essence, it is a question of to what extent language affects the world view of people and to what extent various languages can be considered an expression of different types of thought. This area, too, is controversial. Today, however, various empirical material is available from, for example, the area of multi-lingualism and this can help lead the discussion away from the all too often very speculative level (see below 3.3.2).

One variable in this question is the frequently mentioned role of the environment, and the influence of social structure on language and so on cognition. And so we have arrived at the other extreme – Russian psycholinguistics belongs to this viewpoint – which deviates from Piaget on major points, since thought can not be seen here as an activity isolated from reality. Now we have come to the approach to the psychology of thought of Vygotsky, mentioned earlier, who regarded child language not only as social from the beginning, but also ascribed to it a central part in the intellectual development of a child.

We will discuss the viewpoint of his school and in conclusion will return to the Sapir-Whorf hypothesis.

We have already mentioned Vygotsky's thesis that the ontogenetic development of thought and language has two very different starting points. The development of child language has a preintellectual stage, and that of thought a prespeech stage. Up to a particular time,[7] both develop independently in different ways, until both lines of development intersect at a certain point: thought becomes speech, language becomes intellectual (1962:90, 98).

Although thought and word are not connected with each other at the beginning, and the connection changes during development, according to Vygotsky (1962:119f) it is wrong to consider thought and speech as two parallel, independent forces. He demonstrates in experiments that one must proceed from a union of linguistic thought, and finds, in the meanings of words, a union of both processes which cannot be further dissected and of which it cannot be said whether it represents a phenomenon of language or a phenomenon of thought. Vygotsky (1962:5) considers not only the union of thought and speech as word meaning but also the *union of generalization and intercourse*, of communication and thought.

Vygotsky objects to Piaget's concept of the function of egocentric language, that is, that this does not exercise any useful or necessary function in child behavior, and that this points to a stage of immature child thought, which disappears in the course of further development (1962:16).

His criticism begins with Piaget's opinion of Bleuler's (1963) 'autistic thought'. From the standpoint of phylo- as well as ontogenetic development, this is not a primary mental stage of development. Much rather, according to Bleuler, the autistic function arises relatively late, and there is no biological support for the assumption that autistic thought is primary. It forms neither genetically nor structurally nor functionally the primary stage, on which all other thought forms stand (1962). In reference to Bleuler, he states that a child's autistic thought is closely bound to reality and operates almost exclusively with that which the child experiences in his environment. Vygotsky supports the thesis that egocentric language is a monologue that not only accompanies an activity, but also has a self-orienting function. In his tests, he established numerous examples of mutual connections between the child's ecocentric language and his activities. In them egocentric language has already become a means of thought, when it is a question of solving problems which arise out of a situation conflicting with behavior. The following case should illustrate this.

A child aged 5;6 is drawing a street car. The point of his pencil breaks as he is drawing a wheel. He tries to finish drawing the wheel, by pressing very hard on the paper, but without any success. He says softly: '*It's broken*' and begins another picture with water colors. This time he paints a damaged car, which is being repaired. As he paints, he talks to himself occasionally about the altered object of his drawing. From this situation Vygotsky concludes:

> The child's accidentally provoked egocentric utterance so manifestly affected his activity that it is impossible to mistake it for a mere by-product, an accompaniment not interfering with the melody. (1962:17)

Using examples from a series of experiments, with groups made up of deaf children, or children who spoke a foreign language, but in which all other situational features remained constant, Vygotsky demonstrated that egocentric language changed abruptly. The children stopped speaking or in some cases, restricted their speech considerably. Therefore, Vygotsky concluded (1962:136f) that the illusion of being understood – an important factor in every social language – should in no way be regarded as an accidental or unimportant by-product of egocentric language. The collective monologue, too, is functionally and irreversibly bound to egocentric language, as a further test series showed.[8] Beginning with social language, i.e. speaking with others, the child develops an egocentric language, which is 'a form developing out of social speech and not yet separated from it in its manifestation, though already distinct in function and structure' (1962:138).

The following diagram shows the difference between Piaget's and Vygotsky's models, according to Lawton (1969):

Piaget: Autistic speech → egocentric speech → socialized speech

Vygotsky: social origin of speech → { speech for self →
inner speech, thought external
speech →
speech for others

We should remember Piaget's thesis, that egocentric speech begins to disappear around the age of about seven years, and becomes socialized speech. How does Vygotsky see the fate of egocentric language? For him, egocentric language is a transitional process from outer to inner speech (1962:45f). In its psychological function egocentric language is an inner language for the speaker; its structure is that of an outer language. There is little consensus about what exactly is meant by 'inner language' or 'endophasie'. Vygotsky discusses various standpoints; he considers inner language to be an almost wordless language, in contrast to external language. It operates mainly with meanings. According to Vygotsky (1962:131f), the external language is the transformation of thought into words as far as its materialization and objectivization is concerned. The inner language runs from outside to inside and is an 'evaporation' of language in thoughts. When, as Piaget assumed, egocentric language decreases, its structural characteristics would have to disappear too. The comprehensibility of language for others would have to increase as it approached social language. However, the opposite is the case, according to Vygotsky. The egocentric language of a seven year old is more difficult for others to understand than that of a three year old. Egocentric language does not die out, but develops in a way which is ever more removed from external language – more abbreviated and more difficult for others to understand – to inner language (1962:134f).

Kainz (1962:213) however, demonstrates a monologue function of language (the inner appeal) as an 'action promoting support of consciousness', even in adults. Difficult activities are supported by half-spoken speech. The same can be seen in adults and children in the area of kinesics: in a situation in which it is difficult to express oneself verbally, one paces up and down, or moves about in the chair.

In his developmental model, Vygotsky prefers another direction from Piaget's model. For him, the path of a child's linguistic and mental development does not lead from the individual to a gradual socialization, but rather – since he sets his starting point in the social being of the child – from social to individual (1962:133). Using experimental studies, he divides the development of language and thought into four main stages (1962:16f):
1) The 'primitive or natural stage' which deals with pre-intellectual speech and pre-linguistic thought, mentioned on p. 16.
2) The stage of 'naive psychology'. The child acquires grammatical structures without understanding the corresponding logical operations. For example, he uses a subordinate clause beginning with 'because' correctly before he understands causal relations. Vygotsky's conclusion that a child acquires the syntax of a language earlier than the syntax of thought corresponds to that of Piaget (1924).
3) The stage of external signs and operations, which aid the child in solving a task; for example, counting on his fingers. The use of

egocentric language belongs here.

4) The stage of internalizing, by which is meant the development of the so-called logical memory of the child; the beginnings of mental arithmetic etc, and inner speech.

How do language and thought function in adults? Pointing to Bühler's results, the Würzburg school and his own observations, he states that there is a fusion of the two only in 'linguistic thought'. A large part of thought, such as the technical and tool oriented thought presented by Bühler, the area of so-called practical thought, does not belong here. On the other hand, not all aspects of speech need to be directly bound to thought, for example, when one recites a memorized poem softly to oneself, or when one uses emotionally colored 'lyrical' language (Vygotsky 1962:47f). Quite clearly experimentally based arguments appear here, too, which contradict Watson's (1924) behaviorist identity thesis, that considers thought as soundless speech and speech as audible thought.

Concerning egocentrism, in his commentary on Vygotsky's criticism, Piaget joins him on this issue:

> . . . Vygotsky suggested a new hypothesis: that egocentric speech is the starting point for the development of internal speech, which can be established in a later stage, and that this internalized language serves autistic as well as logical thought. I must agree entirely. . . . (cited by Lawton 1968:41)

Vygotsky and Stern are not the only ones, who, on the basis of their empirical results, turned against Piaget's concept of egocentrism. Studies of child dialogues and variation in child language by Weeks (1971), Berko Gleason (1973), Keenan (1974) and Shields (1976) have shown that small children can react very well in relation to the listeners (see below 3.4.3.2).

According to Church (1961) the child does not originally speak to himself, and is not involved in egocentrism when he holds a monologue. And the child is not indifferent to whom he speaks at first: he may be shy in front of strangers or he may greet them as a desired audience. Church, whose studies concentrated on the child's logical and linguistic operations by which experience is verbalized, and on the ways and possibilities with which children overcome these problems, also criticized the following concept of Piaget. Although he contradicts Chomsky's nativism,[9] Piaget retains the thesis which sees the key to development in biological maturity. This opinion blocks more serious consideration of the part which experience plays in linguistic development (Church 1961).

From what has been presented, the primary part of actual communication in the child's linguistic and cognitive development is evident. For Vygotsky cognitive development is, as we have seen, a social development, in which language takes on a central function. We would like to recall that he differentiates between internal and external language, the functions of which are different: internal language helps in thinking, external language in social communication. On this basis, Vygotsky's followers, among whom we would like to mention the neurologist and psychologist Luria, carried out various empirical observations and experiments, which have led to the further development of his theory.

Like Vygotsky, Luria regards the 'meaningful word' as the end result, in which language and thought are intertwined. In order to establish this, it is important to study the pragmatic or directive function of language as well as the syntactic and semantic one. According to Luria (1959:341), this function is demonstrated in that a word can cause a psychic function such as temporary connections in the brain, and so can guide the child's activity. In almost all of his publications he emphasizes how the child's behavior, which at first requires the help of adults and is subordinate to their directions, is later controlled by the child himself, in that the child supports himself with his language; that is how language becomes a regulator of behavior.

Is the pragmatic function of language so effective with a two-year-old child, who understands words like *fish*, *cat*, and *horse*, that it can direct the actions of the child? Luria (1959) answers this question with the following experiments. A toy fish was placed in front of a 14-month-old infant, with the instruction to hand it to the experimenter. The child did so without any difficulty. Then it was said that he should hand over the cat. The child signalled doubt in his look, began to look among the toys, found the cat, and handed it to the experimenter. From this one can conclude that the words of the adult directed the actions of the child.

In a more complicated situation and with a younger child (12–14 months) the behavior is different. The fish was placed somewhat farther away than a cat (in luminous colors) in front of the child. When he was instructed to hand over the fish he looked at the fish, but his hand stopped halfway, he picked up the cat and gave this to the experimenter. From this Luria concluded that the word *fish* called up an orientational reaction, but that the directive function of the word only remained effective until it came in conflict with the conditions of the situation. Here the word loses its directive force because the orientational reaction is elicited by a nearer, brighter, or more interesting object (1959:343). At the age of 16 to 18 months this phenomenon disappears.

In another experiment, Luria discovered another reason for the elimination of the directive function of a word. Two toys, a horse and a fish, were placed in front of a child (14–16 months), so that they were equally far from the child, and they were the same color and size. The instruction was given to hand over the fish, and the child did so. This was repeated a few times, with the same result. Then in the same tone, he was asked to hand over the horse. Although the child knew the word, he held out the fish. The directive function of the word was cancelled by the dominating impression made by the previous situations. In this experiment, however, it is possible that the child will hold out one or the other object, alternately, which makes it evident that the direct orientation to objects dominates from the beginning (1959:343).

Determining the exact role of language in mental development is accompanied by fundamental methodological difficulties, which according to Luria & Yudovich (1959) can be best avoided by studying linguistically retarded children, whose retardation cannot be traced to organic causes. Such studies are revealing because the situation of the child has not forced the necessity for the development of linguistic communication. By changing the given situation, and by creating an objective necessity for linguistic communication we can cause a rapid development of the child's linguistic abilities, and then study which changes this causes in the structure of the mental processes.

They studied a pair of five-year-old linguistically handicapped identical twins, whose retardation could be traced mainly to their social isolation, although they came from a large family (five other children were all older and normally developed). Both the boys demonstrated complex phonetic weaknesses, many sounds were not pronounced, their vocabulary consisted of a small number of seriously deformed common words, and a few autonomous words and sounds together. Their condition was described as follows:

> as a rule, they understood common language when it was directly related to them. Entirely insufficient, however, was their understanding of grammatically more complex language, particularly when it was not accompanied by explanatory actions. . . . At home, the twins passed most of their time playing together. There was nothing organized to occupy them, and normally they were left to themselves. No one ever read to them from a book or told them stories. They only listened to strangers when they noticed

that their names were said. (Luria & Yudovich 1959).

Luria & Yudovich (1959) also considered the twin situation as a hindering factor, since it did not contain any objective necessity for the further development of linguistic abilities.

By separating them and sending them to two parallel groups in kindergarten they were removed from this 'twin situation' and they had an objective motivation to use language. One of them was given extra speech therapy. Their primitive, action-bound speech receded, and after three months, both of them only had minimal pronunciation deficiencies. Their vocabulary and grammatical abilities were not far removed from those of other children of the same age. A change could be established in the function of their language use: telling and planning speech replaced action-bound speech. After this time, decided changes were also evident in their categories of play, constructive activities, and mental processes. At the beginning of the study, their play was simple and directly related to the situation, and only carried out by actions, not by linguistic means. They were, for example, unable to carry out games which had to be executed according to spoken directions, and which required role playing. They were very restricted in their intellectual operations: for example, they lacked the abilities of abstraction and generalization.

After three months, their mental structure changed too. After the children had adapted an objective linguistic system, they were able to verbalize their wishes and the goals of their actions, and the structure of their previously rather primitive, monotonous play began to change in a more constructive direction.

After ten months, progress was not only visible in this area, but it also became evident that the special language training being given to the one twin had a particular influence on his development. In all three areas, this boy, who had been more retarded, was now more advanced than his brother. In this study, Luria & Yudovich (1959) offer new evidence for understanding the transformation caused by language in the organization of the complex mental abilities of humans (for further studies by Luria and other Soviet psychologists see Lawton 1969; Hiebsch 1969; Hörmann 1976:283–308 and the literature mentioned above on p. 26). Unfortunately, Luria does not go into the details of procedure in his more important experiments. American psychologists have tried to repeat them, but without particular success. The only correspondence was that the execution of the tasks became better as the children got older. Russian psychologists, however, achieved results similar to Luria's (see Miller et al. 1970; Lawton 1969; Dale 1972:225).

The very considerable influence of linguistic ability on early child behavior seen as a result of this experiment, was questioned by Furth, in another experiment with twins. He refers to the development of identical twin girls, the children of deaf parents, who were about the same age as the Russian twins. One was deaf, one had normal hearing, but they were both emotionally and socially developed. The similarity of their behavior was so strong that, after three years during which one attended a school for the deaf and the other a normal school, they still had about the same results in tests. He draws the conclusion that normal socialization, that is, normal active contact with their environment, seems to be a more compelling explanation. For him, lack of social contact is the factor which hinders development and mental maturation in deaf children as well as children with normal hearing (1968).

Since, however, under normal circumstances these contacts are made and supported by language, Furth's statement is not without its problems. All the more so, as he himself points out, since the deaf girl communicated with other members of the family in some form of language, and further, since in an Arthur Point Scale Test[10] with four other pairs of twins, in which one twin was deaf, the deaf twin demonstrated a lag in development compared with the better hearing one.

In this chapter we have not tried to handle such an extensive area as thought and language anything like exhaustively. Rather, our goal has been to point out the most important directions and points of discussion. The discussion continues, and the fact that the obligatory chapter on 'Language and Thought', or 'Language and Cognition' in the various works on psycholinguistics and language acquisition keeps getting longer and longer contradicts Fodor's statement that 'the traditional problem of thought and language now strikes one as slightly uninteresting.' (1972:84). Fodor's (1972) criticism of Vygotsky, which was repudiated by Leont'ev & Luria (1972) shows very clearly how easily unfitting conclusions are reached, partly due to ignorance of the literature, partly due to false interpretation.[11]

The theoretical standpoints of Piaget and Vygotsky's school discussed here, can be criticized in that they do, with the exception of Luria & Yudovich (1959), neglect the purely linguistic aspects of child activity. Even in Luria & Yudovich we do not find an exact structural analysis of the child's utterances. As mentioned earlier, a systematic analysis was not central to their analysis. The whole discussion, however, showed that more clarity in the issue of thought and language can be gained if that which is directly available – the child's linguistic behavior – is recorded in detail. Not only *what* the child said in a certain situation (and whether he said anything at all) but also *how* what was said was structured; for example, such factors as word order, word formation, use of word classes, case, etc. offer a basis for functional evaluation in this area.

A more detailed consideration of language in the Piaget School can be found in the works of Sinclair (1969; 1973) in which an attempt is made to bring Piaget's model of the cognitive structures closer to linguistic structures. In Bever, who analyzes the relations, by which 'specific properties of language structure and speech behavior reflect certain general cognitive laws' (1970:279), speech behavior and speech analysis are represented from the beginning as parallel with cognitive behavior, taking the question of perception strategies into consideration.

A repetition of the experiment, such as Lawton (1969) calls for, would have to include an exact speech analysis. This must be complemented by observations in natural situations.[12] Problem solving through creative processes in real life which are activated, for example, by the need for a word, can in contrast to experimental situations be considered more realistic (see below 4.3.3).

A further area, which is almost as neglected, is the child's awareness of language. What does a child know about language? When will a child make progress 'by the due introduction of language into the processes of his concrete thinking' (Lewis 1963:189), it should be asked, what connection is there between the development of consciousness of language or metalinguistic abilities and the development of consciousness of other cognitive abilities? This question cannot yet be answered. We will return to the child's linguistic awareness in 3.3.3 below. However, we must touch on yet another metalinguistic level, for the discussion of complex thought and language in general. Here, there are still considerable difficulties.

This can be clearly seen in Furth's criticism of Werner & Kaplan (1963), which amounts to the fact that the terminology is not objectively differentiated. When the authors analyze the vehicle-referent relationship, for example, where the sound sequence is considered to be the vehicle of the symbol, one cannot discover any explanation for the relationship of thought and language because one is never sure if vehicle refers to language and referent to thought. But

Framework of Conditions for Language Acquisition

Approach	Supporter	Thesis	Explanation	Model
behavior theoretical	Watson	identity thesis (mechanical)	Thought is developed from language	Ⓓ = Ⓢ
developmental-psychological	Piaget	disparity thesis (idealistic)	Thought and speaking are developed independently at first (prelinguistic thought!), later they run together	Ⓓ / Ⓢ → [S↔D]; phase 1 (egocentric), phase 2 (social)
thought psychological	Vygotsky	convergence thesis	Thought is inner speech, speaking 'sui generis'; the lines of development are separate at first, then they cross	Ⓓ Ⓢ (crossing) → [S / D]; phase 1 (natural forms), phase 2 (social historical forms)
cultural anthropological	Sapir	interdependence thesis (relativistic)	Language is the casting form of thought	Ⓢ ↕ Ⓓ
ethno-sociological	Whorf	linguistic determinism (causalistic)	Language structures and so controls thought	Ⓢ ↑ Ⓓ
social-psychological	Bernstein	encoding thesis (functionalistic)	Speech controls thought and behavior principles	Ⓢ ⇅ Ⓓ

when vehicle refers to the symbol, in its material aspect, and referent the symbol in its meaning aspect, then the reciprocal exchanges between the vehicle and referent only exist in the definition of the terms: they refer to the same event (Furth 1966).

Furth establishes thereby that, in the psychology of thought and the psychology of language, there are many theories on the relationship between thought and language; however, it is not considered an empirically important question that the relationship of two concepts must first name objectively differentiated terms for them.

The criticism of Hörmann (1970:293), too, emphasizes that the problems of the connections between language and thought are made less clear by the circularity of the definitions of language and thought as well as by the methods used to study them.

In summary it can be said that at the present state of knowledge no definite statement can be made on the relationship between language and thought. Just how different the various theoretical approaches are, can be seen in the representation in Table 1.

3.3.2 THE SAPIR-WHORF HYPOTHESIS

The question of the relationship between language and thought was first examined from the viewpoint of cultural anthropology in the debates about the Sapir-Whorf hypothesis at the inter-disciplinary conference on the mutual relationship between language and culture in 1953 (see Hoijer 1954). The history of the idea can be traced to the hypothesis of Herder and Wilhelm von Humboldt. Von Humboldt ascribes to every language a 'Weltansicht', a world view, which exercises a decisive influence on the kind of thought and the emotional behavior of humans. In this respect, Weisgerber speaks of a 'Weltbild' (world picture) which every language transfers to its speakers, and Whorf speaks of a 'world view' (see Hoijer 1954; Weisgerber 1962a; 1962b; Whorf 1956; Gipper 1972:57ff).

Sapir[13] considers language as 'a guide to social reality'. For him, language is not only a means of reproducing experience but also defines and controls human experience 'by reason of its formal completeness and because of our unconscious projection of its implicit expectations into the field of experience'. Language is closely bound to the recognition process. It is seen as an active factor which controls and forms our way of perceiving the surrounding world. Since language systems are not alike, this perception varies for members of different language communities (see Hoijer 1954:93f).

In investigations of the language of the Hopi Indians, Sapir's pupil,

Benjamin Lee Whorf (1956) developed this theory further and formulated it more sharply in relation to the role of language in thought processes. He emphasized that members of various linguistic communities interpret reality differently because of the expressive possibilities of the grammar and lexicon of their respective languages. Their thought is controlled by their language (linguistic determinism). More than Sapir, he stressed the role of grammar in constituting a particular 'Weltbild' which deviates from that of other languages, whereby typically differing observations and evaluations are made of externally similar observations: 'users of markedly different grammars are pointed by their grammars toward different types of observations and different evaluations of externally similar acts of observation, and hence are not equivalent as observers but must arrive as somewhat different views of the world.' (linguistic relativity) (cited by Hoijer 1954:93). According to Whorf, in the Hopi language the time concept cannot be used in the plural as is the case in European languages, in which one can form *ten men* and *ten days* using the same structural pattern. *They stayed ten days* must be expressed *They left on the eleventh day* in Hopi. The manner of linguistic structuring controls the perception and thought of the Hopi Indians.

The hypotheses of linguistic determinism and linguistic relativity have been subject to manifold criticism since empirical testing has not offered any clear results (see Lenneberg 1967; Church 1961; Lawton 1969 and the discussion in Hoijer 1954:216–79). From the fact that one word refers to different objects – such as *file*: 'an orderly arrangement of papers; a container for an orderly arrangement of papers or documents, or a steel tool with a rough ridged surface, for smoothing, grinding down or cutting through something' – it cannot be assumed that they are equated in thought. When someone uses structures such as *my arm*, *my office*, it does not mean that the same relationship is being referred to (see Church 1961, who also emphasizes, that with a complete bond between language and thought it would be difficult to understand how anyone could ever express something new).

These and other arguments are in contrast to discussions such as *Die Macht des Wortes* (The Power of the Word) which the Swedish sociologist Segerstedt deals with in his book of the same title (1947), or that of Chase (1950) which appeared under the title *Tyrannei der Wörter* (Tyranny of Words). Above all, it is the lexical area and its semantic categories which can influence the perception of humans and in the lexical area it is particularly evident that the structure of the areas of meaning is not unimportant in reflecting reality – in grouping and classifying forms. When one language has a single word for a concept, as, for example, in English *grandmother*, and another language has two words, as for example, the Swedish *farmor* [father's mother] and *mormor* [mother's mother], then these languages demonstrate two ways of interpreting reality. The word *grandmother* does not make a difference between paternal and maternal relations, it contains no information on which side of the family the grandmother is related to. On the other hand, Swedish gives information on the relationship between the two generations only with finer differentiation, the general word is missing. Swedish children learn, from the very beginning, to pay attention to such social relationships, when they acquire the correct norms of word use. The same person is called *mormor* by some grandchildren, and *farmor*[14] by others.

In the field of abstracts, the word conditioning of thought is even clearer, since the non-linguistic material reality is missing. What is expressed in two words in German and Swedish, *Gewissen* and *samvete*, and *Bewusstsein* and *medvetande* [in English: conscience and consciousness] is, however, summed up in one word in French: *conscience*. What German and English express in the words *spielen* and *play* respectively, is separated into two clearly marked possibilities, *spela* and *leka* in Swedish. Thus even in more closely related European languages considerable differences can be found. There are numerous examples – one does not have to fall back on the typical examples of the various words for 'snow' in the Eskimo language or the many words for 'camel' in Arabic. Such questions of linguistic relativity cannot be dismissed as trivial or decided only on the basis of a yes/no dichotomy, but rather, the question must be asked: what are the various manners in which language conditions perception? It is necessary, as Luckmann states in his introduction to Gipper (1972), to differentiate between language structure and culturally determined language use.

An extensive presentation of discussion of the Sapir-Whorf hypothesis to date, and a test of the Hopi Indian material can be found in Gipper (1972). He establishes that there are various possible degrees of language conditioning and that every person's thought should be seen as 'relative' to the expressive possibilities of the available language system, as it can only take on form by adjusting to these conditions. This objectivation of human thought in relation to the available linguistic means does not mean, according to Gipper, that it is a question of determinism, since the human mind has the freedom 'to make unlimited use of the limited means of the available language'. However, complete independence can never be achieved, regardless of what one expresses linguistically. In this sense, one can speak of a linguistic relativity principle (1972:248).

The discussion of the hypothesis, however, has in general excluded sociolinguistic aspects, such as questions of socially significant linguistic variations and stability, neither has it sufficiently considered the influence of social structure and social change on language and the various behavior norms of its speakers. Systematic observations of the linguistic behavior of multilingual people – adults and children – must also be undertaken to test this hypothesis. At the Tenth International Congress of Anthropological and Ethnological Sciences in Chicago 1973, Einar Haugen presented an analysis of texts produced by bilingual speakers. He showed that, although radical differences in their world views could not be determined, adaptation to different linguistically and socially conditioned behavior could be seen.

In the language acquisition process, there are many examples showing that language can influence and direct behavior. Among these are all the instances in which 'etymologizing' influences child behavior. Here are a few examples taken from the Hamburg corpus. Martin (4;2) asks at supper *Warum bekomme ich Suppe? Ich muss Brot haben.* – Mother: *Wieso?* – Martin: *Es heisst doch Abendbrot.* [Martin: Why do I get soup? I should have bread. Mother: Why? Martin: But it's called Abendbrot. (This German word for the light evening meal means literally 'evening bread')]. Stephanie (4;1) takes all the handkerchiefs out of the wash and sticks them in all the various pockets in the closet. When her mother asked her why she did this, she answered: *Taschentücher müssen in die Taschen.* [Pocket-clothes (=handkerchiefs) belong in pockets.]

The questions which children ask also illuminate the connections of language perception and behavior. An example concerning interaction rules: when Sven (5;1) hears his mother say *Gesundheit* to someone sneezing, he asks: *What do you say when he coughs?* At the same time he states that in Swedish one says *Prosit* when someone sneezes.

These statements lead to our next section, and to the question of linguistic awareness in children.

3.3.3 LANGUAGE AWARENESS IN CHILDREN

What do we mean when we say that someone can speak a language? Obviously, this statement refers to knowledge as well as to a particular fluency and skill. The linguist regards this proficiency not just as mastery of rules but also as the awareness of this mastery.

The speaker's ability to think about the rules of a language and thereby judge his own language as well as the language of others has played an important part, methodologically, in the development of linguistic theory. In language acquisition research the question of what a child knows about language has not been systematically examined. The development of this metalinguistic ability has occupied only a few linguists, although the question of when a child develops a 'feeling' for grammatical and semantic structures, belongs to one of the central problems of child language research (see Oksaar 1971:342ff).

The ability to make judgements concerning different aspects of linguistic structures seems to be present relatively early in some children. In studies of two-year-old children Shipley et al. (1969) indicate the presence of rudimentary ability to judge grammaticality in American English. In response to an ungrammatical sentence, such as *Gor ronta ball!*, the child asked *Wha' Momma? Gor ronta ball?* This leads to the conclusion that the child regarded the sentence itself as the object of his attention, apart from its communicative function.

Gleitman et al. presented three children, all around the age of 30 months in different role-playing games with their mothers, with 60 short imperative sentences, which were either grammatical, such as *Bring me the ball* or contained deviant word order, such as *ball me the bring*. They were to judge whether the sentences were 'good' or 'silly'. All three found the grammatically correct sentences 'good'; the sentences with deviant word order were more often found 'silly' than 'good' (1972:144). In studies with five-year-olds they determined that the children accepted grammatically incorrect sentences, such as *John and Jim is a brother* as long as the meaning was clear. For children between five and eight years of age, the syntactic correctness alone was decisive. They rejected such sentences as *Boy is at the door* and *John and Jim is a brother* and gave correct paraphrases. In spite of individual differences, according to Gleitman et al., an adult-like ability to complete metalinguistic tasks can be determined in children over the age of five. The acquisition of this metalinguistic ability appears to coincide with the development of other metacognitive abilities, such as memory strategies, which according to Russian observations cannot be determined before the fifth year. More research is necessary in this area in order to establish the connection with Piaget's stages of development (see above p. 79).

In experiments similar to Gleitman et al., de Villiers & de Villiers (1974) determined that children at this age were aware that something was wrong with imperative sentences which had deviant word order. However, they tended to concentrate their attention on the semantic aspects of the sentences when asked to correct what was wrong.

My own observations in natural circumstances, that is, outside a test situation, confirm the assumption that children under five years old react above all to semantic irregularities, which are manifested in word choice. In Estonian it is possible – just as it is in English – to use the word 'go' for movement with a vehicle: *ma lähen lennukiga* [I am going by aeroplane]. When he heard his mother say this, Sven (3;8) corrected her, saying *Sa ei lähe, sa lendad lennukiga* [you aren't going by aeroplane you are flying with the aeroplane]. At this age Estonian, Swedish and German children appear to accept only one possible allocation of an object to an activity, which they learn in a particular situation – an aeroplane flies, a car goes, a train runs etc. The child shows by his reaction that he knows the semantic rules of congruence (see also 4.3.3 below). Chukovski (1968) provides Russian examples.

Numerous earlier observations have shown that a child around the age of three will correct word form as well as word choice in adults and other children. See Stern & Stern (1928:107) and Kaper (1959:8, 21) who also discuss further cases from which the conclusion can be drawn that phonological awareness develops at this time, too.

The language awareness of a child can be determined with relative methodological certainty in situations in which the child corrects himself. Self-correction may occur very early in some children. Pointing at his toy *apa* [monkey], Sven 18 months, said in *Estonian* in the appelative function *Ema apa* ['mother, monkey']. His mother insisted that he say *anna, ema, apa*, ['give, Mother, the monkey'], with the imperative form in the initial position. The child repeated the sentence, corrected himself at once however, and formed the sentences with the vocative in the initial position *Ema, anna apa*, which is the most usual Estonian word order. In addition, the search for the correct form of speech, which can be interpreted as such by hesitation, facial expression, and intonation, is evidence of metalinguistic abilities. Sven (4;5) who had lived in Hamburg since 3;11, spoke Estonian and Swedish at home and heard German from other children and adults as well as on the radio and television, says, in telling German acquaintances about a trip: *Wir hatten auch unser Auto mitgeneemt* [We had also taken along our car] (hesitation) *genimmt* (short pause, some of the listeners smile) *genommt* (correct form: *genommen*). The overgeneralization of the regular past participle form is evidence here of the use of a particular rule, the self-correction points to metalinguistic activities. Expressions which Sven used in his play with his teddy bear, such as *Sind sie gekommen?* (at 4;3) *Wohin sind sie sonst gereisen?* (at 4;4) point to the fact that he was also aware of irregular participles. Kaper discusses a series of examples (1959:137f).

Children who grow up to be multilingual, who correct their own interference errors, serve as evidence that linguistic awareness can also be interlingual. Sven (3;4) calls *Mina olen siin* [knɛ:nade] *pääl* . . . (short pause) *põlvede pääl* [I'm here on my knees]. He replaced the Swedish word for knee, *knäna*, to which the Estonian genitive plural ending *-de* was added with the genitive plural of the Estonian word for knee *põlv*.

A child growing up to be multilingual seems to develop a feeling for different languages relatively early. At the age of 2;4–2;10 Sven often used Estonian as well as Swedish to achieve his goals. The theme of an utterance in the appelative function, when the child wanted something and his parents did not immediately respond, was not infrequently repeated, but in another language. As already mentioned, after the age of 3;11 he also heard German daily. After just two months in Hamburg he frequently compared the pronunciation of German words. In Swedish: *Mamma säger* [fá:tər], *Helmut säger* [fá:ta] [Mother says [fá:tər] Helmut (his playmate) says [fá:ta]] (at 4;1). The following Swedish statement also indicates that the child made metalinguistic observations: *Jag säger* [ekehárt], *han alltid rättar mig* [ekehátt] [I say [ekehárt], he always corrects me [ekehátt]] (4;3). Compare this with the monolingual children in Kaper (1959:17).

Various questions aimed at linguistic elements which are asked by a child may also indicate his metalinguistic interest. At the age of four children may already be aware of the arbitrariness of signs in de Saussure's sense.[15] This is evident from questions like *Why do they call a cow a cow?* (at 3;1) which Bohn analyzed (see also Kaper 1959:90). Noticeable in multilingual children at this age are Why-questions about grammar. Sven (4;3) asked in Estonian why there is *mir* and *mich* in German but only *mig* in Swedish. In general, it seems that awareness of language variety develops around the end of the third year of life, as is evident in the works of Ronjat (1913:81) and Elwert (1960:284).

However, the point in time at which metalinguistic abilities are present cannot be clearly established on the basis of the child's questions. A child between two-and-a-half and four years of age also asks many questions to which he already knows the answer. The reason for these questions lies in his social contact with his surroundings. Lewis (1951:257) finds, that 'it is social sanction for what he already knows that satisfies him' in the use of this type of rhetorical question. He sees this as 'partly a game, the game of question-and-answer . . . and partly a tentative questioning' (1951:254). Kaper also confirms this tendency which finds expression for the child in the playful character of the questions as well as the pleasure of having something he already knows confirmed by someone else (1959:88).

Very little research has been done into the child's knowledge of socio-cultural and pragmatic rules for language use. When Kirsten (1;9) says [fí: dáŋk] when someone offers her something, this is not yet the result of her awareness of this interactive rule in the realm of courtesy. From the analysis of our corpus it can be seen that while playing with their dolls and teddy bears Estonian, Swedish and German children around the age of three years used the most common forms of greeting from the greeting rituals in their respective languages: Estonian *tere*, Swedish *goddag*, and German *guten Tag*. Demands such as the Swedish *säg goddag* ['come, say hello'] (Christina 30 months) are evidence that a certain knowledge of the interactive rules may be present. This can also be clearly seen in the above mentioned situation (p. 96), in which the child wanted to know what was said when someone coughed.

Tests for pragmatic understanding with German children aged two to five years in Hamburg showed that in respect of the polite forms – *bitte* ['please'], and *danke* ['thank you'] and the conjunctive sentences with *könnte* ['could'], and *dürfte* ['may'] – the use of *bitte* and *danke* was found to be more positive than the non-use, and therefore a certain feeling existed for polite expressions and the norms of courtesy. After they heard three teddy bears, which all looked the same, ask in different ways for an apple, the children had to decide which had asked the most nicely and which had said thank you the most politely after he had received the apple. Seven children between the ages of 2;6 and 4;1 found the indicative sentences with *bitte* and *danke* the most polite. The children considered sentences such as *Könnte ich einen Apfel bekommen?* ['May I have an apple?'] or *Ich bedanke mich* ['I thank you] only after the age of 4;3, that is, they reacted to them. Further studies in different languages and cultures are necessary. For more information on the acquisition of the pragmatic system see Bates (1976) and Halliday (1975:102f). On changes of register and partner related variation see 3.4.3.2 below.

3.4 THE SOCIO-CULTURAL SETTING

3.4.1 FUNCTIONAL CHARACTERISTICS

We pointed out above (pp. 27 and 72) that a child who is a member of a group which he has belonged to since birth is exposed not only to language behavior, but also to sociocultural behavior patterns – how to greet, how to ask for something, how to express emotion, what cannot be talked about, etc. The acquisition of these behavior patterns takes place in a socialization process which is continued from birth by means of stimulation from his surroundings. During this he learns to use language in a socially acceptable way, that is, according to the prescriptive and proscriptive norms valid for his society. This process is in no way finished for an adult, since the modes of behavior are never static due to the complex role structure in a society.

In this socio-cultural environment of the group – be it the family or a single reference person – the child is confronted with the idiolectal features of individual languages with phonetic, lexical-stylistic and syntactic peculiarities. He also hears a type of language variety known as nursery language or baby talk (see below 3.4.3.1.2). His first linguistic setting may at the same time be the family language. The term family language is made permissible by lexical as well as syntactic peculiarities found in the language of family members which identify them as members of a group, in spite of individual differences.

So, in many cases, the first linguistic environment of the child is not structured by an interregional means of communication, but rather is composed of numerous individual pieces, which may also be characterized as sociolectal and dialectal features. If this immediate linguistic environment is regarded as a microstructure and the interregional means of communication as a macrostructure, then the linguistic socialization process can be understood as a process of adapting to the conditions of the macrostructure. What Francescato (1970) considers 'the integration of the speaker in tradition' and 'the guarantee for the continuity of the language', we regard as a dynamic adaptation process, and in the analysis of this process it must not be assumed that the socio-cultural framework is fixed and static. Its dynamics are influenced by different social variables, some of which we shall discuss in the following chapters.

3.4.2   SOCIAL VARIABLES
The social variables which normally have the earliest direct influence on a newborn child are family structure and the socio-economic status of the parents. These create the milieu described above in 3.2 which provides the child with either a rich or a poor stimulus environment and sufficient or insufficient emotional attention. We will also discuss the factors of home atmosphere, playmates and sex.

3.4.2.1   STRUCTURE OF THE FAMILY
The importance of family size as one of the factors influencing a child's language development has not been clearly established. Stern & Stern regard the presence of brothers and sisters as an important factor in the speed of language development:

> The whole common milieu, activity and interests, cause the children who are born later to acquire language by playing, so to speak. In addition, the language of brothers and sisters is better adapted to children and is more accommodating to the tendency of language beginners to imitate than the language of adults. (1928:293) (translated by K. Turfler)

Stern & Stern base this on their observations of their third child who, at the age of two years, was completely able to take part in the activities of the two older children, and on Lindner's observations (1882).

On the other hand, studies carried out in the 30s, which are excellently summarized and analyzed by McCarthy (1954:586f), lead to the conclusion that children who spend more time with adults learn to talk more rapidly than children who spend their time primarily with other children. They use longer sentences and more complicated constructions with adults than with other children, and therefore, through frequent conversation with adults, have more practice in better language use (see also McCarthy 1930). This assertion is supported by McCarthy's observation (1954:589) that only children, particularly girls, were the most advanced in all aspects of language development of all the groups which she had studied. Even when it is taken into consideration that only children come predominantly from families with a higher socio-economic status, McCarthy observes that 'their linguistic superiority appears to be out of proportion to what would be expected on the basis of their age, sex, mentality and socio-economic status' (1954:589). Due to the structure of their families, only children have a better chance of coming into contact with adults than do other children, in larger families.

In his study of family milieu and intelligence in 1953 Nisbet, too, concluded that a large family may have a disadvantageous affect on language development. The language model of adults, particularly that of the mother, would have a better influence on language acquisition than that of older brothers and sisters. However, in a large family there is less possibility for direct contact between mother and child than in a small one, according to Lawton (1969).

The question of how much influence brothers and sisters have on the process of language acquisition must be thoroughly studied, taking into consideration age, sex, socio-economic status and other variables, such as place in the family (oldest, second . . . etc.) and difference of age. One can agree with Lawton (1969) when he emphasizes that the size of the family can hardly be considered the decisive factor in inferior success in learning, and that the quality as well as the quantity of the interaction must be studied.

The aforementioned studies do not, for example, take into consideration that in talking to a child a mother often uses the previously mentioned baby talk, which often differs from the common daily language in essential characteristics (see below 3.4.3.1.2). Family habits and the parents' attitude toward children and conversation may also be regarded as significant factors in language acquisition. The interaction between parents and their children should be given particular importance. Milnar (1951) found that children from various social classes in the first year of school who had an extensive vocabulary and were able to carry on a conversation all came from families where they had the opportunity to relate their experiences at family mealtimes and take part in the discussion of questions concerning the whole family. Children who demonstrated a more limited vocabulary and a more limited ability to carry on a conversation came from families which showed little interest in conversation, and in which the children frequently ate alone. Other studies confirm the assumption that talking with any older person, for example the grandmother, may have a positive influence on language acquisition. Concerning this, Britton (1970) mentions a report from the National Council of Teachers 1965, according to which an environment which encourages conversation is most advantageous at the age of two; after the age of five its importance drops off rapidly.

3.4.2.1.1 TWINS AND TRIPLETS
The language acquisition of twins and triplets is worth special attention, not only because twins and triplets assume a special place in a family, but also because they influence each other's language use, as

is indicated above all by the studies of twins. Stern & Stern (1928:294) pointed out that conditions for mutual imitation are nowhere more favorable than for twins. However, as is indicated by the unfortunately meagre research, they seem to be at a disadvantage to other children exactly because of this phenomenon. Stern & Stern (1928:294) record a pair of twins who did not begin to talk until they were nearly four years old, in spite of their having older brothers and sisters.

Day (1932) studied the language of 80 sets of twins, according to the criteria that McCarthy (1930) used for non-twin children. She found that twins lagged considerably behind other children in their language development. The average length of the answers of five-year-old twins was somewhat less than that of other three year olds. Day ascribes this difference to the special social position of twins. Their close bonds limit their opportunities and motivation to learn from one another as would be the case with an older companion.

In addition, because they are constantly together and as a rule have the same experiences, twins are able to understand one another without constant verbalization, which contributes to a delay in language acquisition. This is also demonstrated in the 'twin situation' in the study of Luria & Yudovich (1959) mentioned above on page 88. The combination of two factors: lack of stimulation from the environment and close mutual bonds with each other may also, as Jespersen (1922:185ff) points out, result in an idiom which is not understood by the surrounding world. He records the case of Danish twin boys who were fully neglected by their reference group. They were admitted to an orphanage at the age of four years and, even after some time, did not speak in the presence of others. However, they communicated with each other a lot in their own language, which deviated completely from Danish in that it was non-inflexional and had free word order, foreign sounds and various assimilations among other features. In a short time progress in Danish could be seen as a result of verbal attention from their surroundings.

This delay in language development can also be established in older twins, although it is reduced at school age when children have more opportunity for social contact. This is evident in a study by Davis (1937) which set out to test the validity of the results achieved by Day with twins, non-twins, and only children between the ages of five and ten years. She also established a relationship to the socio-economic status of the family: twins from the upper classes recovered at school more than twins from the lower classes.

Using the same parameters which Day (1932) and Davis (1937)

applied in their studies of twins, Howard (1947) conducted a study of a group of triplets and came to the conclusion that they were subject to an even greater lag in their development. The average length of the answers of five-year-old triplets was, for example, 2.98 words, a result which Day (1932) received from four-year-old twins, and McCarthy from two-and-a-half-year-old non-twins. Since there are not enough studies in this area, the results mentioned here must be considered accordingly. Schaerlaeken's study (1973) with two sets of triplets at the three-word stage does not treat the problem discussed here. McCarthy (1954:590f) discusses a study of the Dionne quintuplets in 1937 by Blatz, Fletcher and Mason. At the age of five, the quintuplets demonstrated a retardation in language development of about eighteen months.

It is evident from the studies mentioned here that not only are twins and triplets subject to special conditions, but these studies also illuminate the influence of the micro- and macro-structure of the environment on language development. One more type of influence should be mentioned here. One of a pair of twins may have an active contact with his environment, develop normally and communicate the information he receives to the other twin by non-verbal means, thereby increasing the retardation in the other's language development (see Zazzo 1960; Hörmann 1970:290; Mittler 1971).

3.4.2.2 SOCIO-ECONOMIC STATUS

The relationship between the family's socio-economic status and the child's linguistic development has been established in a series of experimental studies during the last 75 years. Even considering all the differences in detail which can be traced back to differing methods of observation and evaluation, one central uniform conclusion can be identified: that speech development in children from the lower classes lags considerably behind that of middle and upper class children.

As can be seen in McCarthy's (1954:586) survey of research, Degerando had already drawn attention to a considerable difference in 1847: 'The child of the rich understands more words and less actions, and the child of the poor less words and more actions.' The first important experimental study of milieu dependant differences in language development was carried out by Descoeudres (1921) in Geneva on 300 children between three and seven years of age. In this study upper class children demonstrated a substantial superiority in numerous vocabulary tests (103 tasks). Using this material Stern & Stern (1928:230) computed a difference of eight months in speech development: according to these calculations the level of development of a child from the lower classes corresponded to that of an upper class child around eight months younger. Charlotte Bühler (1928) established retardation in all aspects of development in children from poorer surroundings, but even here, retardation in language development was the most obvious.

Hetzer & Reindorf (1928) studied the effect of different social levels on the earliest stage of language development (0;9–2;6). They showed that children from underprivileged surroundings – 65 children in the Viennese 'Kinderübernahmestelle' [Orphanage] – were from three to six months behind in different areas of language development, and in respect to vocabulary size, as much as 9 to 12 months. Children from families of better social standing used a larger number of meaningful words, more two- and three-word sentences and demonstrated progress in syntax and morphology earlier. However, it is of great interest to note the observation that individual language performance was not evenly influenced by social surroundings.

The works of McCarthy (1930), Day (1932) and Davis (1937) which were mentioned in 3.4.2.1 above also show that children from the upper classes not only used longer sentences earlier than underprivileged children, but also used more complicated sentences and functional forms such as questions. McCarthy (1930) and Day (1932) found that this difference became greater as the children got older. This observation has also been confirmed in more recent studies. The difference increases even more at school age (see Deutsch 1965; Lawton 1969 and the literature discussed there).

In his study of phoneme frequency and type during the first two and a half years of life, Irwin (1948) points out that during the first 18 months no relationship to the status of the family can be established. After this time, that is at approximately the age when language begins to be used meaningfully, the differences between the classes become evident. The best discussion of further studies can be found in McCarthy (1954:587f). On the basis of the discussion of studies concerning language development and socio-economic status as well as her own research, she comes to the conclusion that the less favorable surroundings of children from working class families cause the difference in language acquisition.

McCarthy's view has also been confirmed by more recent studies. Templin (1957) used various tests to study the articulation and differentiation of speech sounds, as well as the sentence structure and vocabulary of 480 children between the ages of three and eight years.

She established a considerable superiority in the language use of upper class children. It is also interesting to note that the children she tested were more advanced in their use of language than children of the same age in the studies of McCarthy (1930) and Davis (1937), a fact which was demonstrated mainly by the use of more complex sentence structures.

As we have just mentioned, the relationship between social status and language behavior in school-age groups has been thoroughly treated in a series of recent studies, of which Bernstein's theory of class based language codes has caused much discussion (see Lawton 1969; Schlee 1973:16–25 and above p. 27). There have been fewer recent studies of preschool children. Although there is generally little doubt that due to the more favorable conditions of their surroundings, middle and upper class children have certain advantages when they learn a language, these 'favorable conditions' themselves have not yet been sufficiently studied.

Since, as we have just seen, appropriate linguistic models and the chance for linguistic stimulation belong to the favorable conditions for learning a language, but on the other hand these are dependent on the family's habits and the parents' attitude toward children, it would certainly be productive if future studies worked with more differentiated sociological and cultural-anthropological evaluation criteria. This is also true for studies of school-age children. As was also shown in the experimental studies of Lawton, linguistic difficulties are directly related to the question of motivation and culture in general. Lawton emphasizes that it is inappropriate to limit the problem to speech 'since language use is the transfer of culture by means of a specific social structure' (1969).

The education, not only of the father as has been customarily assumed, but rather of the father and mother, as well as the income, occupation group, mother's occupation, and leisure and vacation time habits of the family, to name just a few, belong to these differentiated variables. Lawton (1969) established in his discussion of the available research that no attempt had been made to compare subgroups of the lower and upper classes with the same level of intelligence, in order to see if a class related difference could be established between groups among whom the intelligence quotient (IQ) remained a constant. Even so the work needs to be more differentiated. Holmlund (1974:164f) showed in her study of 28 Swedish children aged eight to nine that the verbal IQ of the higher status group dominated significantly at the five per cent level of reliability above the non-verbal

IQ, while this was not the case for children from the lower status group, so these differences were due to chance.

Moreover, the type of situation in which the child speaks must be taken into consideration. Children from the middle classes speak more openly and freely in some situations, and children from the lower classes in others. A good summary of the still rather sparse studies can be found in Cazden (1970) (see also 1972:205ff, and Dale 1972:275–8). Topic of conversation, task and listeners were considered the most important variables of their situation. Also important are the results of Johnson (1974) who found considerably more limited differences between social classes and also between races in analyses of spontaneous speech, as compared to results from standardized tests. Pozner & Saltz (1974) assume that differences in communicative effectiveness can more likely be traced to a more limited vocabulary and not to inability to cope with the communication situation.

In more formal situations, such as an interview in which the speaker is observed and the attention is directed at the language, as Labov (1969) demonstrated, ghetto children tend to be very monosyllabic. In other circumstances, when friends are present and the child is allowed to speak about things which interest him, his inhibitions disappear and his speech becomes spontaneous, fluent and engaged. The important role of the situation had previously been analyzed by McCarthy (1954:594ff).

Holmlund's study (1974) confirmed the observations of Labov (1969) and Lawton (1969), Brandis & Henderson (1970) and a few others, that the linguistic differences of social classes can, to a great extent, be described as a function of the formality of the situation. A status related difference is apparent only in formal situations. Children from families with higher status demonstrated here a far higher degree of elaboration than children from families with lower status, as demonstrated in the complexity of the sentence structure. Holmlund (1974:57ff) classifies elaborateness of speech in three dimensions: degree of complexity (among others sentence length and frequency of subordinate clauses), correctness, and fragmentary expressions. In non-formal situations only very limited differences were evident: children from lower status groups used fragmentary expressions more often.

As can be seen in all of the above, not only the form but also the function of the expression of speech must be taken into consideration even more than before.

The complex question of intelligence and milieu, that is, whether a difference in surroundings has a decided effect on the development of intelligence, cannot be handled in more detail here. A good survey of the important literature can be found in Correll (1974:103–115). When children from upper socio-economic groups as a rule exhibit higher IQ scores than children from lower class families, it can be traced to better opportunities for intellectual development. At the same time, however, it can be argued that the higher IQ's of upper class children are conditioned by heredity. Correll is justified in drawing the conclusion from the numerous studies available that it is not a simple either-or question but rather a combination: 'The inheritance of the pre-disposition to intelligence as well as favorable surroundings work together to make a corresponding development of intelligence possible in the child.' (1970:110). Here, the convergence theory of Stern can be recognized (see above 3.6.3).

3.4.2.3 INSTITUTIONAL ENVIRONMENT

The influence of intellectual and emotional factors in the environment on language acquisition becomes very clear when one regards the insufficient development of small children who grow up in institutions such as orphanages or clinics; who lack normal family contact and the stimulation and security of a family. The factor of security is supposed to have an effect immediately after birth, according to recent findings. At the Paediatrics Congress in Munich in September 1976, the Swedish childrens' researcher Professor Lind emphasized that a baby only five minutes old will seek eye contact with his mother; he must be handled with great care because he is much more sensitive than has been assumed till now.

In numerous studies, the monotonous and impersonal atmosphere of institutions has been considered to be the cause of retarded development. Spitz (1945; 1965) talks about the deprivation and hospitalization syndromes, which appear as a result of the withdrawal of affective (emotional) care. Since the organism of a baby needs not only physical but also emotional care and attention, the lack of this care can cause serious mental and physical damage, and can even lead to death by marasmus, that is a general physical and mental wasting away. A good presentation of studies in the forties concerning this can be found in McCarthy (1954:584ff).

Behavioral differences begin in the very first days. In a series of studies of the daily cries of babies, Aldrich et al. determined that babies in clinics cried considerably more than babies in family surroundings. If, however, the personal attention in the clinic was raised from 0.7 to 1.9 hours per day per baby, the crying was reduced by about 51 per cent (see Aldrich et al. 1964; McCarthy 1954:584). Brodbeck & Irwin (1946) demonstrated a delay in the development of articulation, already apparent at the age of two months. Rheingold et al. (1959) established that vocalization in three-month-old babies in institutions increased when they were given reinforcement in the form of smiles, vocalization and other attention.

Speech sounds, intelligibility of speech and the level of linguistic organization of children who had spent their first three years in an institution remained behind that of children of the same age who had lived in foster homes since sometime during the fourth month. This was shown in a series of tests which Goldfarb carried out in the forties. The same children were tested again at the ages of three and a half, six and eight years, and again as adolescents. Goldfarb (1955) established that the institutionalized children were very inhibited in their linguistic, intellectual and social development, which, in adolescence, was evidenced by aimless behavior, inability in interpersonal relations and a low level of abstract thought.

It must be remembered that the children in institutions lack above all two important factors in development: sufficient emotional attention and the necessary stimulation from the social environment. These factors are also decisive for language development. The milieu of the institution is a typical situation for conditions of deprivation, where there are insufficient behavior reinforcements. According to Correll, there are two other disadvantageous situations:

1) for children who grow up in an isolated area and who therefore must accept insufficient economic (and civilizing) circumstances; 2) for children who grow up in families whose parents suffer from emotional and social disturbances and therefore deny the children the usual contact with other children and things. (1974:132) (Translated by K. Turfler)

3.4.2.4 PLAYMATES, KINDERGARTEN

After a child is about four years old, it becomes a very important factor in his development for him to associate with others of his age. The expansion of his social environment makes it possible for him to expand his range of experiences. For the most part the social interaction of children takes place in play,[16] so that one can assume that a child learns by playing. He not only learns to assume new social roles but also practises language behavior. Therefore the play of younger brothers and sisters develops in a different manner from that of oldest or only children (for more information about language interaction between children see 3.4.3.2 below).

During early childhood, the form of play changes from parallel activity to group play – which can be explorative, imaginative and constructive, just as a child's solitary play. This change brings with its progressing complexity an increase in the command of language (see Lewis 1963:104). This presupposes of course that the child is also encouraged by the parents or older children. The role and effect of kindergarten is particularly clear here, since a child also receives behavior reinforcement from adults. The relevant literature is unanimous in the opinion that the following are among the effective conditions for a child's development: 'that a child has plenty of opportunity to play in the company of others of his own age, and that while he plays, he is speaking, hearing others speak and being spoken to.' Lewis (1963:105).

Cowe (1967) demonstrated that children speak more and in a more advanced way when they take part in group discussion, or 'house-keeping play', than if they play with blocks or woodworking (for more information about the development of sociability in kindergarten see Stern 1967:287ff).

A broader based study dealt with one aspect of language acquisition – articulation – in the social-cultural framework discussed here, but placed it in a larger context. In the years 1966–8 Lejska (1972) did a study with 844 pupils in their first school year in 33 schools in Czechoslovakia. His area of inquiry included the influence of kindergartens, elementary schools and the family, including the education of the parents as a variable, on the development of articulation. The following results are important:
1) the influence of kindergartens on correct articulation of children proved to be positive, when the kindergarten teachers proceed along logopaedic guidelines
2) in schools with several classes in one room, the correct articulation of the older pupils influenced the articulation of the younger pupils positively
3) in cities, the education of the parents should not be considered a deciding factor in the development of correct articulation in children; on the other hand, in the country the education and the social position of the parents still influenced the child's language development, particularly his articulation.

3.4.2.5 SEX
According to a series of American studies in the thirties and forties

there is a slight difference between the language development of boys and girls, whereby girls have a slight advantage. Not only do girls start to talk somewhat earlier than boys, but they retain this advantage – speak more clearly, have a larger vocabulary, use longer sentences – until school age, when the difference tends to decrease.

It is assumed that these differences are connected with the difference in the maturation process of the two sexes (see Karlin 1947). McCarthy (1954:577–81) gives a good critical presentation of the results of 14 studies. She established that a slight superiority can be observed in girls, when groups of boys and girls of equal intelligence and socio-economic status were studied in situations which did not favor the interests of either group (1954:577) (compare McCarthy 1930). Terman & Tyler (1960) also come to similar conclusions.

However, these differences are not significant in all studies. They are more marked in children from lower socio-economic groups (see Davis 1937; McCarthy 1954:579). The only exception apparent at that time was the results of a study by Anastasi & D'Angelo (1952). In this study of black American children, the boys demonstrated superiority in the length of their answers as well as the complexity of their sentence structure. Templin's (1957) extensive comparative study (articulation, vocabulary, number of different words, difference between sounds, and sentence length and complexity) showed only a slight advantage. The values for passive vocabulary were higher for boys in the study groups from three to eight years of age. All significant differences first appear in girls aged five years and up. Berko (1958) did not find any sex related difference in relation to morphological development.

However, Rebelsky et al. (1967) demonstrated that girls at a very young age – they studied the first years – were superior.

The study of twins carried out by Davis (1937) showed that brothers with a twin sister did not lag as far behind in their language performance as twin brothers. With two groups of triplets, studied by Schaerlaekens (1973) at the two-word stage, no difference could be established.

The different opinions appear to depend on the area tested and on the size of the sample group tested, among other things. What results have been reached in more recent studies?

McCarthy & Kirk (1961) tested the largest sample group in this field of research – 700 children, aged 2;6 to 9 years, using the 'Illinois Test of Psycholinguistic Abilities'. No difference was found between girls and boys in 'The Vocal Encoding Subtest' and 'The Auditory Vocal Automatic Subtest'. Only in the 'Auditory Vocal Association Subtest' did girls between the ages of five and six years show any superiority to boys.[17]

A Swedish study of the school readiness of 119 boys and 116 girls, average age 7;2 was conducted by Johansson (1965). It shows a significant difference between boys and girls, whereby girls had better scores in reading readiness and handwriting. In his study of the understanding of instructions which he conducted with 491 preschool children (children in preschool classes), Schlee (1973:73) found no difference (significant to the one per cent level) in boys' or girls' understanding of the formulation of instructions.

On the other hand, the results of Ramer's (1976) study of five girls and three boys between the ages of 1;3 and 1;8 at intervals of three weeks over a period of five months, indicated that the girls' use of syntax developed faster. She established two marked differences in the acquisition of syntax wich are sex and time related. Girls progress faster, but they frequently do not pay attention to word order. Boys progress more slowly, but make fewer mistakes in word order. Other differences also seem to point not only to individual differences but also to sex related styles in this development.

In conclusion, two contradictory results should be mentioned. According to a thorough study conducted by Maccoby & Jacklin (1974), the advantages of girls in language acquisition are smaller than has usually been assumed, or are even non-existent. Many vocabulary tests do not show any difference. According to Nelson (1973), however, girls learn vocabulary more quickly than boys. The average age for a vocabulary of the first 50 words was 18 months for girls and 22 months for boys.

Even from this selection of studies it becomes clear that it is not possible to speak of the existence of global sex related advantages in the language development of girls. Instead, it must be carefully differentiated in what area differences have been established, for which age, and what significance the results have.

It appears, above all, that more fluent, frequent speaking, using a more differentiated vocabulary, has led to this conclusion, whereby numbers of words per sentence, number of sentences per time unit, etc., were measured. There is virtually no information about semantic structures available in this field. In addition, the general cognitive development of the children as well as their personal characteristics, such as temperament, or vitality, should be taken into consideration. There can be various reasons for differences and they should by no means be attributed solely to a sex related socialization process.

113

Bernstein (1971) for example, assumes that girls, more frequently than boys, will be placed in a situation in which they are expected to change role or code and that these factors could influence their orientation toward a more differentiated language use. More research is necessary in order to test the question whether the possible superiority of girls should be regarded 'as a result of the expectations which a child's environment imposes on it', as Schaerlaekens (1973:191) among others, assumes.

When development is being studied, active as well as passive language behavior must be considered. From his results, Schlee comes to the conclusion that the sex related socialization process 'only affects active language behavior, but that boys are not different from girls in their "passive", repertoire' (1973:96).

A further important task would be to ascertain whether there are sex related language styles in school and school-aged children, that is, whether one can refer to girls' and boys' language variations, in the sense employed in the language variation research into men's and women's language in Indo-European languages (see Oftedal 1973). My observations in Sweden and in the Federal Republic of Germany show that even in the first years at school characteristic differences can be established in the use of fill words, invectives and swear words and in paralinguistic behavior patterns such as intonation, tempo of speech, and laughter. For example, girls often speak to pets in a higher tone of voice than boys.

These and other problems we have touched on emphasize the importance of social interaction in preschool children. In the next section we will review some of the central questions in this area, in which our main interest will be the linguistic aspects.

3.4.3 SOCIAL INTERACTION

We have indicated that the family forms the group in the child's socio-cultural framework, in which he learns the fundamental language and social behavior patterns, values, and conventions. This takes place through social interaction. In general, social interaction is considered as the mutual influence of individuals and groups on each other through communication of attitudes and actions.[18] One of the child's first interactions is in the mother-child dyad, which we will examine briefly in 3.4.3.1.1 below. We have examined the means of communication – which are not always verbal – in 2.4. and 2.5 above. Here, we will concentrate more on the verbal means.

Since a child learns and practises a language only in and through social interaction, the quality and quantity of interaction should be considered as two very important variables in this development. Now, we want to cover two types of social interaction more closely from this point of view.

3.4.3.1 ADULT-CHILD INTERACTION

In the seventies it was realized more and more clearly that it is important to differentiate in the investigation of the language environment necessary for a child's language development. This is for practical as well as theoretical reasons. The speculative LAD (Language Acquisition Device) is opposed by the PLD (Primary Linguistic Data) concept, which is based on facts (see pp. 30 and 36 and compare this with Vorster 1975).

With regard to the interaction between adults and children research has been mainly concerned with the function of dialogue. Katz & Katz (1928) considered dialogue as the most important and natural form for a child's development. The form and function of the language of a child in conversational interaction with adults has been examined in a series of studies, for example Slama-Cazacu (1961), Keenan (1974), Ryan (1973; 1974), Rosenthal (1973), and Shields (1976). On the other hand, relatively few studies are available on the language of adults in their interaction with small children although it has been known since the start of child language research that this language is often marked by certain characteristics (see Stern & Stern 1928:381).

Recently however, this topic has received increasing attention at different international meetings, because the answer to the question: 'What sort of language does a child hear from his reference person?' is not only of great interest to linguists, but also to psychologists, educationalists, and anthropologists, with regard to environmental influences. A good summary of the problems and results up to now is offered by the reports read at the conference 'Language Input and Acquisition' which was concerned with this topic, and which were published in Snow & Ferguson (1977).

In this area, it is not just a question of quantitative facts, for example, that adults in interaction with children use considerably more questions, imperatives, and paraphrases than they do with other adults. By using many qualitative characteristics, it has been shown that adults use a very specific register in their interaction with small children and infants.

This register, that is a variety of the language which is socially determined and related to a situation, has a considerably simpler verbal and paralinguistic structure than the register adults use with each other. In German speaking areas this register was known to Hugo Schuhardt and Hermann Paul as 'Ammensprache' and Jespersen (1922:179) analyses it under the name 'nursery language'. American child language research first took notice of the phenomenon in the sixties; however, in the last few years it has expanded and systematized the problem through a series of studies (see 3.4.3.1.2 below).

Interaction, which is most important for the social, emotional, and linguistic development of a child, starts with the mother (or some other adult who is close to the child) in a relationship known as the mother-child dyad.

3.4.3.1.1 MOTHER-CHILD DYAD

In his thorough study of the mother-child relationship in the first year, Spitz indicates that this relationship, which sociologist Simmel had already regarded as a special group formation – he called it a 'dyad' – offers a unique opportunity to observe 'the beginning and development of social relations, as it were in statu nascendi' (1965).

As was shown in sections 2.1 and 2.4 above, the child who does not yet talk, successfully communicates with his reference persons by vocalizations and kinesic means. Mueller & Lucas (1975) have shown that children at this stage demonstrate a difference between person and object related behavior. This means, among other things, that the adult, usually the mother, interprets the messages 'correctly'. Spitz is justified when he asks: how to explain the almost clairvoyant way in which a mother understands the meaning of her child's cries and babbling? He states that, we talk about the mother's intuition, intelligence and experience, when we actually know very little about what goes on in a mother in this respect (1965). One thing is clear, that mother and child influence one another mutually. The special nature of the relationship in this dyad lies in the fact that it is isolated to a certain degree from the surrounding world, and is held together by exceptionally strong emotional bonds (Spitz 1965).

Stern & Stern emphasized that the first sound utterances, which they consider a special form of expressive movement, serve at first as an expression of negative emotions, only later do they express feelings of desire. According to them a child cries when it is hungry, wet or tired or in pain – as soon as it is a few months old, it also cries when its need for change is not sufficiently answered (1928:152). The different types of cry can be exactly differentiated by means of a spectrograph (see 4.2.1).

The emotional signals which the child receives from the mother lead to a communication. Consciously or unconsciously each partner recognizes the feelings of the other and reacts with emotions, so that a continuous, mutual exchange of emotions takes place (Spitz 1965), and so the process of relationship to a human partner, which should be regarded as basic for the further emotional and social relations of the child, begins in the mother-child dyad. The social behavior of older children in wider surroundings is positively or negatively influenced by their experience in the family, which according to Argyle (1973:56) can be traced back to the fact that children make generalizations about the behavior of other adults based on the behavior of their parents.

From the beginning, the attention of the mother is verbal, too; it is through her speech that the infant receives very early a value and motivation system. Positive and negative expressive actions such as those of satisfaction, joy, contempt, disdain, etc., are verbalized in different forms. Not only direct experience, but also verbal – *That's right! That's a good baby, you may, you should* – can serve to strengthen a motivation. This is almost unrestrictedly true in western cultures, in which a single mother figure is the infant's main interactive partner. Culture specific effects of child care can already be established in three- to four-month-old infants. A comparison of mother-child interaction in Tokyo and Washington, in which vocalizations were analyzed as 'happy' or 'unhappy', was carried out for this age group by Caudill (1972). It was demonstrated that in families with a similar background, the American baby had a higher tone of voice than the Japanese baby. This was most evident in 'happy' vocalizations (for further information see Bullowa et al. 1976). Spitz (1965) discusses cultural determinants of the mother-child dyad; however, the language aspect is not touched on.

3.4.3.1.2 LANGUAGE SPOKEN TO CHILDREN

In this section we will consider more closely the question of what the language that the child hears is like. We have mentioned that there is reason to speak of a special register. This register, which is known as 'baby talk', 'mother's speech', 'parental speech', and 'nursery language' in English literature, is called 'Ammensprache', 'Kindersprache' and 'Babysprache' in German.[19] There is a lack of systematic studies in this area concerning the German language. My material covers observations of five mothers and three other reference persons in connection with our longitudinal study of language acquisition. This material confirms earlier, sporadic observations in the German area.

In general, the language directed to children is marked by a typical intonation, and other paralinguistic patterns. It is spoken more slowly, the articulation is clearer than the language used with adults, intonation contours and pitch are exaggerated, and a higher tone of voice is used. Further, speakers – adults and older children – use phonological and grammatical modifications in speaking to a small child. They avoid difficult consonant groups, use mostly two syllable words and simple syntactic structures: *Hier Buch!* Not only is there duplication of syllables, such as *wauwau*, but also of words, as can be seen in the following example. A mother points to a bird on a pond and says to the two-year-old Peter: *Dá Vógel, macht schwimme, schwimme* [There's a bird, going swim, swim].

Also common is the use of the third person, when the adult refers to himself or to the child in direct speech: *Mutti kommt gleich! – Wie gross ist das Kind? – Wo ist Hansi?* [Mommy is coming! – How big is baby? – Where is Hansi?]. Further, the sociative *we* is found considerably more often than in the language used with adults: *Wir waschen uns nun die Händchen* [Now we'll wash our little hands!] where there are certainly alternative meanings, either *Wir waschen nun deine Händchen* or *Du wäscht dir nun die Händchen* [Now we'll wash your little hands, or Now you wash your little hands].

In communicative acts in this register, diminutives of the type *mein kleines Mäuschen!*[20] [my little mousy!] are used more frequently than in standard language.

The language which is spoken to children can be recognized as a special register in various cultures. Ferguson (1964) studied 'baby talk' in six languages – in English, Spanish, Arabian, Giljak, Marathi and Comanche. He established that it can be considered a conventional part of the various languages, that is, as one of the various styles which has survived several generations, and was not developed spontaneously by each new set of parents. At the present stage of research, it has not yet been determined whether one can speak of universals for this style – or 'simplified register', as Ferguson (1977) calls it – as was recently discussed[21] (compare this to the discussion in connection with the problems of universals above 2.1).

A good outline of studies in the field can be found in Farwell (1973), Vorster (1975) and Snow (1977). Up to now 34 characteristics of nursery language have been demonstrated (see Blount 1972). It is characterized as an expressive-emotional register, which seems above all to unite two functional goals: to ease communication and to express intimacy and tenderness.

Most of the studies concern themselves with the language of the mother, the child's main conversation partner. Mothers are simple and redundant in their conversation and use many questions and imperatives, few preterite forms, and few coordinate and subordinate phrases. Their speech is fluent, the tone of voice is often higher than usual and the intonation is exaggerated. These characteristics can be divided into 'measures of prosody, of grammatical complexity and of redundancy' (see Snow 1977:32). In Estonian, Spanish and the Slavic languages the use of diminutives is particularly conspicuous, as is palatalization in Estonian.

According to a series of other criteria – which, however, have been studied less – this register seems dynamic and flexible. The flexibility depends on the age of the child, the type of adult activity during which speech occurs and on social differences, etc.

Snow (1972) studied 42 middle-class mothers. With two-year-olds their conversation was simpler and more redundant than it was with ten-year-olds. In talking to two-year-olds, significantly fewer third person pronouns were used, nouns were repeated, and considerably more verbless sentences were used. Mothers hardly differed from non-mothers however, in their speech with two-year-olds. Sachs, et al. (1976) on the other hand, found significant differences in the conversation of a group of non-parents with a child (1:10) in comparison to communication with other adults (see also Broen 1972).

Bakker-Rennes & Hoefnagel-Höhle (1974) found differences in different situations. The language of a mother was more complex in freer situations (reading aloud, playing) than in situations where she cared for the baby (dressing, bathing, feeding).

Fraser & Roberts (1975) found similar situation dependant differences. In their study of 32 mothers and children (1;6 to 6;0) the language of the mothers varied according to the task and the age of the child.

An analysis of the manner in which 18 Dutch mothers from three social classes adapted their way of speaking to the needs of their children learning to talk does not lead to any significant social difference (for this unpublished study see Vorster 1975:304). Further studies are necessary in this area, as well as on the important, and scarcely researched question of how adults interpret the language of children. (Compare the problems of the prelinguistic period 3.4.3.1.1 above.)

Almost no research has been done on the language of fathers and other men talking to small children. Berko Gleason (1975) found that fathers in a home environment also had the typical characteristics of the simplified register. Among other things, fathers used more imperatives than mothers, particularly with their sons. Their language, however, was not as exactly adapted to the level of the child as the mothers' was. The language of male and female teachers in a kindergarten, however, demonstrated qualitative and quantitative similarities.

According to my observations, fathers speak in a considerably higher tone of voice and use a more exaggerated intonation when they are alone with small children than when other members of the family are present.

Although the register discussed here shows wide ideolectal variations, and not all of its elements are used by all the adults who talk with infants and small children – although the paralinguistic elements are used almost all the time – from the cases discussed here, it can still be concluded that it plays an important role in the process of language acquisition, which not only has practical but also theoretical consequences. The basis of language acquisition is, therefore, not just any adult language, but rather a very specific variation of it, whose structure leads to the conclusion that it can ease the children's learning process. According to Brown, in his introduction to Snow & Ferguson (1977), the old opinion about the order in this process 'AS→CS (adult speech→child speech)' must be replaced by a new one, that is 'AS→BT→CS (adult speech→baby talk→child speech)'.

The manner in which adults talk to children, the existence of the register discussed here, offers a valid argument against Chomsky's observation that natural speech always demonstrates 'numerous false starts, deviations from rules, changes of plan in mid-course, and so on' (1965:4) which, again, served him and his school as proof that language acquisition should be regarded as inborn and preprogrammed, since a child could not learn language on the basis of the defective data of natural speech. Brown & Bellugi had already pointed out expressly that a child in no way hears a phonologically or grammatically deviant language, but rather a 'simplified, repetitive, and idealized dialect' (1964:136).[22] This is not considered, however, by the supporters of the nativist approach (see 3.6.2 below).

Although a mutual influence can be established here through different sorts of interference, one should not equate this register with the subcode of a small child, as is so often done. Common examples of children's language, such as over-generalization of the irregular verb forms of the type *singte* and *gesingt* [singed], do not occur in this register; neither does violation of the linguistic or semantic congruence occur. In various languages, the mutual influence between the language of the adult and the child leads to, for example, proper names and nick names: *Bob*, *Peppo* (Giuseppe), *Nenne* (Sven), *Pelle* (Per), *Lulu*, *Lili*.

There are divided opinions over the use of the typical vocabulary in this register. Now and then it is assumed that the acquisition of standard words is retarded by the use of baby words. In fact Stern & Stern (1928:281) found that those who find it unacceptable to teach a child words like *bow-wow* and *pipip*, *ticktock* and *puffpuff* first demonstrate a complete misunderstanding of the nature of children. These onomatopoeic words encourage thinking in language in its developing stage, during which a child is not yet ready to understand words such as *dog*, *clock* and *bird*. A child then quite naturally and automatically progresses through the phase of *bow-wow-dog* or *ba-sheep* to *dog* and *sheep*. The onomatopoeic word, which first expresses the whole object, is reduced to an adjective (bow-wow-dog = dog, who says bow-wow) then disappears entirely (Stern & Stern 1928:382).

According to my material, children who use such expressions know very early the corresponding words in the adult language since it is part of the dynamics of this register that adults do not only use *bow-wow*, but also *dog*. Without a doubt, the child then has the opportunity to try 'exercises' in style. Sven (2;5) called his various teddies by the Estonian children's word *mõmmu*: *valge mõmmu* ['white teddy'], *pruun mõmmu* ['brown teddy'], but in picture books, he identified teddies either with *mõmmu* or with the normal word *karu* ['bear']. 'Rabbit' was called in turn either by the children's word *jän'ku* or by the normal adult word *jänes*.

In 2.4 above we mentioned non-verbal behavior in the communication process. With this register, which is so important for the development of language, it is an important element also. In what way do non-verbal aspects of interaction, for example different gestures, function in communication? This part of the communicating world around the child is still little known, and must be studied from different viewpoints. For example, one interesting question would be whether the gestures which accompany this register are different from the gestures that adults use in interaction with each other. Another question would be how gestures and actions accompanying the conversation of adults, such as pointing, providing or moving toys and other interaction strategies are understood by children, how they react to them, etc. Further, are they used because the adult wishes to impart more information, or in order to adapt to the child's level of understanding? There are signs that this could be the case. Mothers give their one- and three-year-old children about the same number of verbal invitations in play situations, as Garnica (1975) established. However, these verbal signals are accompanied by gestures considerably more often for one-year-olds than for three-year-olds, for whom the gestures are also not as well differentiated.

There are, however, still far too few experimental studies from which the details of the effect of 'inputs' in language acquisition can be learned. The Hess & Shipmann study (1965) is still regarded as one of the best attempts to find the relationship between these aspects; they come to the conclusion that the language which children hear, and which is qualitatively insufficient, that is, the 'input [is] insufficiently adapted to the level of complexity the child could process', hinders the development of language (compare this to Ervin-Tripp's 1973:262f 'environmental input' and Snow 1977).

Macnamara (1972) assumes that children learn to speak, among other things, because they have the ability to grasp the meaning of the sentences that they hear, independently of the sentence itself. This hypothesis could be supported by the characteristics of the register discussed here, among which is its 'here and nowness' according to Phillips (1970), since it mainly verbalizes that which the child sees, hears, or directly experiences. Most studies confirm the observations of Brown & Bellugi (1964), that the speech of adults often contains expansions; these are considered to be an effective stimulus in language acquisition:

> It seems to us that a mother, in expanding speech, may be teaching more than grammar; she may be teaching something like world view. (Brown & Bellugi, 1964:148)

The proportion of expansions is relatively large: 30 per cent of the entire speaking time of the mothers (academic women) of two of the children Brown & Bellugi studied. Without a doubt the children receive important information through such expansions, since they encode aspects of reality which the child itself did not verbalize. Compare this to the thorough study of the interactive cycles of 22 mothers with their children conducted by Moerk (1975) (see also Moerk 1972).

Brown & Bellugi (1964:145) have shown that the mother-child

interaction is, for the most part, a cycle of reduction and expansion (compare this to 3.6.4 below). As Snow emphasizes, mothers make 'very predictable comments about very predictable topics' (1977:41). This makes the semantic process much easier for the child. More research is necessary in this area, but the results up to now clearly indicate that the role of adult-child interaction is much more important than has been indicated in linguistic theory.

3.4.3.2. CHILD-CHILD INTERACTION

After family interaction, interaction among peers is among the most important sources which can influence the child's manner of behavior. Peer-groups are known in various cultures, and their importance as a basis on which the child carries out various social activities increases at school age. As a rule, American children take part in peer-group activities earlier than European ones (see Argyle 1973:60). A dyadic interaction with another child can already take place very early, through non-verbal means. An infant between eight and nine months may offer another child a toy; among the earliest forms of social interaction is the conflict over a toy (Jersild & Markey 1935); at the age of two years, however, children already play cooperatively together (see Argyle 1973:58f). According to Bühler et al. (1972), while a two-year-old can only interact with one other child at a time, interaction in groups of three children is already common at three and four years of age.

Our knowledge about the behavior of small children in groups of peers is still rather limited; information about children under three is particularly scarce. A summary of the most important studies can be found in Schloon (1976), whose work deals with individual differences in social interactive behavior in 18 to 30-month-old children. Most studies deal with children three years old or older, and a multitude of behavior categories are studied: aggressive and defensive behavior, competitive and cooperative behavior etc. Honig et al. (1970) used up to 100 discrete units of behavior in the observations of 32 children between the ages of one and four years, for example, ten different units for each main category, such as 'environmental contact, information processing, food behavior, manual activities, negative reinforcement, positive reinforcement' etc. The different category systems of social interaction for preschool children are clearly presented by Schloon (1976:30ff) (see also the ethological study by Blurton Jones 1972b).

These studies did not deal with the linguistic aspects, as, conversely,

123

the non-linguistic aspects were also excluded in the study of the language of child-child interaction (on the importance of coordination in this area see 2.4 below).

In contrast to child-adult communication, very little research has been done on the question of how children use language with each other to achieve different interactive goals. Very nearly all studies are case studies.

Keenan (1974) observed the conversations of her twin sons (2;9) and found that – contrary to the opinion of Piaget and his followers – they were quite able to carry on a continuous dialogue and to react to reciprocal utterances. Her results speak, among other things, against the high proportion of egocentric language for children of that age which Piaget (1923) claimed. In one conversation period of 257 conversational exchanges ('one or more utterances bounded by long pauses or by the utterances of another speaker') only 17, that is six point six per cent, were of the type of utterances not directed at the other conversation partner. Keenan summarizes the conversational strategy of the children as follows:

> Extended stretches of cooperative talk are achieved by reproducing exactly or modifying slightly each other's utterances. . . . Novel utterances may appear as topically relevant comments on an antecedent utterance. (1974:183)

Mueller (1971) studied the spontaneous conversation of two children between 3;6 and 5;6 in play situations. Eighty-five per cent of all utterances between the children belonged to successful communication, that is, to the type that either received an answer, or at least aroused the attention of the listener. Maratsos (1973) and Garvey & Hogan (1973) established considerable communicative abilities in preschool children.

The study by Shields (1976) also deals with conversational abilities, above all with the development of dialogue in three- to five-year-old children in kindergartens. Shields interprets the following complex of characteristics as the most important constituents of dialogue: 1) inter-individual participation, exchange and cohesion between the speakers and 2) thematic and contextual cohesion. She finds considerable communicative skills in children at this age:

> They can maintain an interpersonal communicative relationship, they can adapt their language to their notions of the understanding of others, and they are using the main systems of language to induct and organize not only as interactive relationships but as interpersonal field. They can focus attention on a topic and maintain it by non-specific reference over chains of

exchanges. They can use many of the common cohesive devices such as ellipsis and tagging. (1976:25)

Garvey (1975) also established an important communicative variation in kindergarten children between the ages of 3;6 and 5;7. Next to dialogue research, which is just beginning, and perhaps even more promising for the study of cognitive and operational abilities, is variance research, which is beginning to interest the child-child interactive researchers.

The observations of Weeks (1971) and Berko Gleason (1973) have shown that children are able to vary the manner in which they speak to different adults and children considerably. Features of baby talk can even be observed in preschool children when they talk to younger children. Shatz & Gelman (1973) demonstrate that four-year-olds use shorter sentences and more modifications from nursery language when they talk to a two-year-old, for example about a toy, but that this did not occur when they talked to their peers or mothers.

Sachs & Devin (1976) studied the conversation of four children (aged 3;9 to 5;5) with an adult, a peer, a baby and a baby doll in various situations. All of them spoke differently to the babies and the dolls than they did to their mothers and peers, and they showed phonological and prosodic characteristics of baby talk. Since dolls were spoken to in the same way as babies, it is assumed that feedback is not necessary for the modification in their speech. It can be seen that children have a feeling for an age dependent adaptation of their language by the fact that they simplify their way of expressing themselves when they play-act being a baby.

From this kind of register switching it can be concluded that children can acquire an awareness for partner related language variation in communication acts very early on and can acquire the ability to judge a situation in which variation could occur. So we have reached a point where it seems proper to ask: what does a child have to learn, when he learns to talk?

3.5 WHAT IS ACQUIRED?

As indicated above, a child not only acquires the ability to make and understand grammatical and acceptable utterances, but also learns to judge situations in which they are proper. This process takes place together with the interactive process, in which linguistic and non-

125

linguistic behavior patterns may be coordinated, and often occur as one functional unit.

3.5.1 LANGUAGE AS A MEANS OF EXPRESSION AND COMMUNICATION

Language, as a typical human and social phenomenon, serves as a sign system for thought, recognition and social behavior processes; it reflects the activities of a society and so is the most important means of expression and communication for its members.[23] It must be emphasized that a child does not learn language alone, as an end in itself, but rather – in every society in a different way – in order to establish contact with other people and in order to express his feelings and thoughts. This includes the acquisition of the sound system, the grammar, the semantics and various sections of the lexicon of a language, but it also goes beyond these into the pragmatic systems, because they include the functions of these parts. Language not only makes contact between people possible, but also determines even group membership. So language becomes a part of the speaker's identity, and for the listener, it becomes an identification factor. 'He speaks differently' often implies 'He is not one of us'. With time, a child also learns this side of language; and even though this does not yet seem to be very marked in preschool children, this aspect must be studied too.

Language can be regarded as a socially conditioned convention, but is at the same time also a norm, which must be accepted by everyone who grows up in a linguistic community. If he deviates from this norm, he runs the risk of being misunderstood, or not understood at all. In the socialization process, many social norms are communicated to the child, through the medium of language which is itself a norm. A clear presentation of the problems of norms can be found in Segerstedt, or for further comparison, in Parson & Shils (1951). According to Segerstedt, social norms have three functions: '1) to create dispositions of behavior or emotions 2) to release behavior, and 3) to release emotions' (1966:104). This is true of language, too; however the functions of language can be handled much more concretely, as can be seen in the models which we will now consider.

3.5.1.1 THE FUNCTIONS OF LANGUAGE

Models of the functions of language are based on Bühler's *Organon-Model* (1934:24–30), which he derived from 'concrete linguistic experience' and the conversation situation. His model arose from Plato's statement that language is an 'organum' [tool] for one person to communicate something to someone else about things. Based on these three fundamental relations, Bühler constructed a model of the causal observation of concrete linguistic processes. He gives the following example. Someone notices a rustling, looks out the window and says *It's raining*. The other hears the words and also looks out the window. So, according to Bühler, when something is said about objects or facts, the concrete sound phenomenon is converted to a sign by three kinds of factor. Each of these have three functions, which should be regarded as semantic functions:

1) The concrete sound phenomenon is a *symbol* on the strength of its attachment to objects and circumstances. Therefore, the word *rain*, for example, has a *referential*, cognitive ('Darstellung') *function*.

2) It is a *symptom* (signal, indication) on the strength of its dependence on the sender, whose inner feelings and thoughts it expresses. Therefore the word takes on an *expressive* ('Ausdruck') *function*, whereby it also refers to the speaker himself.

3) It is a *signal* on the strength of its appeal to the listener, whose inner and outer behavior it directs like a traffic signal. Therefore the word also has an *appelative* ('Appell') *function*, since it speaks to the listener, and works as a signal to his behavior.[24]

Bühler presents these relations in the following figure:

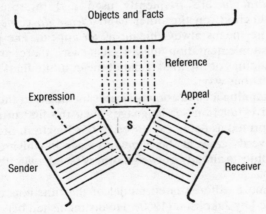

Figure 1: Bühler's Organon Model (*After Bühler 1934:28*)

The circle refers to concrete sound phenomena. The triangle illustrates the three functions, by which the sound phenomenon becomes a sign. By drawing the triangle so that it stretches out over the circle,

Bühler wanted to show that what is materially present always receives a perceptive supplement (1934:28). The intention of the speaker never completely coincides with the interpretation of the listener, since he, the listener, supplements what he hears through the background of his own experience. But, at the same time, the triangle covers less than the circle. In this way, Bühler indicates the principle of abstract relevance, that is, that the sign in all its concrete characteristics does not have to agree with the semantic function. Rather it can be relevant to only this or that abstract moment (1934:44). The listener not only supplements what he hears perceptively but at the same time he also makes reductions in what the speaker intended.

Bühler's three part division of the semantic functions of the sign included that part which we like to call pragmatics today. When someone says *It's raining* to someone else, he can interpret it purely as a reference to something outside the sender's being; however he can also interpret it as an expression of the sender's joy or dissatisfaction – usually by paralinguistic features – he can also understand it as an appeal, for example for him to take along an umbrella, etc. This sort of interpretation through functional domination depends in part on the situation, and on the socio-cultural framework in which something is said. Expressions such as *There's a draught* are frequently used and interpreted in the appelative function; on the other hand *Please do come and see us again* is by no means always meant as an appeal. The principle of perceptive supplementation makes clear why there are so many misunderstandings of the kind 'I didn't mean it like that!' or 'I didn't understand it that way!'

At the beginning a child communicates by means of the expressive and appelative functions of language: even the first utterances are mostly interpreted as being expressed in this function. Stern & Stern (1928:182f) verify cases at the one-word stage in which examples of pointing to objects already outweigh others (see Lewis 1951:202f and 4.3.1 below).

An even more differentiated model of the functions of language was developed by Jakobson (1960). He distinguished between the six following factors in the speech act, each of which corresponds to a specific function:

The *addresser* sends a *message* to the *addressee*. To be operative the message requires that a *context* be referred to ('referent' in another, somewhat ambiguous, nomenclature), siezable by the addressee, and either verbal or capable of being verbalized; a *code* fully, or at least partially, common to the addresser and addressee (or in other words to the encoder and decoder of the message); and, finally, a *contact*, a physical channel and psychological connection between the addresser and the addressee, enabling both of them to enter and stay in communication. (1960:353)

These six factors, *addresser*, *addressee*, *message*, *context*, *code* and *contact* are assigned the following linguistic functions:

1) The *emotive* or *expressive function* expresses the attitudes, the emotional and volitional state of the speaker.

2) The *conative function* is directed at the addressee; grammatically it is expressed in the vocative and the imperative which belong to the first grammatical forms that the child acquires.

3) The *poetic* or *aesthetic function* of language is marked by the focus on the message, on the linguistic medium. It can be found not only in poetry, but also in a subordinate role in political and advertising slogans, and in children's language (see Holenstein 1975:168).

4) The *referential* or *cognitive function* dominates in the usual conversation: this function designates objects in the external world.

5) The *metalinguistic function* makes it possible to talk about language with the help of language. Jakobson emphasizes its importance in language acquisition: without metalinguistic explanations this would hardly be possible.

6) The *phatic function*[25] appears when the utterance should establish, lengthen, interrupt or reinforce communication. According to Jakobson (1960:356) this is the first function which a child learns and masters successfully.

Jakobson's emotive, conative, and referential functions correspond to the expressive, appelative and referential functions in Bühler's model. Most linguistic utterances seldom fulfil only one function, but as a rule there is one which dominates and so determines the structure of the statement (see Holenstein 1975:158ff, and compare the language functions in Leont'ev 1968, and Ervin-Tripp 1966:85ff, and Halliday's 1975 six functions listed above in 2.2.3. Kainz 1962:173ff gives a good summary of function theories).

Kainz differentiates between primary or elementary linguistic functions – these are divided into dialogue and monologue – and secondary functions. Kainz regards the dialogue as the main function of language, since language serves as a means of communication, as a means of making the contents of consciousness which are to be communicated understandable. As a result of its secondary functions, language plays a role in such areas as the magical-religious, the ethical and the aesthetic, and in intellectual fields, since, although it is first and foremost a tool, it is also a cultural sphere with its own regularity and a place and area for creativity and value judgements of the intellectual, aesthetic and ethical sort (1962:220). The ethical functions can be seen, for example, in language conventions such as adaptation to the personality of the conversation partner in different areas of language (grammar, polite language, comparison and metaphor). Research in language acquisition must concern itself with the acquisition of these aspects, too. A three-year-old girl who, upon entering a doctor's waiting room, points to a woman and cries out *She looks like a witch!* has not mastered these functions yet, although, considering the stereotype of witches, the comparison may have been rather fitting.

What does it mean, when it is said that a child has successfullly mastered this or that function – and with time has mastered them all? From empirical evidence, it can be inferred that he has learned to use various linguistic and paralinguistic means in accordance with these functions in interaction with other people – adults and children. He acquires various communicative abilities, which can be summed up as communicative competence. This competence will be discussed in 3.5.3 below, after the problem of competence and performance has been briefly treated in the following section.

3.5.2   COMPETENCE AND PERFORMANCE

We established that a child learns a language as a means of communication. Learning a language as a means of communication requires not only that a child master the linguistic material according to the rules of grammar, but also that he acquire the ability to judge the conditions for using this material and that he master the rules of these conditions, including change of register and strategies of code switching, as is the case for many multi-lingual children.

The child must also develop the ability to recognize the linguistic demands for each different situation and to react appropriately to them. If the child understands the semantic structure of, for example, the word *man* and he can use the sentence *Here comes a man*, correctly, he must still learn that socio-cultural rules do not allow the sentence *Hello man* and demand instead *Hello, Mr X*. To use a language as a means of communication requires a certain competence which is much more than pure linguistic competence, that is, the mastery of a system of verbal signs. These considerations already show that Chomsky's narrow concept of competence and his differentiation between 'competence' and 'performance' are not sufficient for the problems of language acquisition; they are even misleading. Chomsky (1965:4) deliberately does not consider any examples which are dependent on language variation; he operates with an ideal speaker-hearer, and regards language use as a direct reflection of linguistic competence (which in reality often does not exist) (see 2.2.2 above and compare the criticism of Hymes 1971:5f, Oksaar 1972d:130f, Derwing 1973:259ff and Hörmann 1976:33ff).

Since competence can only be analyzed through performance and performance research is still very much in its beginnings – although members of the Prague School, like Skalička (1948), had long ago emphasized the necessity for a linguistics of 'la parole' – the linguist is confronted with a dilemma today. Intuitively, he differentiates between linguistic ability and language use, but the relationship remains obscure. At least, it should have been clear that it was necessary for linguists to concern themselves with language use when they started to occupy themselves with semantics and context theories for determining meaning.[26] Greenberg has already indicated that 'It would now be generally agreed that meaning is to be understood functionally, i.e., that meaning is to be described in terms of a rule of use stated in terms of the environment, (cited in Hoijer 1954:14). To the linguist, this shows that such a sharp division between linguistic ability and language use as has been normal in linguistics, particularly since de Saussure, is hard to uphold and in any case, hardly productive methodologically, until more is known about the rules or norms of language use.

For language acquisition, a sharp division cannot be maintained from the beginning, because the only material that can be analyzed is the language produced by children, and the linguist cannot use his adult intuition to judge the developing language of the child. For information on the possibilities of acquiring knowledge about the linguistic abilities of children see 3.3.3 above. Furthermore, the concept of deep and surface structure cannot be used in the same way as it is for adult language. Surface structure has already been shown to be an important factor in problems of intelligibility: 'It is often noticed that certain recursions (self-embedding, for instance) are difficult to understand because they make stringent demands on immediate memory' (Smith 1970:132).

From what has been said, it can be concluded that the concept of competence cannot be explained without taking socio-cultural and situational data into consideration (see Oksaar 1972d; 1976b:13). This interpretation of linguistic ability brings it closer to social reality than does that of transformational grammar. Hymes (1967; 1971) calls this competence *communicative competence* and speaks of 'competence for use' (1971:10).

3.5.3   COMMUNICATIVE COMPETENCE

When Hymes states that a child acquires three abilities – a repertoire of speech acts, the ability to take part in speech acts, and the ability to judge the speech acts of others – he wants this to be understood as a competence 'which is integral with attitudes and values concerning language and integral with competence for the interrelation of language with other codes of communicaton' (1971:10).

Appropriateness plays a central role in this concept, and further, the inadequate term 'sentence' is no longer used but rather the term 'speech act', which refers to Austin's (1962) speech act theory. Hymes (1967:17), however, considers communicative competence to be the abilities which make it possible for members of a society to use language and to interpret the use of language (see 2.5.1. above). This competence is based on two factors: (tacit) knowledge and (ability for) use (1962). This differentiation makes it possible for him to assume a more differentiated competence, according to different degrees of knowledge. The details of this, however, have not yet been made operational. This is no reason to abandon the whole concept, as Hörmann recommends for communicative competence as defined by Hymes. Hörmann recommended:

> Instead of special competence, one should regard a comprehensive style of speech as a (general) language game, whose choice is conditioned by the repertoire of language games which the speaker has at his disposal. The idea of the language game allows us to see the fluent transitions which exist between the choice of a particular formal style which is generally fitting for the whole discussion on the one side and on the other side the choice of the sort of communication 'appropriate' to a particular speech act. (1976:328)

But Hymes tried to solve this problem too; his concept of competence included 'knowledge of rules of style and knowledge of rules of social interaction'. The difficulties of establishing a terminology are not swept aside by the vague term 'language game'; on the contrary, it creates more. Wittgenstein (1967:§51; 57) considers the language game to be the speaking of a language as a part of an activity or way of life. He counts the following as part of language games: giving commands and acting on commands; describing an object; inventing a story; making a joke; translating out of one language into another; asking, thanking, swearing, greeting and praying. He, too would call the whole – the language and the activities with which it is connected – the language game (1967:§7).

Apart from the fact that the game analogy does not readily imply regulated acting and speaking, since 'game' also includes actions which are not guided by rules, i.e. the games of children, the term is also extremely misleading in its suggestive figurativeness: one can always, and at any time do without games, interrupt them or give them up. This is not true of language. But even when what is meant by language game is clearly established by definition, the dichtomy of language and speech is unavoidable.

There is, therefore, no necessity to abandon the term 'communicative competence for language' in favor of 'language game'. Anyway, it can be seen that Hymes's approach is similar to the idea of competence.[27] The concept must, of course be more differentiated, since there are different sorts of communicative abilities. In a direct (face to face) interaction, oral communication includes not only verbal but also paralinguistic and kinesic abilities. Communicative abilities can be divided not only into verbal and non-verbal opponents, but also into actional and non-actional, since one can also communicate by silence. Naturally that kind of categorization depends on how broadly communication is defined. Watzlavick et al. (1967) considered all behavior in an interpersonal situation to be communication, i.e. as having informational character. However, this implies that one cannot 'not communicate' in such a situation (for information on newborns and babies see Bullowa 1974 and Bullowa et al. 1976). The linguistic components of communicative competence are summed up as socio-linguistic competence by Erwin-Tripp (1972) and also van der Geest (1975).

3.5.3.1 INTERACTIONAL COMPETENCE

A suggestion for the differentiation of the term 'communicative competence' is made in Oksaar (1977). I consider interactional competence to be the ability of a person, in interactional situations, to perform and interpret verbal and non-verbal communicative actions, according to the socio-cultural and socio-psychological rules of the group. A child learns the rules gradually, and at the same time must also learn to synchronize verbal acts (*Hello, Mr Miller*) with non-verbal acts (look at Mr Miller, extend hand,[28] etc.). *Hello, Mr X*, belongs to the so-called routines: greetings; polite expressions; beginning a conversation, for example on the telephone, or asking the way, and the like. The question of how and when a child learns these routines has hardly been considered in the research. Berko et.al. (1976) found that the acquisition of such routines seems to progress in a different direction from the rest of language acquisition. When a child hears *Give me the ball. That's the ball, The ball is red* and the like, he learns the concepts; first comes the competence, then the performance. Routines are learned the other way around, performance comes first:

> The adult marks the routine by the use of some device like *Say*, and insists that the child perform. Only later, long after he has learned to say *Bye bye* or *Thank you* or *Trick or treat* might he come to know what, if anything, it all means. (1976:134)

Further studies are necessary.

In the linguistic area of interactional competence, the roles of speaker and listener are not equally divided, and cannot be summed up in one system of rules. The listener has a different grammar from the speaker,[29] as we already know, and as has been emphasized by Ščerba and the Petersburg school just as by the Prague linguists. For example, homonymy exists only for the listener. The division of roles in the communication process is demonstrated in the function of syntax and semantics. For the speaker semantics dominates communication; and syntax, the manner of combining words, is guided by the type of message. For the listener, this manner of combination is primary; it guides the semantic interpretation. Modern linguistics has hardly considered this important difference. In paedolinguistics, however, this relationship must be included from the very beginning: a child first receives language in the role of a listener, long before he is active in the role of a speaker.

After we have given a rough outline of the problem of what a child acquires when he learns a language, we will consider the question of how language is acquired. In light of the diversity of positions in learning theory only those which are directly relevant for language acquisition will be treated.

3.6 HOW IS LANGUAGE ACQUIRED?

At the present stage of research, there is no generally accepted theory of learning. In answer to the question of how language is acquired the views of two contradictory theories of cognition are usually cited: the behaviorist (empirical) approach, and the nativist (rationalist) approach. Both find themselves in the frame of reference already marked by the Intellectualism–Voluntarism controversy between Preyer, Oltuscewski, Lindner and Ament on one side, and Wundt, Meumann and Idelberger on the other (see above, 1.2.1).

3.6.1 THE BEHAVIORIST APPROACH

Classic behaviorism, which goes back to Watson (1924) regards learning as a connection of a *stimulus* to a *response* by a conditioning. Learning theory differentiates between classic or reactive, and operant or instrumental conditioning. The first goes back to Pavlov (1927) who became famous for distinguishing between two signal systems. The stimuli of the outside world affect the organism through the primary signal system. The famous Pavlov dog was trained to react to certain bells by salivating. The bell was the signal that food was coming, and the flow of saliva – the typical case of 'conditioned reflex' – was the response. This process – at a particular stimulus, here the sound of a bell, there is a conditioned response, here the flow of saliva – is known as classical conditioning. The construction of the response is dependent on the reinforcement. If the bell is rung repeatedly without being accompanied or followed by food, the flow of saliva will eventually cease to occur.

Pavlov then applied the principle of conditioning to people: words act like stimuli, and yet the verbal stimuli are not qualitatively the same as those of the animals, because language, the secondary signal system, exercises its influence as a 'signal of the primary signal'.

In contrast to classical conditioning, operant conditioning assumes that a human does not need to be be activated first by a stimulus. He 'constantly' releases bits of behavior into the world, and then experiences the reaction of the world in the form of either re-inforcement or of withheld reinforcement (Correll 1974:19). From his experiments with animals, Thorndike (1914) concluded that a stimulus is not necessarily followed by a single response, but rather, based on the principle of trial and error, one response which is rewarded is chosen from a number of possible responses. This behavior is then learned.

Skinner (1957), too, regarded the process of learning from a similar standpoint. He talked about verbal behavior which, for him, is always controlled by a stimulus. A pattern of behavior is learned when its execution is reinforced. A child, who first forms non-reactive sounds, imitates sounds for which it is rewarded by the attention of its reference person. Due to this selective reinforcement from the reference person, the child's sound system gradually approaches that of the reference person. A detailed criticism can be found in Chomsky (1959).

In contrast to Thorndike and Skinner, Mowrer's (1960) autism theory does not necessarily presuppose the necessity of reward – it is also possible that a child acquires the habit[30] of saying a certain word, not through his own speech, but through hearing it in pleasant situations (as Mowrer concluded from his experiments with parrots). These situations form a primary reinforcement. The word, which is heard, becomes the secondary reinforcement: the child wants to imitate the word himself and feels an autistic satisfaction in so doing (for a detailed discussion of these conditioning theories, see Hörmann 1970:244ff; 278ff; 1976:22ff; Bergius 1971:30ff; 82ff; Jenkins 1965; Correll 1971:18ff). By means of operant conditioning it is possible to explain the imitative tendency, earlier regarded as instinct, in language acquisition (see Correll 1971:20). Between a verbal stimulus and a verbal response, however, there can also be a verbally transmitted association, which influences the act of learning. This relationship is explained by the mediation theories (see Osgood 1957; Hörmann 1970:189ff). They play a central role in discussion of the acquisition of meaning.

We would like to emphasize the following criticisms of the assumption that the behaviorist approach can explain language acquisition. Hörmann (1970:278ff) points out that the usual understanding of reinforcement cannot explain either the speed of language acquisition, or the stability of meanings, once it is acquired. In language acquisition it is very hard to prove that, by trial and error, certain behavior leads to a reward.

Peizer & Olmstead (1969:60f) emphasize that if only negative or positive reinforcements are important to a child then it must be asked: what happens during correction? Correction undoubtedly leads to a modification of what is acquired; quite often however, it only carries the information *that* something is wrong, not *what* is wrong. Bergius (1971:82) explains that it may be possible that conditioning plays a part in the acquisition of words and their meaning, but that not all speaking is stimulus controlled. Church (1961) points out that learning also takes place without reinforcement.

In regard to autism theory, cases in which understanding of speech is present without any self production, as for example in the case of mutes (see above p. 81), already demonstrate that this theory cannot explain the whole process of learning, either. However, it did draw attention to the role of imitation (see below 3.6.4). Furthermore, this would imply that a child's first words would always have to be spoken in a pleasant situation, which is not always true. Hörmann (1970:284) states that autism theory, which is based wholly on the emotional component of language learning, reaches its limits where language takes on its instrumental character. Without a doubt, the emotional component exists. However, language is employed primarily as a means of communication, and therefore language acquisition cannot be explained only through the emotional component. In any case, it can be established that sounds, and even difficult sound combinations, are learned more easily and quickly in words that symbolize what the child likes particularly well (see Oksaar 1972c:194 and below 4.3.2).

3.6.2 THE NATIVIST APPROACH

While the behaviorist approach regards language acquisition as stimulus controlled, and therefore subject to outside control, the nativist approach works on the assumption that language acquisition is not the acquisition of habits, but rather the development of innate linguistic abilities. This approach received special attention through the spread of transformational grammar. According to Chomsky (1969), and McNeill (1966) a child has at his disposal a set of rules similar to those of transformational grammar. This childish ability manifests itself in language universals. We discussed some principles of this concept, which belongs to the rationalist tradition, above in 2.2.2 in connection with methodological questions. Here it will be handled with respect to some theoretical questions and to criticism of the nativist approach.

Chomsky assumes that knowledge of language – a grammar – can only be acquired by someone who

> is 'preset' with a severe restriction in the form of grammar. This innate restriction is a precondition, in the Kantian sense, for linguistic experience, and it appears to be the critical factor in determining the course and result of language learning. The child cannot know at birth which language he is to learn, but he must know that its grammar must be of a predetermined form that excludes many imaginable languages. (1968:78)

According to Chomsky, however, we are at present hardly able to formulate a hypothesis about this innate preconditioning 'that is rich, detailed, and specific enough to account for the fact of language acquisition' (1966:27).

How does Chomsky imagine the procedure of a child? The Language Acquisition Device (LAD) (see above p. 30) makes the following possible:

Having selected a permissible hypothesis, he can use inductive evidence for corrective action, confirming or disconfirming his choice. Once the hypothesis is sufficiently well confirmed, the child knows the language defined by this hypothesis, consequently, his knowledge extends enormously beyond his experience and, in fact, leads him to characterize much of the data of experience as defective and deviant. (1968:78) (See also Chomsky 1975:13ff on the 'innateness hypothesis'.)

Lenneberg, who sees language as an aspect of the biological nature of man, expresses himself somewhat more carefully, and also with more differentiation. At present, very little is known about the inner organization of language processing in children. Only indirect keys are available – language universals, normal age of starting to talk, and a universal strategy for language acquisition – from which one could infer 'a great specificity for the underlying matrix'. The central question 'Just what is postulated as innate in language behavior?' can be answered as follows: 'Essentially the modes of catergorization. . . . This is an aspect of the latent structure. Innate also is the general mode of the actualization process but no particular aspect of the realized structure.' (1967:394)

Lenneberg did not regard features which are only characteristic of certain natural languages, whether they are particular to syntax, semantics, or phonology, as inborn. However, he states that there are many reasons to believe 'that the *processes*, by which the realized, outer structure of a natural language comes about, are deeply rooted, species-specific, innate properties of man's biological nature' (1967:394). Unfortunately, he also speaks of language universals, although language acquisition has only been studied in a very limited number of languages. In her criticism of nativist theory, Slama-Cazacu (1976:132) justly points out that far-reaching conclusions have been made based only on data from English, French, Japanese, and sometimes Russian, which in no way really justify a generalization.

As an argument for an inborn disposition to language, and against empiricism, nativists emphasize (among other things) that children develop their competence relatively quickly and uniformly, although only imperfect language material is available through spoken language. The primary linguistic data, i.e. the language presented by the child's environment, triggers language acquisition, but does not influence the manner of its function (see Chomsky 1965:4, 33). This statement is not supportable. In 3.4.2.1 above we stated that the language spoken with a child is of a very special nature, which undoubtedly simplifies his introduction to the sound system, the lexicon, and the syntax. Furthermore, 'speed' and 'uniformity' cannot be made to agree with the empirical facts, and belong to the methodological weaknesses of the theory, which were discussed in detail by Slama-Cazacu (1976:132f).

It can be added, from the criticism of this approach, that even the hypothesis that a child 'possesses' a system of rules similar to a transformational grammar, that is that the basic categories and their functions, as well as the relation between deep and surface structures, are present in a child, rests on grounds that make the serious, scientific consideration of the whole very questionable. It isolates language acquisition from other areas of knowledge and from the socio-cultural environment of a child (see Oksaar 1975a:73ff).

Peizer & Olmsted (1969:61) emphasize that, according to this model, a child does not even need to speak himself, in order to achieve the adult model. The present state of reseach into linguistic universals cannot offer any evidence for the assumption that a child has only to fill the pre-existing categories with the realization of the language of his environment. It cannot be concluded from the fact that a child at a particular time has control of a particular mechanism of rules, either that it was born with this mechanism, or that it only acquired it by conditioning (cf. Derwing 1973:55ff; Church, 1961).

Strangely enough, the present critics of this model have not introduced the evidence of the so-called wolf-children into the debate. The case of Genie, described above in 3.2, about which scientific results are available, offers unique material for establishing the role of environment in activating development, naturally without questioning the basic biological functions. This leads us to a third approach, convergence, which does not accept the 'learned–innate' dichotomy.

3.6.3. CONVERGENCE

While the modern empiricist–nativist controversy continues among linguists – Chomsky (1975:28ff) for example, sticks by his main concept without considering the criticisms – developmental psychology has achieved a reconciliation of viewpoints (see List 1972:75; Leuninger et al. 1972; Morton 1971). Those who hold to the nativist hypothesis fail to consider that the question of linguistic ability, which is species-specific for humans, cannot be separated from the question of socialization, enculturation and cognitive development. The fact that a child not only has to acquire linguistic competence, but that a human in his social context must begin to learn the communication rules at the same time as he learns the linguistic rules has not yet been adequately considered in language acquisition research.

Much of the discussion in the empiricist-nativist controversy should be regarded as speculative, as Slama-Cazacu explains:

> . . . because on the one hand, there are no convincing facts that may support either position, and on the other, the existing facts are presented by both schools as arguments meant to support their theory. (1976:128f)

Still, it seems remarkable to me that hardly anyone in the modern empiricist-nativist debate has responded to Stern's convergence theory. Stern had already presented this theory as uniting the standpoints of the two schools in 1914 in his *Psychology of Early Childhood*. He stated:

> Mental development is not just an 'appearing' of inborn characteristics, but it is also not merely a receiving of external influences, but rather the result of a *convergence* of internal factors with external developmental conditions. This 'convergence' is valid for the larger characteristics as well as for individual features of development. The question should not be 'Does this come from inside or outside?' but rather 'What part of this comes from inside and what part from outside?' since both influences always work together, only with differing amounts of influence. (1967:26f) (Translated by K. Turfler)

Stern also calls language development 'a convergence product . . . between the continuous influence on the child of the speech utterances of his surroundings and his internal language needs and capabilities' (1967:123). This idea is mirrored in, for example, the well-known work of Lewis, without direct reference to Stern:

> The linguistic growth of a child in his social environment moves forward as the continued convergence and interaction of two groups of factors – those that spring from within the child himself and those that impinge upon him from the community around him. (Lewis 1963:13)

Not an 'either-or', but rather a 'one-as-well-as-the-other' principle promises to be a more realistic starting point for forming a hypothesis in the area of *how* in language acquisition. However, not speculation but many-sided collections of facts should be the basis, according to the methodological standards presented in Chapter 2 (for more information on species-specificity in language see Dingwall 1975; on behavior as neither 'purely innate' nor 'purely acquired' see Mayr 1974).

The organizer of the symposium 'Biological, Social and Linguistic Factors in Psycholinguistics' in London in 1969, John Morton, regards three factors as decisive for the development of language, in the individual as well as in the species. They are 1) physical make-up 2) the relationship between man and the outside world 3) the relationship between individuals – the social factor (1971:7). But what remains uncertain is 'the way in which they interact, and which, if any, is dominant'. The present controversial standpoints can be traced back mainly to the difference in emphasis placed on these factors (1971:7). Systematic, empirical basic research which could bring this uncertainty closer to certainty, still needs to be done (see Slama-Cazacu 1976:138). However psychologists do recognize the importance of a multi-factor model of linguistic development (for examples see Bever 1970; Campbell & Wales 1970; Slama-Cazacu 1976:144).

3.6.4 IMITATION

The role of imitation in language acquisition and in learning theory in general is one of the most controversial questions and, to explain it, many individual studies are necessary, just as is an exact explanation of terminology. Many difficulties are connected with the fact that there is no universal definition of 'imitation' and that 'imitation' and 'repetition' are often used synonomously, for example, by Ervin (1964) and Bloom (1973:67). In psychology, imitation is generally understood as a process in which behavior is acquired by copying the behavior of a model (McNeill 1970). We can differentiate between *spontaneous imitation* in which the child himself imitates someone, usually the parents, and *non-spontaneous* (elicited) *imitation*, which takes place through the initiation of adults (see Dale 1972:91f). Differentiation between spontaneous imitation and repetition is a difficult undertaking (for information on more categories and a discussion of them see McCarthy 1954:517ff; on imitation as a collective term for different mechanisms for learning see Bergius 1971:126f).

Stern sees imitation as 'that factor which makes language learning possible in the first place' (1967:123). This is also the standpoint of the Piagetian School.[31] Sinclair emphasizes: 'the main factor in learning to talk is being able to imitate . . . language learning is also bound to imitation since in Piaget's theory all representation is considered to stem from imitation.' (1975:228)

The nativist approach negates the role of imitation in language acquisition, although the fact that a child imitates the speech of adults is not questioned. The process of acquisition is, however, not made up of imitation according to McNeill (1970), who also emphasizes that the contribution of parents' conversation to language acquisition is not just to offer a basis for the children to imitate. The role of imitation should, however, by no means be underestimated; just as, as we have seen in the discussion of Skinner and the autism theory, it should not be overestimated, until more is known about its function. There are different opinions about this.

Lewis (1963:25f) differentiates between three stages of imitation in the first year, and regards them as decisive in the understanding of linguistic signals.

From his empirical data, Kaper (1969:51f) states that children discover a system in spoken utterances, which they imitate. He also points out that even when a child's sentence deviates from the rules of the adult's language, it by no means proves that the child is not imitating adults. He notes that his son (3;2) used the sentence *Och, is het pijn*, instead of *het doet pijn*, but he also notes the same deviation in his own language use in the form of a question *Is het pijn*? He regards the word order of his son's sentence as imitation of his own question (see Brown & Bellugi 1964), but with the exclamatory tone instead of the question tone.

Brown & Fraser (1964) were the first to concern themselves with the structure of imitative sentences. In children between the ages of 2;1 and 2;11, they established that there were no differences between imitated and free spoken sentences of medium length.

Ervin (1964), too, compared spontaneous imitation and the free speech of five children about the same age as those Brown & Fraser studied. She also comes to the conclusion that they do not deviate structurally from free speech and draws the careful conclusion that 'there is not a shred of evidence supporting the view that progress toward adult norms of grammar arises merely from practice in overt imitation of adult sentences.' (1964:172) She does, however, find imitation important in acquiring a phonetic system and vocabulary; Stern & Stern have also discussed the matter in depth (1928:132ff).

After Brown & Fraser, Brown & Bellugi (1964) were among the first to operationalize imitation in research into children's syntax, and to employ it as a factor in triggering reduction-expansion activity in mother-child interaction. The children's sentences (ages between two and three years) were seen as selective imitation of the surrounding language, and it was established that at first only the strongly emphasized words of the adults were used. Articles, auxiliary verbs and most function words – which have a limited semantie content – were lacking: *That's an old time train* is imitated as *old time train*; *he's going out* as *he go out*. The word order is retained; for longer sentences the words at the end of the sentences were used (1964:137).

This type of utterance, which Brown & Fraser (1964) called

telegraphic speech, is called systematic reduction of the model by Brown & Bellugi (1964:143), that is a reduction of the adult sentence. Adults imitate the sentences of a child in that they repeat them as complete sentences. For example: *baby highchair* is repeated as *baby is in the highchair; sat wall* as *he sat on the wall* (on expansion see above 3.4.3.1). The child can now try further imitations with reduction. Brown & Bellugi are of the opinion that syntactical development at least cannot rest on imitation (1964:188).

On the other hand, Braun-Lamesch (1972:415) emphasizes that it is an error to maintain that imitation does not play a role in the acquisition of syntax. It is only that it has a lesser role here than in other areas. According to Church (1961) direct imitation plays a more limited role in learning grammatical and syntactic rules because the use of rules demands a transposition of the respective given. It can be added, that the reduction-expansion cycle gives the child the opportunity for syntactic exercise and understanding practice. Schlesinger (1975:220) assumes that the child practises new grammatical constructions in this way. Brown advocates another hypothesis: new grammatical forms, which the child does not yet have under control, are left out; however, when they are used it is according to the norms. Therefore, they can be recognized and imitated, but are not always available (see Slobin in Ferguson & Slobin 1973:463). Slobin interprets his data in the expansion-reduction situation similarly: Child: *Papa name Papa*. Mother: *Papa's name is Papa, uh-hum*. Child: *Papa name is Papa*.

It would certainly be wrong in such cases, which have often been documented in my Estonian, Swedish and German material, to deny that imitation has a furthering influence on the development of syntactic and morphological structures. The child also hears words with morphological elements, for example the word *Papa's* in the sentence quoted above, and these may be used metalalically.[32] The fixed word order of the noun-noun relationship at the two-word stage, according to Schaerlaekens (1973:150), can only be convincingly explained as the imitation of the word order of adults.

According to many studies in the sixties and seventies imitation belongs to an area which must be taken into consideration in the various questions of language acquisition (see Menyuk 1969; 1971; Bloom 1970; Jones 1970; Oksaar 1971; Bielefeld 1972; Francescato 1970; Schlesinger 1975). More research must be done however to determine which roles it plays at the various linguistic levels, and at the various stages of the learning process. In connection with this, another

143

question is important, which was touched on by Menyuk (1971:167): Which comes first – understanding and then imitation, or does imitation lead to understanding?

Another, as yet unexplained question is whether a child can imitate *sentences* without making his own.

Apart from the fact that imitation plays a different role for various children (Bloom 1973:144) there are two opposing views about sentence imitation. Fraser et al. (1963) and Turner & Rommetveit (1967) are of the opinion that imitation is a sensori-motor ability and is not dependent on understanding. On the other hand, Slobin & Welsh (1971) emphasize that imitation must function through understanding the sentences i.e. the meaning system. When the sentence overextends the direct memory span of the child, he must understand it, i.e. know the grammar of the sentence, in order to imitate it correctly. In this way only sentences which are within the limits of the direct memory span can be imitated in the way presented by Fraser et al. (1963). Slobin summarizes the results of various studies:

> Children may rote imitate sentences without understanding but within clearly definable limits of length and complexity. However, they also tend to reduce sentences in imitation to their level of ability – often revealing comprehension which goes beyond the evidence of their spontaneous speech. Furthermore, in natural settings, imitation itself may be an indication that the child is attempting to comprehend ongoing speech (in Slobin & Ferguson 1973:464)

Shipley et al. (1969) point out that a child's repetition of adult utterances helps him to understand. That sentence length influences sentence imitation in the way suggested by Slobin & Welsh (1971) can be seen in Miller's study (1973).

The viewpoints discussed here are built exclusively on verbal means of expression. At the same time the paralinguistic and kinesic means of expression must also be studied, even more since it is known that the child tends to imitate very early (see Stern 1967:64; Spitz 1965). Church (1961) reports that the earliest known imitation in children's development is sticking out the tongue at the age of 10 to 20 days.

Many of the statements discussed here are the results of test situations. The question whether imitation and repetition could also have other functions than those discussed here in the framework of linguistic abilities is seldom asked. However, it is important since spontaneous imitations can have a communicative function, too, and belong to the phatic function of language (see 3.5.1.1 above). In adult interaction, which does not usually involve language acquisition, imitation not only has the function of marking difficulties in understanding, but also, as

Ryan (1973) among others explains, an emphatic agreement with the speaker or an expression of mutual feeling. We can also establish that on the other hand, expressions in the area of routine – greetings such as *Good day*, *Good-bye* – only appear as apparent repetitions. They are, however, conditioned by socio-cultural norms.

Children's imitation should not, therefore, be considered only from the linguistic point of view, but also from the communicative standpoint. When Martin (2;0), pointing to something, asks: *What is that?* and gets the answer *Coffee*[33] and then repeats *Coffee* it may also – although it cannot be established with certainty – be imitation, which functions to imprint the new information on his mind; different observations point to the fact that children imitate unknown linguistic elements more frequently than known ones (see Brown 1973; Ryan 1973). However, when father says *Martin, Mommy is coming!* and the child answers *Mommy is coming!*, besides being an utterance of the expressive function, it may also be a means of the phatic function of language, in order to further communication, since it is not a question of new elements in the linguistic possession of the child.

Studies of child-child interaction have also shown that repetition frequently occurs and, as Keenan (1974; 1975) states, should be interpreted as a means of recognizing and agreeing with a conversational contribution just heard. Keenan finds that over 50 per cent of the answers in the dialogues of her twin sons (2;9) consisted of repetitions of statements. Between 2;9 and 3;0 years, substitutions appear: 'The child stops relying primarily on repetitions as a means of acknowledging a previous conversational contribution. Substitution operations create discourse that is intermediate to these stages. It is a form of repetition, and it is based on background knowledge.' (1975:85) (on Keenan's study see also above 3.4.3.2).

Shields (1976) explains that the sequences imitated in the dialogues of children can be considered as an exercise in theme cohesion, which is an important feature of dialogue (on imitation in playing, see Stern 1967:267f).

While we have emphasized an expanded function area of imitation in the process of language acquisition, in conclusion we should mention Guillaume (1925:24), who points out that no imitation is completely passive. A selection takes place, the child does not repeat everything which he heard. In addition, Jakobson stated that:'on the one side, the child's creation is not original, not an invention out of nothing, but on the other side imitation is not a mechanical helpless acceptance. The child creates as it borrows . . . what is borrowed is not a copy; every imitation requires a selection, and so, a creative deviation from the model' (1972:8).

Creative deviation mirrors its own system formation. The influence of the models – in which the frequency of what is heard, according to my studies, should not be underestimated – and the discoveries and realizations of a system can be observed in the overgeneralized forms in children's language, such as *grandfather sitted and readed*, which are formed in analogy to the regular verb forms acquired earlier (see 4.3.4 below).

3.7 WHEN IS LANGUAGE ACQUIRED?

This is not here a question of the timing of the development of individual stages; these have been discussed in 1.2.2 above and we will return to them in Chapter 4. At this point, we are more interested in the question of whether there is a critical age for language acquisition, that is, how old a human being can be before it is too late for him to learn to talk. The concept of a critical period in animal behavior, which has, for example, been established in birds and dogs, was applied to language acquisition by Penfield & Roberts (1959). They emphasize also that it is very difficult to learn a second language after puberty. Lenneberg (1967) has considered the biological basis for this assumption the most carefully. His neurophysiological explanations are not, however, uncontroversial (see 3.1 above).

According to Lenneberg (1967:142) there is much evidence that primary language acquisition is dependent on a certain stage of development. An individual leaves this stage at puberty. Numerous observations of the causal relationship between recovery and age in cases of brain damage, such as traumatic aphasia, offer evidence that a critical age can be set. The younger the injury is suffered, the better the chances of recovery. Lenneberg concludes that '*language learning* can take place, at least in the right hemisphere, only between the ages of two to about thirteen' (1967:153; see also 3.1 above). Lenneberg's explicit presentation of language in the context of growth and maturity (Chapter 4) leads to the conclusion that the critical limit for language acquisition can be set around the time of puberty. This time limit does not seem to be valid for many other kinds of human learning; for the acquisition of numerous general capabilities there do not seem to be any age linked limits.

Concerning the ability to learn a foreign language, Lenneberg emphasizes that this is also possible as an adult, because 'the cerebral organization for language learning as such has taken place during childhood' (1967:176). Still, there are two conspicuous differences after puberty: accent-free speech is no longer possible even with conscious learning in normal instances, and even the ease with which one can learn a language before puberty, just by living in a country, seems to be lost.

These statements concerning pronunciation can easily be supported. However, concerning other linguistic levels, one cannot necessarily assume that foreign language acquisition (second language acquisition) is generally so limited as Penfield & Roberts and Lenneberg emphasize. Observations of emigrants have shown that by no means all of those who emigrated young always demonstrated a good command of the language, and on the other hand, many of those who first had contact with the new language as adults spoke it very well (see the discussion in Huxley & Ingram 1971:268). Although more exact studies are necessary, these statements alone are sufficient to lead to the conclusion that neurophysiological explanations are not enough. In exactly such cases psychological factors such as motivation, attitude toward the language and country, prestige, etc., play an important role (see Oksaar 1972a:501f). They are factors which may possibly also be connected with forgetting the mother tongue.

In principle, observations in the area of foreign language acquisition should not be brought into the discussion of primary language acquisition, since if the languages are not acquired at the same time, there are different prerequisites. However, on the question of a critical period, second language acquisition offers the only opportunity to carry on studies of the different factors which could affect the ability to acquire language in and after puberty, in which cognitive and emotional factors seem to play an important role.

The case of Genie (see Curtiss et al. 1975) demonstrated, however, that puberty does not necessarily need to be the end of the critical period. Genie made progress in English although she had not heard any language during what Lenneberg called the critical period. Further studies are necessary which examine more closely the recently discussed connection between Piaget's stages of Formal Operations (see 3.3.1 above), and the accepted limit for primary language acquisition in puberty. Rosansky (1975) asks:

> What in the nature of Formal Operations might be an inhibiting factor to further language learning? Does some operation compete with language acquisition so that the child is no longer able to learn language? Perhaps the

problem is not in any single operation but rather in the whole nature of cognitive development, i.e. the process of decentration, progress from the static to the dynamic, and the flexibility brought on by reversibility.

3.8 SUMMARY

In this chapter we presented the requirements and conditioning factors of language acquisition. While there is still a series of open questions concerning the neurophysiological foundations, which makes further studies of intraorganic communication necessary, there has been agreement on the central questions of the complex problem of socio-psychological requirements, such as the role of emotional and social stimulants in the human environment. Among the most important factors in external conditions for language acquisition is the socio-cultural framework, whose social variables, such as family structure, socio-economic status, institutional environment, playmates, kindergarten and sex were fully discussed in relationship to the linguistic development of children.

This was preceded by a detailed discussion of language and thought, from the perspective, amongst others, of the relationship between linguistic and cognitive development. The presentation of the major research approaches, most importantly the two opposing models of Piaget and Vygotsky, leads to the conclusion that a more exact conclusion cannot be reached about the relation between language and thought, in the present state of research. This will first become possible when a systematic analysis of children's language behavior, which has generally been ignored by both sides, has been drawn into the model. The discussion of the Sapir-Whorf hypothesis makes it clear that in previous discussions sociolinguistic aspects, such as questions of socially significant linguistic variation and stability, were excluded; and the influence of social structures and social changes on the language, and of different behavior norms on its speakers were hardly considered. The language acquisition process offers clear examples of the manner in which language can affect the reflection of reality and the behavior of children.

Up to now little research has been devoted to what a child himself knows about language, i.e. his language awareness or meta-linguistic capabilities. Three-year-olds already seem to develop an ability for phonological analysis; children under five, however, react most strongly to semantic irregularities, which is demonstrated mostly in their choice of words. A feeling for certain pragmatic rules can also be found relatively early, soon after 2;6. Multi-lingual children may demonstrate an interlingual language awareness by two to three years.

The important interactional factors for language acquisition were discussed. The interaction basic to social, emotional, and linguistic development takes place in the mother-child dyad. The language spoken to children is a specific expressive-affective register, characterized by typical intonational and other paralinguistic patterns, and by phonological and grammatical modifications with the function of making communication easier, and of expressing intimacy and tenderness. This register has, however, theoretical consequences, since its existence contradicts the conditions of language acquisition postulated by Chomsky. Discussions of child-child interaction direct attention to the fact that children may develop an awareness for partner-related variation of language in the communication act relatively early, and acquire the ability to judge situations in which variations can be undertaken.

There were three questions which it was important to touch upon in conclusion. The first question: *What is acquired?* was answered by means of an analysis of the various functions of signs, and of communicative, particularly interactional competence. *How is language acquired?* led from critical observations of the empiricist-nativist controversy, to convergence theory, which, because of its principle of inclusion, makes a more realistic formation of hypotheses possible, in which the importance of multifactorial models of language development was emphasized, and 'telegraphic language' and controversial views of the role of imitation were discussed. Children's imitation should not, however, as has been usual, be observed from the purely linguistic point of view, but rather, its communicative function should be taken into consideration too. In response to the question *When is language acquired?* the idea of a critical age for acquiring language was discussed, during which second language acquisition was touched on.

QUESTIONS

3.1 What arguments does Lenneberg list in support of biological foundations for language?
What is lateralization, and what part does it play in language acquisition?
3.2 What is the importance of the social context in language acquisition?
3.3 What were some of the earlier arguments concerning the interdependence of language and thought?

3.3.1   What is 'tool thinking' and what relation does it have to the language and thought debate?
Contrast the theories of Piaget and Vygotsky.
3.3.2   Trace the development of linguistic determinism.
3.3.3   What evidence is there that a child has a certain metalinguistic awareness?
3.4.2   What are some of the social variables which affect language acquisition? State briefly the importance of each.
3.4.3   What major types of social interaction with children does the author mention?
Describe the language used by adults in speaking to children. What are its main features, and what significance does it have for language acquisition?
3.5   Describe two models of the functions of language.
What does a child learn when he learns to talk? That is, to what purpose does a child learn language, and what function does it serve?
3.6   Describe the two major theories of how a child learns language. What approach does the author suggest?
What role does imitation play in language acquisition?
3.7   When does a child learn a language? (At what age). What evidence is there for or against the idea of a critical age for language acquisition?

4 Stages of language development

4.1 PRELIMINARY REMARKS

In the following, we will consider some stages of language development. Here, it must be emphasized that the classification, if representative, comparable data from many different languages had been available, could have been done in more exact profiles. Further, it must be observed that different schools do not agree when and according to which criteria the beginnings of speech should be set. While the communication oriented school sets the beginnings of language at birth (see Truby 1969), the syntax oriented transformational grammarians set it at the two-word stage. According to Lenneberg (1967:158, 377) language development cannot start until after two years of age since he presupposes a certain stage of physical maturity and growth. For our classification we will use a method practised by the psychologists, whose criteria is the first word used with a fixed meaning (see Ervin-Tripp 1966:57; Stern 1967:122). It is advisable, however, to regard the beginning as a zone, since establishing the first word which has meaning does involve a number of difficulties (see 4.3.1 below).

Data from the languages of the major cultures yields the following average time for the stages of development. Around the third month the babbling period begins; about the tenth month the first word which is understandable in the environment may appear. The times given here have also been supported by my Estonian material, as well as by the Japanese studies of Murai (1963) and Nakazima (1966). One-word sentences are followed by two-word sentences and shortly thereafter by multiple word sentences. Inflexion appears around 2;6 (see Stern & Stern 1928, also above p. 9f and the comparative presentations of Lewis 1951:265–369, and McCarthy 1954:499ff).

These generalizations can only serve as a very rough average for a particular cultural circle, and individual deviations must always be expected, corresponding to the reality of human performance. As

Truby stated: 'Every child is different . . . Not only is the *language* of every child unique, but so is the developmental pathway associated with the establishment and accomplishment of that language.' (1976:84) Since most studies do not offer a stable base for comparison, a series of problems arises here, which we mentioned in 2.1 above. Among the unanswered questions, is the influence of structural differences of languages on the development of the categories. The presentation in this chapter can be restricted in general to purely verbal questions, since the related non-verbal and socio-cultural aspects were covered in Chapters 2 and 3.

4.2   PRE-STAGES AND BEGINNINGS OF LANGUAGE LEARNING

The stage which precedes the stage when the first word with a stable meaning occurs, and which includes approximately the first ten months can be divided into two periods according to sound production: 1) the earliest stages and 2) the babbling period. Research on prelanguage sound development involves great difficulties, since analysis without instruments is never faultless. Lewis (1951) presents the best survey of the beginnings of language learning from the first cries on. For more information on these stages see McCarthy (1954), Lenneberg (1967) and Truby (1976).

4.2.1   THE EARLIEST STAGES

Two sorts of vocalization are included in the earliest stages. Among the first are the birth cry and all other sounds connected with crying. Liebermann (1967:41) emphasizes that children communicate from birth on by means of sounds. Newborns already demonstrate different types of cry (see Lind 1965, and Truby 1976, who deal also with prenatal development, and on this question see McCarthy 1954:505). In the earliest stage, in spite of individual differences, the cry of hunger can be differentiated from the cry of pain.

According to Lenneberg (1967:276f) the second sort of vocalization appears some time after the sixth or eighth week, and consists of weak short 'gr-' sounds. In my material they can often be observed from 0;4 on, mostly in pleasant situations, and continue to appear occasionally as late as 0;9. Lewis (1951:30ff; 1963:18ff) distinguishes in utterances which are not crying, between sounds of discomfort and those of comfort, and establishes several stages of development (1963:15ff).

The more exact the technical possibilities for observation are, however, and the more many-sided the examination, the more differentiated the functional interpretation of early vocalization promises to be. Bullowa et al. (1976:85f) state that non-cry vocalization appears considerably earlier than has usually been assumed. Already in the first days they observed a series of sounds which did not seem to be connected with discomfort, and were often of low intensity. As can be seen in films, a typical sound might appear over a period of six days, always in social interaction between adults and the baby. Further research by Bullowa and her colleagues at MIT, with the goal of establishing a relationship between sound categories (studied spectrographically) and the behavior patterns of the child, also in interactive situations, promises to yield important conclusions about the forms and functions of earlier vocalization.

In contrast to Lenneberg (1967:277) who wanted to divide sounds into vowels and consonants only after the sixth month, the child's earliest utterances have been studied by a series of researchers, among others, Irwin and Lewis, on the basis of those sounds regarding which there is general agreement that they can be classified as vowels (see McCarthy 1954:506). According to the studies of Irwin (as presented by McCarthy 1954:508f), a child uses an average of 4.5 vowel-like sounds and 2.7 consonants during the first 2 months. Eighty seven per cent of the consonants which appear first are glottal, ten per cent are velar.

In the analysis of early vocalization, excepting the cry, it must not be overlooked that in the first year, difficulties in the co-ordination of breathing, oesophagus and mouth-throat mechanism can be established (see Lenneberg 1967:277).

4.2.2 THE BABBLING PERIOD

As Bühler (1930:105) states, two-month-old babies demonstrate certain specific gestures and sounds – experimental movements and babbling – which, in contrast to their previous impulsive activities, they notice and repeat. The beginning of babbling is connected to the child's positive experiences: when he feels satisfied, he repeats a series of sounds. Stern & Stern (1928:153) consider babbling as a sort of expression of comfort. Lewis (1963:19f), who differentiates between babbling as an expression of comfort and babbling as a sort of playing with sounds, explains this by means of the satisfaction the child receives from the utterances. This is similar to certain principles of Mowrer's autism theory, (see above 3.6.1). Mowrer assumes that the child does not begin to babble until the secondary reinforcement for his vocalization has been established. However, this assumption is contradicted by the fact that even children who are born deaf babble.

The structure of sounds produced by babbling is predominantly characterized by reduplication, i.e. repetition of consonant and vowel, such as *dada*, *nana*, *bebe*, or *tada*, *mibi*, *kaga*, where the consonant is formed at the same position. Babbling may also include sounds and sound sequences which do not appear in the linguistic environment of the child. Jakobson states that a babbling child may accumulate articulations which never occur all together in one language, or even one language family: consonants formed at any given position, palatalized and rounded, fricatives and affricates, tongue clicking, complex vowels, diphthongs, etc. (1972:20; see also Stern & Stern 1928:157). A word of caution from Truby should be mentioned here, however. He emphasizes that the description of any vocalization whatever, whether it can be linguistically identified or not, 'must be deferred to a visible-sonic analysis if there is to be physical validity for the description' (1976:94). The difficulties of describing children's sounds had already been discussed by McCarthy (1954:516).

Functionally seen, the child is not only practising different articulations, but also fulfilling communicative demands, since expressive utterances of comfort or discomfort may be connected to certain complexes of sounds (see Stern & Stern 1928:156). In this respect, the interpretation of an adult should be regarded as an important variable (see 3.4.3.1.1 below). Hoyer & Hoyer (1924) have pointed out the expressive value of the intonation of babbling monologues. Among other things, they establish an intonation of command, of attention getting, and of tenderness.

In the question of which role babbling should be given in the linguistic development of a child, there are two opposing opinions. Jakobson (1972:31f) denies it any influence on phonological development and makes a sharp division between it and the actual first stage of language, which is expressed not only in the deduction of phonetic means, but also in that the vocalization may cease for a short period. Neither does the psychologist Carroll see any relation to further development, (see Ervin-Tripp 1966:58). Lenneberg (1967: 140f) also speaks against a connection.

On the other hand, Blount (1970) explains that babbling should in no way be considered as unplanned, but rather as a period in which development is connected with the whole process of forming adult words. This can be seen particularly in studies of imitation abilities in the first year and a half. Based on their study of five children aged 0;6 to 0;8 and five others between 1;0 and 1;1, Oller et al. (1976) prove that the same preference for certain sorts of phonetic elements and sequences can be established in babbling as in children at a later stage of development. Irwin's research also supports a continuum; Bühler (1930:224) regards babbling as the basis for further development of the spoken language, and Leopold (1947), Murai (1963), Weir (1962) and Jones (1970) find further research results and arguments for this relationship. Lewis (1963:34f) states that the first words include sound combinations which frequently occur in the babbling period: *mama*, *papa*, *baba*, *tata*, an observation which Stern & Stern (1928:351–73) discussed thoroughly in a contrastive context.

These statements are all built only on the production of the child, and so observe the perspective of the sender. We know very little about the perspective of the receiver, particularly the perception of speech and comprehension in the earliest years of life. It is generally accepted, as has already been stated, that the child understands the language of its reference person much earlier than he himself speaks. However, there is no systematic research on how and when this ability is developed, and what linguistic consequences this has for the child's own production. Church (1961) discusses the principal problems; Eimas (1974), Morse (1974) and McCaffrey (1975) offer a survey of the literature.

Experimental studies have shown that the child at the age of one month recognizes the difference between two synthetic syllables [ba] and [pa]. However, according to McCaffrey (1975:211) such statements can only be interpreted as statements about physical-phonetic differentiations, which are not yet part of a linguistic system. Such studies, which are carried out with the help of synthetic language stimuli by, among others, Eimas (1974), do not correspond to the natural conditions of a child when he hears language. Furthermore, the ability to differentiate does not alone explain how and when a child recognizes sounds as elements in a language system conveying meaning. The studies do show that a child can differentiate quite early between phonetic patterns.

However, it is generally assumed, particularly since Lewis (1951:43ff 115f), that children first learn to differentiate between patterns of intonation and then between phonetic patterns. The first differentiation includes the different voice qualities; friendly or angry voices, etc. While a two-month-old child reacts with a smile when it is spoken to, regardless of what tone is used (Lewis 1951:54), Bühler &

Hetzer state that nine out of ten children in the third month react positively to an angry tone, and in the fourth and fifth month only four, the rest react negatively. In the sixth month all react negatively, and the response to a friendly tone is not only positive, but also neutral (see Lewis 1951:45). The question of when a child differentiates between a human voice and other sounds, such as striking a spoon against a china plate or the rustling of a piece of paper, was studied by Bühler et al. (1927). In the first two weeks there was a considerably more positive reaction to sounds. In the fourth week, however, the reaction to voices was more frequent; this was regarded as the first social reaction.

A further step is to study the differentiation of certain phonetic forms and the recognition of their use. The first reaction is demonstrated when, for example, the child turns his eyes in the direction of the wall clock when he hears *tick-tock*. Lindner's (1882) son did this for the first time at 20 weeks, after being lifted to the clock every day and hearing the words and the loud ticking.

In summary it can be said that the contrary opinions in judging the role of the babbling period in further linguistic development can be traced to differing starting points. Using formal criteria, Ervin-Tripp states:

> We may summarize the prelinguistic period by saying that the child's vocal output during this time has no known formal relation to his later phonological and grammatical patterns, though the comprehension system lays the groundwork for these patterns. (1966:60)

From the functional point of view the following hypothesis can be established according to which, as Menyuk states, the babbling period is not only a period in the development of language

> for vocalizing to obtain pleasure or to 'tune in' on the communication process, but also serves a useful linguistic purpose and is probably necessary for later development. (1971:69)

Research concerning development from the babbling period to the period of the one-word sentence, or holophrase, has mostly been concerned with the sound repertoire. However, since the one-word sentence is a sound-meaning unit leading to the surrounding language, but the babbling words are not, it must be asked when the ability to connect sound sequences with content is acquired. From the expressive utterances mentioned on p. 75 and further observations on child language reasearch from Lindner (1882) to Leopold (1939) and Lewis (1951) it can be seen that children already use sounds and sound combinations consistently in recurring situations and that although they are not identifiable words from the adult language, they are used successfully in communication.

When Lewis's son, aged between 1;0 and 1;4 wanted something out of his reach, he always stretched out his hand and said *e-e-e* (Lewis 1951:334ff). In such situations, Sven, aged 0;9 to 0;10, used *áta*, or also *áta áta*; the Estonian *anna* [give] may have functioned as a model. However, it is not possible to find a model for *krrr*, which was used during the same time when the wish was fulfilled, or for *geba* which was often used between 0;8 and 0;10 as a global expression for identification, looking at toys, the window, the door, a clock, etc., but without reaching or pointing gestures. All these examples, which can easily be multiplied, are evidence for the fact that a child is creatively active and shows the ability to form his own expression-content correspondences. Halliday (1975:33) established expressions for 12 different contents for his son at the age of 0;10,5. For more information on the analysis of such vocables – the term coined by Werner & Kaplan (1963), who designated such expressions on the border between babbling and conventional words – see Dore et al. (1976:15ff), who regard them as 'phonetically consistent forms'.

Most studies of language acquisition do not draw any methodological consequences from such observations. However, this suggests to us that a transition period should be set between the babbling period and the one-word stage, since this period seems to be of central importance for the development of semantic abilities. The Estonian repertoire of the child Sven at this stage contained 1) pure babbling: *tatata* (0;8), 2) babbling words i.e., phonetically and semantically identifiable sound sequences: *mämmäm*, expressing displeasure, underscored by paralinguistic elements (0;7), 3) adult words: *ema*, Estonian ['mother'] after (0;9); *amp* ['lamp'] Estonian *lamp*; *auto* (1;0) ['car']; whose correct use was established in many situational contexts.

How adult words and linguistic structures develop will be discussed in the next section.

4.3. DEVELOPMENT OF LINGUISTIC STRUCTURES

4.3.1 ONE-WORD SENTENCES
Between the tenth and the twelfth month, the stage of so-called one-word sentences begins, during which the child uses more and more meaningful expressions in the one-word form. As has been

mentioned, considerable individual differences in time can be expected. This stage can last some months, or even a year (Stern & Stern 1928:180). The debatable term 'one-word sentence', which has been suggested by Stern & Stern in the first edition of their book (1928:180), refers, according to Bühler (1934:72f), to the fact that those so-called global expressions cannot be regarded either as words or as sentences. Strevenson pointed out that the first words of a child correspond to a whole sentence:

> though an infant's first words are commonly such as are used by us in nominal relations, yet in the infant's speech these words are not nouns, but equivalent to whole sentences. When a very young child says 'water', he is not using the word merely as the name of the object so designated by us, but with the value of an assertion something like 'I want water' or 'There is water', the distinction in meaning between the two expressions being shown by the child's tone of utterance. (1893:120)

Stern & Stern (1928:179f) also see sentence-like structures in one-word sentences, which the child does not use 'in order to express an idea itself, but in order to express an opinion about it, or to demand that someone else say something about it.' Spitz (1965) also expresses himself in a similar way. And Lewis states:

> when the child first uses and responds to adult words referentially, he is referring not so much to an object – a thing within the situation – as to the situation as a whole . . . A word that the child speaks is . . . one means by which he responds to a situation, as an essential part of his total reaction to it. (1951:159)

The theoretical status of one-word sentences – which is not un-important in the question of grammatical development – is still controversial today, since there are difficulties involved in regarding isolated one-word utterances as sentences. However, this discussion was first driven to extremes by child language researchers who were influenced by transformational grammar and the thesis of inborn syntactic structure, such as McNeill (1970), who assumed that children, 'when they are limited to one-word utterances are still able to contrive something like complete sentences'. On the other hand, Shipley et al. (1969) argued against the assumption of sentences as holophrastic speaking and warned against overinterpretation on the side of adults. Brown (1973:153f) also sees the danger of this breadth of interpretation and suggests, with Bloom (1973), that the term 'sentence' should be avoided altogether in this connection: these words could not be sentences, but could express semantic intentions of a greater complexity.

In the arguments for and against, clearly presented by Dore (1975), one could find a way out of the theoretical dilemma by returning to Bühler's definition, according to which one-word utterances are regarded neither as sentences nor as words. That is to say that they do not yet belong to the double class system of words and sentences by which language, according to Bühler (1934:70), contrasts with other systems of more efficient traffic signals such as flag signals. Bühler compares the one-word stage of the child roughly to the single class universal signal system of sailors which has the feature 'that nothing of any kind of structuring of the meaning of the signal appears in the materially perceptible signs' (1934:71). This explanation seems to be better adapted to the primary facts than the one offered by Stern & Stern (1928:180), which refers to the stage where 'the sentences consist of only one word'. The fact that one-word utterances can be paraphrased by sentences should not lead to their being regarded as sentences themselves. Stern & Stern emphasized that

> The childish *mama* is not translated into the complete language by the word 'Mother', but by the sentence units 'Mother, come here', 'Mother give me', 'Mother, put me in the chair', 'Mother help me', etc. (1928:179f.) (Translated by K. Turfler)

Here, the child language uses a means foreign to its own system – translation – and this is not an innate characteristic of the child's language system.

What do we know about this stage? First, that the child can communicate with his surroundings relatively unhindered in communicative acts, by means of holophrastic speaking with the help of paralinguistic and with or without kinesic means, because, in spite of multiple reference relations, the situational context makes interpretation easier. Further, global expressions always have a situation dependent reference, in which the prosodic characteristics take on a particular role. According to Menyuk & Bernholz (1969 cited in Brown 1973:153), three semantic modalities can be distinguished in children between 1;6 and 1;8: statement, question and emphasis. The first utterances are still phonetically unclear, their meaning is not yet fixed. A word like *papa* often has a wider range of application than later, it is overgeneralized in its use, as for example when the child says *papa* to various men. However, the child seems to achieve the same thing, in principle, as the adult, only on a somewhat less differentiated level, as Lenneberg proved (1963:281). Hilde Stern's use of *mama* and *papa* clearly illustrates how dynamic this period is:

after 0;10 she began repeating words, at first without any understanding. After 1;0, she always answered the question *Who am I?* with *mama*, regardless of who asked, mother, father or nursery maid. *Papa* was still difficult to imitate at 1;1. After 1;1.5 Hilde used *papa* spontaneously and in answer to questions; it came in conflict with the word *mama*, which was gradually pushed into the background. Mother too, was now mostly called *papa*. A time followed in which both names existed in continual confusion (Stern & Stern 1928:19; see also Lewis 1963:37).

It is interesting not only that Hilde Stern (1;1.5) answered the same question with *papa* – with apparent hesitation and consideration – but also that she, after she had used both words correctly at 1;2.5, at 1;4.5 still often calls her father *mama*. This illuminates a general character-istic of language development, which Stern & Stern (1928:178) designate as wave movement: 'a continuous exchange between times of quicker and slower progress'. There are of course considerable individual differences, which vary from a short pause to a six month pause in learning words, to forgetting a part of the words already learned.

We have shown that there are arguments against using the term 'one-word sentence' in the way suggested by Stern & Stern but in favor of the way suggested by Bühler. Statements that one-word utterances function in the same way as sentences do later (Lenneberg 1967:283) are also not sufficient reason to regard them as sentences, although it does illuminate some aspects – since, as Jespersen (1922:134) explains, sentences presuppose a certain grammatical structure which is missing in the utterances of the child. Positions which go to the other extreme should also be repudiated; Bloom (1973:20,31) maintains that children at the one-word stage have almost no knowledge of linguistic structures and sentences. The child's efficiency as a listener, and the ability of children to understand the sentences directed at them clearly speaks against this idea.

As already mentioned, from the reactions of a child one can decide very early whether or not he has understood what was said. The following case shows that this is not just comprehension of intonation patterns, but rather that a certain ability to segment what is heard can develop relatively early.

Sven knew, at the age of one year, what sound a cat makes, and at the age of 1;1 gave the correct answer to the Estonian question *kuidas teeb kassike?* ['what does the kitty say?']. In the weeks thereafter, the correct answer was given after the first two words of the question. Nor did he answer with another familiar animal sound, since the question form came only in the context of the word 'kitty'.

Many more such cases can be found in my material from this period, and lead to the conclusion that the child had stored the question and can already visualize it structurally after hearing the first words: the emphasized key word is missing, but the sentence is correctly answered. Therefore, the influence of intonation, which is generally given an important part in language understanding, cannot have been decisive in this case. (see. p. 155, and for observations at this stage Stern & Stern 1928:167ff; Lewis 1951:113ff; Dore 1975:29).

There are various opinions on the function of intonation in conveying meaning in a situation, in which children do not use a certain word actively. Grégoire (1947:28) states that intonation is the deciding factor in understanding a sentence. Based on his son's reaction to the question, (asked in French), *Where is the window?*, Grégoire was able to conclude that he had understood the question. The same reaction followed when the question was repeated in English, but with French intonation. Meumann (1902:29) refers to Tappolet's experiment, in which he asks his children, aged between 0;6 and 0;8, the same question, first in German, then in French with German intonation, and both times received as an answer 'seeking gestures' in the direction of the windows.

Leopold analyzed the behavior of his daughter (0;11) who correctly understood her mother's question *Where are your shoes?*, since she pointed to her shoes in answer. He asked her in German and received the same reaction in answer. Leopold, however, concludes that the positive results depended on the fact that the two languages are closely related, the more so because he received no reaction to the question in Spanish. He concludes therefore, 'Intonation alone does not suffice in such a case; at least the keyword must be formally assimilated, minor divergences being still negligible' (1939:27). However, we established just the opposite: Sven (1;0) pointed correctly to his new boots when he was asked in Estonian: *Kus on Nenne uued saapad?* ['Where are Nenne's new boots?']. He reacted in the same way to the question in Swedish, with Swedish intonation: *Var är Nennes nya skor?* The keywords in both of these unrelated languages are completely different (see Oksaar 1971:345).

Intonation or keyword or both – further studies are necessary. Anyway, it appears to me that Leopold may have ignored an extra-linguistic factor: not wanting to react! A case from my material on imitation demonstrates the effectiveness of this factor and the 'consequences' of the child:

Sascha's Mother: *Sascha, say Sven!*

Sascha (1;2): [pi:ʃ]
Mother: *Sascha, that's Sven. Say Sven!*
Sascha: [pi:ʃ] (smiling.)
(After two hours they meet again.)
Mother: *Sascha, say Sven!*
Sascha: [pi:ʃ] (seriously.)
Mother: *Sven!* (louder, somewhat excited.)
Sascha: [ppi:ʃ] (with very clear aspiration.)
(After three hours, they meet again.)
Mother: *Sascha, say Sven!*
Sascha: [pi:ʃ]
Mother: *Sven! Sven!* (excited.)
Sascha: [pi:tʃ] (smiling.)

The one-word stage, according to Lenneberg, represents a transitional phase, 'during which the rules are extended from the interaction of articulatory movements to the interaction of larger language units, namely morphemes and words' (1967:283). He sees 'primitive syntactic units' in it (1967:283). Another aspect is semantics. Brown (1973:154) is justified in pointing out that assumptions such as Greenfield makes, that semantic relations, which are found at the two-word stage, already exist at that stage, rest only on the interpretations of adults. What facts would actually be evidence for semantic development at this stage? Brown (1973:154) gives clear examples. When a child, who uses the word *hat* correctly no longer calls a certain hat – father's hat – *hat*, but *father*, and when the child proceeds in the same way for several objects, that is, he sometimes uses the class name and sometimes the name of the owner; then the following conclusion can be drawn: it is evidence of the formation of the morpheme for '*procession*'.

How is the child's lexicon structured at this stage? Nelson (1973) studied 18 English children and found that most of them used at least 50 words at the one-word stage. They can be divided into six categories:

1) 51 per cent were 'general nominals': *ball*, *doggie*, *snow*
2) 14 per cent were 'specific nominals': *mommy*, and names of pets
3) 14 per cent describing or demanding activities: *give*, *byebye*, *up*
4) nine per cent were modifiers: *red*, *dirty*, *outside*, *mine*
5) eight per cent belonged to the personal-social words: *no*, *yes*, *please*
6) four per cent were function words: *what*, *for*.

In the following sections we will discuss three areas of linguistic development: phonetics and phonology, semantics and the lexicon, syntax and morphology.

4.3.2 PHONETICS AND PHONOLOGY

The literature on linguistic development in this area is very extensive (see Slobin 1972). The second volume of Leopold's studies, which were mentioned above on p. 19, is still regarded as the most basic work in the field. In the third chapter of her book, Menyuk (1971) gives a good summary of the important work in phonology done since Leopold. Among the best of the newer summaries are Ferguson (1976), and the second chapter in Ingram (1976).

Of the four theories of phonological development – the behaviorist (Mowrer 1960; Olmsted 1971, among others); the prosodic (Waterson 1971), which follows the tradition of Firth's prosodic analysis; the theory of natural phonology (Stampe 1969), which is based on a universal, inborn system of phonological processes; and the structuralist theory (Jakobson 1972; Moskowitz 1973, and others); the latter theory is the best known. We will base our discussion on Jakobson's theory, and will refer to Ferguson & Garnica's (1975) comparative presentation of the four approaches.

The structure of the sound system was first discussed by Jakobson in 1941 in his panchronistic models (see above, p. 14). This model is based on the principle of maximum contrast and minimum energy use. The hierarchy of the phonological structure determines the order of acquisition. The simplest structures with the widest contrast – *a, i* and *u, p, b,* and *t, d,* – are acquired first, then the more complex structures of contrasting sound classes are developed. Using data from all the studies of children's language published up to 1941, Jakobson constructed the following rules, which were to be valid for all languages:

> On the threshold of the first stage of language development, vocalism is built up around a wide vowel and, at the same time, consonantism is introduced by stops in the front of the mouth. Usually, *a* appears as the *first vowel*, and a labial stop as the *first consonant* in children's speech. (1972:61) (Translated by K. Turfler)

The contrast for consonants first appears between labials and nasals: *papa–mamma*, only later between labials and dentals: *papa–tata: mama–nana*. For vowels, the first contrast can be established between a lower and a higher position of the tongue – *a* and *i: papa–pipi*. The next step brings a division of the higher vowel into a 'palatal or velar, for example, *papa–pipi–pupu*, or a third middle degree of openness, i.e. *papa–pipi–pepe*' (Jakobson 1972:62–4). Vowels at the mid-tongue position – *e* and *o* – are learned later, since they are in a double contrast with lower and higher vowels.

It has often been observed that children replace the front consonants with back ones and say *dut* [dood] instead of *gut*, [good], or conversely, replace *d* and *t* with *k* and *g*. Leopold traces this to the undifferentiated stage of the phoneme system. The child is phonetically capable of pronouncing velar consonants, but phonemically he only commands the difference between two sets: labial and non-labial, and lacks the differentiation into three sets: labial-dental-velar. In his material, the sharper division between the three sets first started around the third year, the differentiation between voiced and unvoiced around the end of the second year; so that *t* and *k*, *d* and *g* all together form one phoneme. Fricatives, such as *s* and *f* do not belong to the elementary sound system, according to Leopold (1956/57:121) – *f* is therefore often replaced by *p*, and *s* by *t*. The affricates *pf* and *ts* are acquired even later.

Jakobson's famous theory, linguistically obvious as its basic principle seems to be, cannot however claim any general validity, because of the narrowness of the data it was based on. It must be tested against material from many languages, even if it seems to explain a general tendency of development (see Oksaar 1971:339). Because the data which is available at present cannot be compared, it also cannot be used to support the conclusion that the development suggested by Jakobson is the most frequent (see Ferguson 1976:17; and Olmsted 1974:105f for a critical evaluation).

Velten (1943) and Leopold (1947:199ff, 204ff) had already found important deviations from Jakobson's sequence of development in their material. To take an example from Leopold's material (1947:205), it was shown that the bilabial *w*, which Jakobson had not considered, was learned very early (1;1) and functioned as a fricative. Therefore Jakobson's statement that dental fricatives appear before labial ones cannot be maintained. He also did not consider that *h* and *f* are among the first sounds acquired by a child (see Ferguson & Farwell 1975:435; Ingram 1976:17). In his Czechoslovakian material, Ohnesorg (1959:151) also presents a sequence of development which deviates from Jakobson's. Further, it must be stated that Jakobson did not include children's onomatopoeic words (which have a more complex structure) in his study. In my material, there is evidence for the word [hafθl] as an onomatopoeic form, which uses the voiceless dental fricative [θ], not present in the native language, in the complex [fθ1]. For about a month, Sven (aged 1;1 to 1;2) used this word, frequently doubled [hafθlhafθl] to designate a functioning radio.

Now the central question is whether, as Jakobson suggested, there is evidence of phonological contrast between classes of sounds at an early stage of the child's development. My data (Oksaar 1971:334f; 1972c:194ff) speaks against it, and leads rather to the conclusion, that a child 'contrasts' words. That is sounds, even difficult sound combinations, are learned more quickly and easily in words which refer to something which seems to be of particular interest to the child. The brand name of the car NSU Prinz was always pronounced correctly, while otherwise [nts] appeared as [ns] (2;6); the Swedish dillkött [diltʃøt], which designated Sven's favourite dish had a stable pronunciation from the start, while [ʃt] was avoided in all other Swedish words, or was replaced by [s]. These statements suggest that if the functional aspect is taken into consideration from the very beginning, by asking which expression is used in what situation and for what reason, the resulting picture may deviate from Jakobson's. Sound acquisition – which does not occur independently of words – must also be considered using a complex of controlling factors which take the development of a semantic system and communicative-functional aspects into consideration.

Ferguson & Farwell found a series of variable forms in their material (*c.* 1;6) – words, which began with *m* or *m~n*, others with *n* only – and conclude: 'it is often impossible to make well-motivated claims about phonological contrasts in the usual sense at these early stages, as some might wish to do.' (1975:431) Crutten-den, whom they refer to, explained in 1970 that at the beginning it only seems possible to establish contrasts between words. However, because it excludes functional aspects, this approach cannot explain why contrasts arise between certain words and not others.

The relevance of the communicative-functional aspects can be clearly seen in the analysis of quantity in acquiring the Estonian phonemic system, which I discussed in Oksaar (1971;1972c). Usually languages have at the most two phonemically different degrees of quantity. They have a binary system, which differentiates between long and short vowels, for example. In Estonian we find the unusual case that consonants as well as vowels appear in three degrees of quantity: short, long and extra long.

The three degrees of quantity have a phonemic function, as can be seen in the following words. Vowels: 1. degree: *sada* [hundred] 2. degree: *saada* [send] (imperative) 3. degree: *saada* [I want to have (it)].

165

Consonants: 1. degree: *lina* [sheet] 2. degree: *linna* [the city's] (genitive) 3. degree: *linna* [into the city] (illative). (Oksaar 1972c:195) (Translated by K. Turfler)

At the age of 2;1 to 2;3, this system of quantity was fully developed in the six children studied, while at the same time the complete sound system was not yet completely developed. Sven differentiated, for example, between the three degrees of quantity for *i* in 1) *pime* ['dark'] 2) *piima* [milk] (genitive) 3) *piima* [milk] (partitive) and for *l* (at 1;7) in 1) *pala* (adult form: *palav*) [hot] 2) *kolla* (adult form: *kollane*) [yellow] 3) *alla* [down]. After the age of 2;4 no further deviations from this competence in the system could be observed. The fluctuation before this time occurred between the second and third degrees, and never between the first degree and the other two.

This fact brings to light another aspect of Jakobson's law of the gradual acquisition of the phonemic system. Jakobson refers to sounds when he states that 'contrasts, which are relatively infrequent in the languages of the world, belong to the last sound acquisitions of the child.' (1972:76) However, since he is dealing with the phonemic system, and the Estonian quantities, which are phonemic, belong to contrasts which seldom occur in world languages, one *could* assume that they would be acquired rather late. On the contrary, however, they are among the earliest acquisitions. This can easily be explained when the semantic-communicative aspect of the words are taken into consideration. It is important for the child to learn the differences in quantity from the very beginning, since they distinguish very frequent word forms; the child hears them constantly in his environment. The question of frequency in communication must therefore be taken into consideration, too.

Other results also lead to the conclusion that Jakobson's statements cannot properly be regarded as rules. According to Jakobson (1972:77) – in reference to Benveniste – the child develops either *l* or *r* as one of the last sounds because there are many languages which do not make a distinction between them. Weir (1962) however, indicates that her English speaking son (2;6) had full command of *l* and *r* while his use of other sounds still fluctuated. Statistics in my Estonian material show that at the same age *l* was dominant, but that *r* was fully developed, too. These statistics must be brought into connection with text analysis, however; the phenomenon should be observed as part of sentences or other larger units, since the fluctuations could be context dependent, that is, assimilative, as shown in the following Estonian sentences:

1) *Pane tuli äla* (correct: *ära*) [Switch off the light]
2) *Onu Berti para kardi ära = onu Bertil parandas kardina ära*
[Uncle Bertil had fixed the curtains.] (2:1).

In the first sentence, *äla*, instead of *ära*, seems to be the result of the influence of the *l* in the preceding *tuli*; in the second sentence, the correct sounds are used, probably supported by the distribution of *r*-sounds in the whole utterance.

Moskowitz (1973) attempted to explain phonological development using syllables as the basic element. Her explanation is considered an expansion of Jakobson's theory. It retains a universal order, to which is also added reduplication. A child uses CV (consonant-vowel) words and reduplicated CVCV words first, then they are followed by words with either harmony of consonants or of vowels, that is with repetition of the same consonant or vowel. The phonemic segmentation first begins when CVCV words are produced without the phenomenon of harmony. This approach is also an idealization, which is not based on empirical observation. Evidence which does not fit this pattern can be found in many languages. Among their earliest words Estonian children frequently learn words with a VCV structure, which do not even have vowel harmony, for example Estonian *ema* [mother] *isa* [father] (Oksaar 1971:339). Rather in many cases, Jakobson's observation that a child can use a word with two different consonants or vowels at first, but not both differences at once, holds true. Here, too, there are many individual differences.

The fact that not only *ema* [mother] but also *geba* (0:8), which has a completely different distribution, belong to the first words which a child learning Estonian acquires (Oksaar 1971:339) and that one of the first words of German and Estonian children, is *auto* – to name only a couple of examples which contradict the rule for the sequence of sound acquisition postulated by Jakobson – leaves the following questions still open in research today: 1) Is there a general sequence of acquisition of sounds and oppositions? 2) What status does the phonology of child language have in the system? To what extent is it autonomous, that is, to what extent does it demonstrate structural relations which deviate from adult phonology? As in other areas of language acquisition, according to Lenneberg (1967:280), the basic principle is that patterns and structures, not individual elements, are acquired. In my opinion, however, the interaction between elements and system or structure in the learning process must be studied more closely. Studies such as that of Smith (1973), which argue for universal categories based on generative phonology, although they only describe English data, do not contribute towards answering these questions.

Studies of phonological development must include phonetic development, since at first a child can only identify the words which he hears by using phonetic characteristics. On the other hand, an adult, who already has command of a phonological system, filters every acoustic perception and interprets it according to his system (see Francescato 1970). A series of empirical observations, discussed by Ferguson (1976), leads to the conclusion that phonological development takes place by means of changes in the pronunciation of individual words. Lindner's son (1;10) first used *daka* for 'danke' [thank you], then in the same month *ganke*. He added the nasal segment but then assimilated the dental consonant *d* with the velar one.

The sound system of the first vocabulary may contain elements which are lacking in the surrounding language (Grégoire 1947:101). A French speaking child may use palatalized dental sounds, which disappear in time. Russian, Polish and Estonian children, whose lingistic surroundings do have the phenomenon of palatalization-nonpalatalization as a binary opposition, retain them. Jakobson's (1972:108) explanation that the earlier palatalization of the dental sounds can be traced to the child's linguistic tendency to achieve an optimum separation of the sounds, seems theoretically plausible, since the difference between labial and dental sounds is thereby increased. However, individual cases must be subjected to more careful observation. Sven (1;7) first pronounced the Estonian word *muna* [egg] with a palatalized nasal, [mun'a], however, on the next day the form [mul'a] was used, with a lateral, and on the following day the correct pronunciation [muna] occurred. On the other hand, it must also be considered that adults often tend to use palatalization in their speech with children, even in languages where it does not have any phonetic function (see 3.4.3.1.2 above). The influence of the surrounding language must therefore be taken into consideration as a factor.

It is known that the simple structure of the phonological system of a small child leads to numerous homonyms, i.e. the same sound form is connected to contents which are not related to one another (see Velten 1943; Ervin-Tripp 1966:69; Oksaar 1971:341f). There are still only a few exact descriptions of the process; Ervin-Tripp assumes that it appears to a greater or lesser extent in the phonological development of every child. The following case illuminates the connection between homonyms and the development of the phonetic and phonological units.

At the age of 0;11 Sven used [á:pa] to designate his toy monkey[1] and for the lamp, in Estonian *lamp*. The new Estonian word *saabas* [boot] (1;0) received at first the pronunciation [á:ba], but there was often very little distinction between [p] and [b]. After one week of frequently designating all three objects, supported by kinemes, the phenomenon of 'disturbing homonym' became evident, so that 'lamp' and 'boot' were excluded from communication, and [á:pa] only functioned as the designation for monkey. Only when the opposition /b/:/p/ was achieved with clearer articulation, at 13 months, was the word for 'boot' [á:ba] brought back into active use; in isolated cases, also with the final sound of *s*. About the same time, the sound complex [mp] was stabilized in [ampa]. It is interesting that [ampa] had already been used several times (0;9), but was then abandoned. This is connected to the phenomenon which Ferguson (1976:27) summarized as *phonological idioms* i.e. that there are words which are pronounced better or worse than the typical words in the child's phonological system. They are called *progressive* or *regressive idioms*. Developments must thus also be expected which move away from the adult model, and result in regressive idioms. They correspond to overgeneralizations at other linguistic levels.

In contrast to earlier studies, such as those by Templin and Irwin, and also Jakobson's description, in which the material is presented as if a phoneme is learned once and for all, Olmsted emphasizes, from the results of his study of 100 children between 1;3 and 4;6 that:

> A phone is not learned at once and for all. In fact its usual course of development appears to consist of a mixture of success and errors in successive attempts at a given phone with gradual increases in the percentages of success and decreases in the relative numbers of errors. (1971:244)

According to Irwin's (1947) studies in the first 30 months vowels occur with greater frequency than consonants. The curve for the use of vowels rises continuously until the second year; the curve for the use of consonants is parabolic. At 2;6 a child uses practically all the vowels, but only two-thirds of the consonant repertoire. Back consonants, particularly glottals, and front vowels dominate in the first months, but at the age of 2;6 the ratio is reversed (see McCarthy 1954:509).

In comparison with the research on a child's production abilities, considerably less research has been done concerning his perception abilities. Shvachkin's study in the year 1948 (1973) is still regarded as one of the most extensive experimental studies done in this area. He stated that the ability to recognize differences between all vowels and consonants was developed in Russian children between the ages of 0;10 and 1;9. The experiment required 18 children to react to monosyllabic nonsense words, which differed by one distinctive characteristic in each task. It led to the conclusion that the order in which the differences are acquired in perception is similar to that suggested by Jackobson for production. However, since not all of the important details are presented – how often the children were tested, which criteria were used to establish that a child had perceived a certain opposition, etc. – objections can be made to the validity of Shvachkin's results, as Garnica (1973:216) correctly points out. The results of Garnica's (1973) own experiment with 16 children aged 1;5 to 1;10, carried out as a test of Shvachkin's hypothesis, leave many doubts about a universal ontogenetic order of phonemic perception. The order of development is considerably more variable than appears in Shvachkin's data.

Using the same technique as Garnica and Shvachkin, Edwards (1974) studied the perception and production of English fricatives and glides (/l/, /n/, /w/, /j/) in 28 middle and upper class children aged from 1;8 to 3;11. Her basic hypotheses were that the correct phonemic perception of an opposition is acquired by its correct pronunciation, and that the unmarked sounds, i.e. orals are acquired before the marked sounds, such as nasals. Her results only partially support the hypothesis; the most important results are that three-year-olds do not have a complete phonemic perception, that it develops gradually, generally earlier than production, and that the order of acquisition displays a tendency to uniformity, in which the details vary widely (1974:218f.).

Even if nothing definite can be said about the order of the development of sound perception, and many studies must be carried out – with younger and older children, larger samples, with various sound positions and in various languages, – there still seems to be much evidence that sound perception precedes sound production. A series of observations made in natural situations supports the results gained in test situations. A child can, for example, as Smith (1973) states, perceive the differences between [s] and [ʃ], although he himself pronounces *ship* as [sip]. He protests when an adult uses the same pronunciation. The following dialogue demonstrates how a child orientates himself on the (here imperfect) model of an adult – Smith's child uses the form [maus] for both *mouth* and *mouse*, although it can recognize both without error in pictures.

Adult: *What does* [maus] *mean?* – Child: *Like a cat* – Adult: *Yes: what else?* – Child: *Nothing else.* – Adult: *It's part of you.* – Child: (disbelief) – Adult: *It's part of your head.* – Child: (fascinated) – Adult: (touching child's mouth)

What's this? – Child: [maus] (1973:137).

Another dialogue, which is found in Dingwall, illustrates the relationship between [r] and [w]:

> Adult: (pointing to a picture) *What's that?*
> Child: *That's a* [wæbɪt].
> Adult: *No, say* [ræbɪt].
> Child: *But I didn't say* [wæbɪt], *I said* [wæbɪt]!

In any case, Shvachkin (1973:113) finds that sounds which a child cannot pronounce are differentiated later than those which the child can pronounce. Peizer & Olmsted (1969) and Salus & Salus (1974) maintain that sounds can be correctly pronounced only when they can be recognized.

In the first stage of development, based on the first 50 words, Ferguson (1976) discovered a series of characteristic features: the child plays a very active and creative part in this process. His first words form a connection between babbling and adult language. The child's phonological systems for production and perception are relatively independent. The following observations are also important:

> In the child's construction of a phonological system for production he begins with structural constraints in selecting adult model words and in producing his own words . . . The child invents and applies to his repertoire of phonetic word shapes a succession of phonological rules which regularize the pronunciation of phonetically similar words. The child gradually relaxes his constraints of selection and production to allow greater structural complexity and diversity within words. Each child follows his own distinctive route in phonological development. (1976:36)

Between the ages of 1;6 and 4;0, this development is intensified by a series of phonological processes, for example progressive and regressive assimilation, dissimilation, substitution, reduction of sound complexes, omission of initial or final consonants and so on. Particular individual articulations are not learned but rather 'categorical sound contrasts which approach the sound system of the native language step by step' (Leopold 1956/57:121). Good summaries can be found in Leopold (1947:207–235), Lewis (1951:177–88), Ingram (1976:29–44) and Pačesová (1968:200– 205). Her study of her son's structural development of Czech phonemes is also interesting from the methodological point of view. She does not divide her material into time periods, but rather into three periods of lexical units – the first 50, the first 100, and the first 500 words. This method allows for the fact that children develop at different rates, and offers a better basis for comparison in further studies than the usual differentiation according to the child's age.

4.3.3 SEMANTICS AND THE LEXICON

The discussion of the development of the sound system demonstrates clearly that the word is genetically primary, when sounds function phonemically, since 'the child does not imitate sounds but rather *words*, which it simplifies according to the state of its own sound system' (Leopold 1956/57:122). He must learn that these words mean something – that adults connect certain sound forms with certain contents, that is, that the expression and contents are inseparable. As has already been mentioned several times, the child communicates with his environment before he can talk (see 2.4 above). He can also understand adult utterances before he can use the words himself. Evidence of this is offered when Kirsten (0;11) can point to the right object in answer to the question, 'Where is Mommy's nose (eye, ear)?' and 'Where is Teddy's nose (eye, ear)?' Macnamara maintains:

> Infants learn their language by first determining, independent of language, the meaning which a speaker means to convey and by working out the relationship between the means and the language. (1972:1)

That is, a child first learns to understand what the speaker means, and uses 'this intention as a key to the final mastery of the linguistic code' (Hörmann 1976:352). There is no consensus of opinion as to how this happens; each theoretical standpoint from which the question is approached is already mirrored in its formulation. For example, the question 'How does the child assign utterances to meanings?', as presented by Hörmann (1976:343f), already makes the primary assumption of a semantic deep structure, while Macnamara's statement assumes that cognitive structures precede linguistic ones. It is important, however, to ask what knowledge the child has already acquired before it begins to operate with word meanings. Clark summarizes the most important features of a child's knowledge:

> He has been gathering a large amount of nonlinguistic knowledge about his environment. He can identify objects, their properties (e.g. shape, size, texture), their usual orientation, their customary or possible relations to each other in space and so on. He is also setting up primitive notions of causality and learning to relate events in time, e.g. the customary sequence in his everyday routines. (1975:78)

The child acquires this knowledge by means of his perception system, communication takes place on several channels of the sensory qualities at once (see 2.4 above). There is much to support the assumption that 'It is his organization of this nonlinguistic knowledge that seems to provide the child with his first hypotheses about what words might mean.' (Clark 1975:78)

We have already discussed different theoretical viewpoints in the sections on 'Language and thought' (3.3), and 'How is language acquired?' (3.6). Certain aspects of semantic development were analyzed in connection with semantically oriented grammar models (2.2.2.2 above). Here we shall deal with some of these questions more closely.

Too little is known about the development of the semantic system and the semantic structure. The factors which would lead to observations such as, for example, Lenneberg's (1967:336), who sees a similarity between the cognitive mechanism behind semantics and that behind syntax, in the process of categorization, differentiation and interrelation (transformation) are still unexplained. According to Leopold (1956/ 57:122) words are almost always learned together with meanings, during which 'it is clearly a progression from coarse to continuously finer differentiation'. In order to operate with vocabulary the child must learn to identify situations, too, in which the various differentiations function (see above p. 72).

The child learns the necessary semantic features[2] in the situational context as well as in the linguistic context of the communicative acts, which a child who still cannot read hears. Important questions in this connection are: 1) Which elements are selected? 2) Is it possible to establish the grounds for this selection, which passes through the filter of the cognitive process? The ability to transform the so-called objective reality – the variety of the complex of features – into the linguistic reality, can best be observed in children (Oksaar 1975a:734f).

Differentiation is developed from coarse to very fine, during which the principle of over-generalization is frequently observable. The basis for this process was already clearly illustrated by Leopold (1949a), when he emphasized that the selection of the surrounding vocabulary which the child undertakes, according to cognitive abilities, is 'at first governed by his needs and wishes'.

The child strides from coarse, partially unacceptable groupings of meanings through expansions and restrictions of meanings, step by step to the acquisition of the adult categories. Along the way, he finds complexes of meanings which adults reject or laugh at. They are disappointed when the child calls all men 'Papa', but think it perfectly all right when he calls all

173

strange men 'Onkel'. The laughter or disapproval of the surrounding adults is an incentive to subconsciously check and reform the categories. (1956/57:122) (Translated by K. Turfler)

Principally important are the conclusions which can be drawn from this observation. First, that there are two contradictory forces at work in this process – expansion of meaning, and restriction of meaning – and secondly that the reaction from the surroundings influences this development. Jespersen has already emphasized: 'A child is often faced by some linguistic usage which obliges him again and again to change his notions, widen them, narrow them, till he succeeds in giving words the same range of meaning that his elders give them.' (1922:117) Lenneberg assumes that at first a child uses a word for 'a general and open category, stimulus generalization is prior to stimulus discrimination' (1967:332).

In a series of examples Leopold (1956/57:422f) illuminates the arbitrariness of the categories in adult language, which the child must deal with in the process. We choose one of those concerning objects. A child learns what a *Bürste* [brush] is by observing that in spite of all the differences between *Zahnbürsten* [toothbrushes], *Schuh-bürsten* [shoebrushes], and *Haarbürsten* [hairbrushes], they are all referred to with the same word because they are all used with a similar motion. Then it is only logical when a child refers to a similar object, which a painter uses with a similar gesture, as a *Bürste*. (In German, a paint brush is called a *Pinsel*.) English speaking children can make this generalization, since 'brush' includes both the German *Bürste* and *Pinsel*. Children learning French and German must learn another word (see above 3.3.2).

It should not be overlooked that for the child, the reality which he 'classifies' is not static, but dynamic. As early as 1894, Dewey pointed out that a child's tendency to use the same word form for a series of objects, for example *ball* for orange, ball, moon, etc, can only be understood if we ask to what extent *ball* has an active meaning for the child. 'Ball' is something to throw, just as much as it is a round object (cited by Lewis 1951:197). From another point of view, which still includes this aspect, Lenneberg (1967:333) states 'categorization is a creative process of cognitive organization rather than an arbitrary convention.'

Lewis (1951:194–209) offers a systematic analysis of the situations in which over-generalizations occur, also taking the older literature such as Meumann, Stern & Stern and Dewey into consideration. He classifies the conditions discussed by Stern & Stern (1928:186ff) as objective similarity of situation, but those of Meumann and Dewey as affective in respect to functional similarity. According to Lewis (1951:199), however, it is not sufficient only to analyze the situation, but rather one must consider the function of the word used by the child, since the child:

> is both expressing the feeling aroused in him by the situation, and drawing attention to it, with the result that the bystander is brought into his circle of activity. (1951:206)

The same driving force, which stimulates expressive activity in a child who does not yet talk, is effective in the expansion of word use, according to Lewis:

> As before, the child finds himself confronted with new situations which rouse him to speech: but now instead of using one of his own primitive cries he uses a tool which he has found effective in a similar situation. Urged then by this declarative impulse, he uses an acquired word, and in doing so extends its use. The need for declaration has helped to bring about extension (1951:206)

With systematic observation, it becomes clear how the child tries to identify the unknown verbally by using features he already knows. When he uses the same designation for different objects, it can be attributed to sameness of function or reality, or similarity of colour and/or form. My material shows, however, that it is frequently more than one feature which causes the over-generalization, and that the process can be judged only in terms of the entire communicative act. A typical example: Sven (1;3) found a pointed paper clip, picked it up and had a similar painful experience to his first encounter with a needle, and said in Estonian, but without turning to his mother, *nõel* [needle]. Here, the paralinguistic elements – some hesitation, frightened-asking tone of voice – lead one to classify the whole as a sort of identification-question. From the entire situation, it can be seen that the effect of the object – a painful prick – was the dominant feature for the over-generalization, but that it could have been influenced by the size as well as the nature of the material, that is, the visual features. A classification of over-generalization such as Clark (1973:78–83) attempts, using data from older material, in which the extension is classified according to one criterion – 'movement, shape, size, sound, taste, texture' – is questionable. Quite often features from different classes can work together, as was seen in the example above.

Before we turn to the discussion of Clark's hypothesis I would like to present some further examples for designating an object seen for the first time, in which the object is named by identifying certain features or bundles of features (Oksaar 1971:353ff). Such observations made in the child's natural linguistic milieu should always be preferred to observations made in experimental situations, although they are not mutually exclusive (see above 2.3).

1) Feature class: Form. A *cow* in the field is called *elevant* (Estonian) [elephant], after the largest animal known (1;10) – A stone *lion* in front of a museum is called *lambake* [lamby], after the child's stuffed toy; here the similarity rests on the similar pose. – When Sven (1;8) saw the midnight sun on the horizon in north Sweden, a completely new experience for him, his prompt reaction was *kolla* (=*kollane*) *pall* [yellow ball], accompanied by a dash in its direction (see Dewey above p. 174) – *Raindrops* on the window are called *vihma tükikesed* [little pieces of rain] (1;8).

2) Feature Class: Form and Color. White asparagus stalks cause him to ask *Mis see on? Küünal?* [What is that? Candle?] (2;4); the child was familiar with white candles. – Big foamy *waves* on the Baltic sea are identified as *lumi* [snow] (2;6) – Every light colored car is called *pappa auto* [Daddy's car] (1;4 to 1;5).

3) Feature Class: Function, Movement, Form, Location. Sven (1;4 to 1;5) called his baby carriage [mæ':auto] – he called the nurse maid Mai [mæ:]. It seems that three factors mainly contributed to this: a) sameness of function – the child rides in the carriage, just as he does in his father's car, Mai 'steers' it, just as father does his car, b) movement – the carriage and the car are both objects which can be moved, c) form: both have four wheels. The child showed a great interest in all kinds of wheels at that time. Location may also have played a role: both were in the garage.

4) Feature class: Absence of Substance. Sven (1;6) learned the Estonian word *auk* [hole] in connection with the keyhole. The next day the key which was connected with it was also called *auk*. After two weeks, however, the word was applied to a series of other empty places: the hole left by a drawer which had been removed, boxes without lids, empty spaces between the pages of an open book. The common feature of all these items is 'absence of substance'. It is interesting to note that these categories, which are harder to recognize than objects such as a ball or a car, and for which, in many cases, there is no word in the adult language – for example for the empty space between the pages of a half open book – are recognized so early by a child.

With the help of different types of cases of over-generalization – which usually occur between the ages of 1;0 and 2;6 – the process of combinations in the area of semantic development can be recorded and analyzed. Expansion of the possible uses of a word result logically and consistently from features and bundles of features which can be found and identified in reality. What is called 'metaphoric' in adult language can be regarded as primary use here.

As the empirical data shows, the features which are important for the identification of meaning cannot always be nearly as easily established as Clark (1973; 1975) asserts in her 'Semantic Feature Hypothesis'. According to this hypothesis, the extension of words to include new objects is primarily based on perceptual similarities. Word meanings are learned in succession: at first the child identifies them with the help of only one or two features which are perceptual. According to this hypothesis then, the child might understand 'dog' as 'four-legged' and therefore call cows, sheep, zebras, and all other four-legged animals 'dog'; most over-generalizations are based on this form. The word is gradually given more and more new features, which lead to a gradual adjustment from the more general meaning to the more special meaning of the adult use (see Clark 1973:72f).

Leopold (1949a:102–154; 1956/57) had already proved how complex the process is, and how it is marked by continuous expansions and contractions of meaning. His presentation does not however, speak for Nelson (1973; 1974) who criticizes Clark's hypothesis using arguments from Piaget's theory. She is of the opinion that children are not able to analyze the features of an object, such as form. They experience objects and people in the network of relations in which they occur:

> From the child's interaction with people and objects, specific concepts emerge, each of which is composed of a functional core synthesized from the various relationships and acts into which each concept enters. (1974:278)

According to Nelson, children regard those items as similar, which have similar functions; a point of view which Dewey had already supported (see above p. 174). A functional feature of ball, for example, could be 'can be rolled', while a perceptive feature would be 'round'. Our examples clearly showed that both are possible; although, when the whole material is taken into consideration, it can

177

be said that over-generalizations based on similarity of function are much less frequent than those which arise from perceptual features.

In contrast to Clark, Hörmann (1976:130f) states that the features of a word do not form an additive sum, but rather show a dynamic relationship. The question still remains, for example, as to where the more linguistic features 'time', 'simultaneous', 'before', in the meaning of *before* and *after*, come from, if the child only infers features from perception as the theory postulates.

In respect of the question whether over-generalizations also occur in understanding, the studies of Hutternlocher (1974) and Thomson & Chapman (1975) lead to the conclusion that there are individual differences (for details see Clark 1975:81f).

How does a child learn opposites – adjectives such as *hot* and *cold*, *long* and *short*, *more* and *less*; adverbs such as *above* and *below*? At first they are often confused. Leopold (1957/57:123) explains this by saying that at first the child operates with a two part contrast – 'normal' and 'not normal'. The three part opposition, which underlies antonyms, 'hot–normal–cold', is learned later. Leopold only found five or more parts such as 'hot–warm–(normal)–cool–cold' at a much more advanced stage of development. Donaldson & Balfour, Donaldson & Wales and Clark have carried out studies of this sort and other sorts of rational designations since the end of the sixties. They tested English speaking children betweeen the ages of three and five (for a more detailed discussion see Clark 1973; 1975). While at that age the over-generalization discussed above occurs only infrequently, another sort of over-generalization can be established with relational words, in which both words of a pair like *more–less* are used synonymously. One result which should be regarded as important is the fact that both words are used synonymously in the meaning of 'more'. From this, and from the observation that the meaning of the unmarked word is chosen from pairs of dimensional adjectives, that is, the meaning of *large* and not that of the marked *small*, it can be concluded that words with general features are acquired first. Children between 3;5 and 4;1 can understand the unmarked adjective of a pair of opposites much better than the marked one.

Using her own and other studies, Clark (1973:94) established that the pair *big–small* was over-generalized as the unmarked pair in the semantic field of more specialized dimensional adjectives such as *long–short*, *high–low*, *wide–narrow*. From that it could be concluded that the pair *big–small* is acquired before the pair *long–short*. Further studies are necessary to test the hypothesis. From the studies of Eilers et al. (1974) with 14 children aged between 2;6 and 3;6, it can be seen that individual variations in the learning strategies for these adjectives must be expected.

That children between the ages of five and eight years still do not seem to differentiate between *tell* and *ask* and interpret *ask* as *tell* can be seen in Carol Chomsky's (1969:63f) experiments; we will come back to them later. However, in natural situations it can be observed that a child tries very early to bring the various features of a situation into line with his vocabulary; that is, he gives it a greater flexibility than the 'Semantic Feature Hypothesis' would imply. This can be seen more clearly when the child is missing a word.

Sven (2;2) goes into a dark room, and wants a light. Apparently he does not know the expression, since he hesitates, after calling his mother, and says, in Estonian, 'Dark go 'way'. It is interesting to note here that the child expresses his communicative goal by using the minus marker of the given situation, and not the plus marker of the new one, i.e. by an over-generalization. The following utterances demonstrate the combination of semantic features as well as the early expansion of the nominal phrase. Sven (1;9) sees his neighbor (who has a small daughter) mowing the lawn: *Teine pappa niida . . . onu niida*, [the other daddy mowing . . . uncle mowing]. (The verbal endings in the Estonian are still missing.) The child 'practises' the tendency to differentiate on objects in his surroundings, as can be seen in the following example. Two lamps, which look alike, were usually switched on in the bedroom. Sven (2;10) describes his observations, introducing them with a question:

> *Isa, kas sa paned tule põlema? Samad tuled põlevad. Samad lambid põlevad. Pirnid.* [Father, do you turn on the light? The same lights (=source of light) are burning. The lamps are burning. Light bulbs.]

Except for *samad* [the same], all of the words fufil the conditions of semantic congruence in Estonian. The order *tuled–lambid–pirnid* – 'lights–lamp–light bulbs' – demonstrates differentiation in 'part of' categories.

The general question which Hörmann asks '. . . does a child learn the features which belong to a word, or does he learn the word for a concept, which can be translated as an aggregation of features?' (1976:389), in which he seems less inclined to the first position, can hardly be answered from the 'either-or' perspective, in the present state of empirical research. Rather, it seems that the assumption is justified that both occur in the semantic identification process. How they are divided in the various areas of meaning must be studied more closely.

A further question which must be studied is: When does the naming system turn into a relation system? How and when does the child learn the semantic congruences, that is, the necessary concurrence in the classifications of verbs and substantives which refer to an object (Leisi, cited by Oksaar 1976b:208, principles 68–71), for example, that *flowing* can only be used for liquids? In 3.3.3 above we pointed out that this occurs in certain situations, and that a child between three and four years old already reacts to the non-observance of rules of semantic congruence. Further observations in various languages are necessary, among other things, in order to answer the question of when awareness of the metaphoric use of language develops. In the second chapter of his book, Chukovski (1968) gives a series of examples of children's reaction to the figurative and idiomatic language use of adults.

In 3.3.2 above we discussed the arbitariness of the semantic categories. This can be seen not only by contrasting various languages, but also in the semantic development in child language in a language community. In German, the usage norms for *Blume* [flower] and *Blüte* [blossom] are determined by the features of place. However, a child, using the features of form and color, identifies for example a *Blume* [flower] on a cherry tree. In Swedish, there is no comparable differentiation – everything which blooms is *blomma* [blossom and flower]. Swedish children make the same identification but in this case it is not a deviation from the adult model.

The semantic identification process is connected with the principle of *Sinngebung* ('giving sense'), which four- and five-year-old children demonstrate in such questions as: *Meerettich – ist er aus dem Meer gerettet?* or *Restaurant – gibt es da Reste?* (Oksaar 1975a:735). It is well known that this principle is the basis for the popular etymology of adult language. It presumes the ability to segment (on this question see also Brown 1973:390). Stern & Stern (1928:417ff) offer a series of examples for this age. The instinct for play and the poetic function of language in the sense of Jakobson (see above 3.5.1.1) can also be seen here. Such statements as *the cat barks* can be traced to the play instinct. Jakobson regards this case as a manifestation of the 'freedom of a child to use language'.[3]

As we have seen, not only the expressive ability of a child, but also his interpretation is connected with his ability to segment. We know much too little about what a child, even a school-age child, understands. Difficulties arise even for adults, since the question of understanding is inter- as well as intra-linguistic, and can depend on age differences, sex, education, etc. (Oksaar 1976b:135) There is however, a much better possibility of establishing this in experiments with adults than with children.

△One must always take into consideration that the interpretations of utterances by a child as well as by adults are based on the background of their experience. The area of interest seems to be an important factor which offers the first level for interpretation (Oksaar 1975a:735). The following examples from the Hamburg corpus may illustrate this point. A six-year-old boy, who can read and who very much likes riding in a bus, but seldom has the opportunity, sees a half empty bus go by with the advertisement, *Wir suchen Fahrer. Hamburger Stadtwerke* [We are looking for drivers. Hamburg City Works]. Astonished, he asks *Warum hält der Bus denn nicht öfter?* [Then why doesn't the bus stop more often?] For the child *Fahrer* [driver] means *Mitfahrer* [rider]. A seven-year-old boy was asked what the following sentence meant *Müssiggang ist aller Laster anfang* [Idleness is the beginning of all vices]. His answer: *Das ist der erster Gang. Den legt der Laster ein, und fangt an zu fahren* [That is the first gear, the driver shifts into it and starts to go]. (Note: to understand this example, it should be pointed out that it involves two unconscious puns: *Müssiggang*=lazy, but *Gang*=gear; *Laster*=vice *and* truck or lorry.) All such examples, which cannot be simply explained as anecdotes,[4] are evidence that in studying children's semantic systems one must look for a linguistic behavior schema, in order to explain socio-psychological and cultural behavior. The following example from a tape recorded protocol should serve to illuminate a part of the meaning system and level of argumentation of a 4;3-year-old twin girl.

Ute (sich vom Spielen unerwartet an den Erwachsenen wendend): *Ulf und ich sind Zwillinge.* – E: *Was bedeutet Zwillinge?* – Ute: *Kinder.* – (2 Stunden später) E: *Was seid ihr, Ute und Ulf?* – Ute: *Zwillinge.* (Ulf schweigt) – E: *Was ist das, Zwillinge?* – Ute: *Kinder.* – E: *Aber dein Bruder Sven ist doch auch ein Kind. Ist er ein Zwilling?* – Ute: *Nein.* – (1 Stunde später) E: *Wer sind Zwillinge?* – Ute: *Ulf und ich* – E: *Was bedeutet das, Zwillinge?* – Ute: *Kinder . . . sind das.* – E: *Aber Sven, dein Bruder?* – Ute: *Ist auch ein Kind.* – E: *Aber ist er auch ein Zwilling?* – Ute: *Nein.* – E: *Aber . . . wie geht das . . .* – Ute: *Es sind gross und wir sind klein . . . Zwillinge.* (Sven ist 7;0) – E: *Was ist denn das, Zwillinge, was meinst du noch mal?* – Ute: *Weiss ich nicht mehr . . . Kinder vielleicht.*
[Ute (turning unexpectedly to the adults): *Ulf and I are twins.* – E: *What does that mean, twins?* – Ute: *Children.* – (two hours later) E: *What are you, Ulf and Ute?* – Ute: *Twins* (Ulf is silent) – E: *What is that, twins?* – Ute:

181

Children. – E: *But your brother Sven is a child too. Is he a twin?* – Ute: *No.* – (one hour later) – E: *Who are twins?* – Ute: *Ulf and I.* – E: *What does that mean, twins?* – Ute: *They are . . . children.* – E: *But Sven, your brother?* – Ute: *is a child, too.* – E: *But is he a twin, too?* – Ute: *No.* – E: *But . . . how is that . . .* – Ute: *He is big and we are small . . . twins.* (Sven is 7;0) – E: *What does it mean, twins; what do you think?* – Ute: *I don't know any more . . . Maybe children.*] (translated by K. Turfler)

At the beginning of the dialogue the child equated *twins* with 'children'. This could be evidence for the acquisition of the meaning of an unmarked word before a marked one. In the course of the conversation, however, it can be seen that it is a more differentiated process than that: 'small' appears to be an important feature in her understanding of the word *twins*.

There are a great number of studies, based on English, concerning the extent of vocabulary and vocabulary growth at the preschool age (for a critical discussion see McCarthy 1954:526–37). Unfortunately, most vocabulary tests offer very little opportunity for comparison, because of their varied methods of sampling. Smith's study (1926), based on Thorndike's word lists, is basic. Passive and active vocabulary were tested, but not evaulated seperately. See Table 2 on vocabulary growth.

Age	Test Person	IQ	Number of Words	Growth
0;8	13	—	0	—
0;10	17	—	1	1
1;0	52	—	3	2
1;3	19	—	19	16
1;6	14	—	22	3
1;9	14	—	118	96
2;0	25	—	272	154
2;6	14	—	446	174
3;0	20	109	896	450
3;6	26	106	1222	326
4;0	26	109	1540	318
4;6	32	109	1870	330
5;0	20	108	2072	202
5;6	27	110	2289	217
6;0	9	108	2562	273

Table 2: Vocabulary growth in relation to age (*from Smith 1926; cited by McCarthy 1954:233*)

In spite of the relativity of the results, caused by the procedure – Grigsby's test in 1932 showed 1507 words for three-year-olds, 2148 for four-year-olds, 2527 for five-year-olds, and 3054 for six-year-olds (McCarthy 1954:533) – an approximate picture can be formed of the growth of vocabulary at different ages. The most considerable growth occurs between the ages of 1;6 and 2;0 and between 2;6 and 3;0.

Templin (1957) carried out a series of tests concerning the distribution of word classes. Nine word classes and one mixed group were considered. It was shown that this distribution remained remarkably stable in relation to the total number of words. The following extracts, using six word classes should illuminate this:

Word Class	Age 3	3;6	4	4;6	5	6	7	8
Noun	17.7	17.1	16.4	16.5	16.1	17.1	17.0	17.0
Verb	22.6	23.0	23.1	23.6	23.5	25.0	24.0	24.3
Adjective	6.3	6.9	6.7	7.7	7.5	7.6	7.3	7.4
Adverb	10.0	9.9	10.1	10.0	10.6	10.0	10.4	9.1
Pronoun	19.4	19.2	20.3	18.9	20.0	19.3	18.0	17.8
Conjunction	1.5	2.3	2.8	2.5	2.6	2.6	3.3	3.7

Table 3: Percentile distribution of word classes (*cited by Templin 1957:101*)

It should not be overlooked, however, that Smith's data is over 50 years old. It can be assumed that today vocabulary is developed more rapidly (see Dale 1972:138). For various data on vocabulary size see Stern & Stern 1928:225ff; Kegel 1974:52–60 also offers a good survey.

Spontaneous word building by means of composition or derivation can be found in a child's lexis after two years. Some examples from Stern & Stern (1928:394f, 407f): 1) *brennlicht* (burn light) [star] (2;5), *kindsoldat* (child soldier) [a soldier who looks small because he is standing far away] *dunkelweiss* (dark white) [said of a yellow-grey dog] (3;11) 2) *kloppe* (hitter) [meat pounder], *schliesse* (closer) [door knob], *kaffrig* (coffeeish) [napkin with a coffee spot] (4;1). These examples lead to the question of morphological development which will be discussed in the next section along with syntactic development.

4.3.4 SYNTAX AND MORPHOLOGY

At an average age of 1;6, two-word sentences are used as well as one-word sentences, and even sentences of several words; a development which seems to be dependent on memory span and brain capacity (Lenneberg 1967:168ff; see also Wanner 1974:112). Two-word sentences dominate up to 2;0. At this time, syntactic differentiation, a jump in the expansion of vocabulary and further development of the phonological and semantic systems also take place .

The first stage of the two-word utterance forms the so-called word-sentence-block, i.e. two one-word sentences are used together with the same intonation and a pause between them: *auto.go* (1;6) [The child saw a car go by]. From the situational context it is clear in such cases that the child is aware of more than one aspect of the referent, but is not yet able to express the relation syntactically. In the second stage the words are uttered together in an intonation that also shows that they belong together: *mommy brush* (1;7).

Stern & Stern (1928:199) had earlier stated that every word in such an utterance still has the value of a sentence, and maintained that one should really speak of 'a primitive sentence chain'. Leopold (1956/57:123) too, regards two one-word sentences used together as a transition stage to sentence formation. However, it is important even at this stage to establish individual differences. While Stern & Stern (1928:199f) record such expressions at the time that they find utterances such as *There see bow-wow* (1;5½), this development takes place successively for Leopold's daughter – to mention a corresponding study, in which the child's language was observed continuously. The following data illustrates the development of a subject–predicate sentence.

Transition forms, such as *mama? sch!*, which Leopold interprets as 'What is mama doing? She is sleeping', are uttered at the age of 1;6. Two months later, he notes that in such utterances, where the first word is a noun and the second a verb, the question tone of voice disappears: *Daddy wash!* (1;8), in which the intonation of both parts can easily be recognized as a one-word expression. During 1;8 both parts are bound together into one unit: *Lady m* [the lady (in the picture) is eating] compared to 1;11: *Fritzchen steht* [Fritzchen is standing] (Leopold 1956/57:123; 1949:28).

Methodologically this sort of statement leads to the conclusion that child syntax should not be considered in isolation from the phonetic and phonological systems. First words and word chains are affected not only by mutual relationships in the phonological hierarchy, that is, the phonemes and their groupings, but also by prosody. Phonetic difficulties can delay the learning of certain models.

Leopold (1956/57:123) also found examples of three- and four-word utterances around the end of the second year, as well as sentences with subject–predicate–object. Stern & Stern (1928:203ff) also found examples of contracted sentences: *hommt die mama und der papa auch* [comes mama and papa too] (Hilde 1;11). Of course, statements of this sort cannot be generalized; here – as in other areas of language acquisition – their value lies in the presentation of individual paths and strategies which it is important for linguists to study (see Ferguson 1976:33).

Brown & Hanlon (1970:30) established, as a basis for comparison, that the average sentence length offers a good index of language development in the first years. The index which Brown and his colleagues use – the MLU (mean length of utterance) – which is used by Bloom (1970), Bowerman (1973) and in most of the American studies, is based on morphemes. For example, all the inflectional endings are also counted as units (see Brown 1973:54). This index can be very misleading for a language such as Estonian which is rich in inflectional endings (14 cases), since the children may use many endings, but quite often do not use them according to the adult pattern. For similar reasons, Park (1974:8) found MLU unacceptable for German. To function as an instrument for measuring linguistic development this index must be further developed to include expressive styles in various communicative acts, and this has not yet been done. For example, in dialogues about picture books children often answer questions with one word sentence questions: *What is the doll doing?* – answer: *sleeping*. The subject is already contained twice in the situation context: in the question and in the picture. On the other hand, in other communicative acts, in which the child says something himself, longer utterances are used. Kirsten (2;0): *Onkel hat Bonbon. Mehr Bonbon dann!* [Uncle has candy. More candy then!].

As was already explained in 2.2.2.2 above, the basic semantic relations which are expressed in the two-word sentences used by children include: agent–action, agent–object, action–object, possession, etc. However, it cannot be established whether they want to convey the same meanings as adults convey with grammatical morphemes, articles, prepositions, and auxiliary verbs.

A comparison of functions in two-word sentences in six languages, English, Russian, German, Finnish, Luo and Samoan, which Slobin presents, offers the following common categories. I list English and German examples:

1) Locating: *there book*; *Buch da*
2) Demand, Wish: *more milk*, *bitte Apfel*
3) Negation: *no wet*, *nicht blasen*
4) Description of an Action, Activity or Situation: *hit ball*, *baby highchair*, *Puppe kommt*, *Tiktak hängt*
5) Possession: *my shoe*; *mein Ball*
6) Modifies (qualifies): *big boat*; *Milch heiss*
7) Question: *where ball*; *wo Ball* (1971a:178f)

The following should be noted about these functions. Concerning category 3 Bloom (1970:172) differentiates between three semantic categories of negation: 1) 'non-existence' – *no wet* = dry 2) 'rejection' – *no wash* = don't wash me 3) 'denial' – *no girl* (negation of a previous statement that a boy was a girl). Concerning category 4, there are different types of descriptions; see the relations agent–action, agent–object, etc., mentioned above.

There are three principal directions in the description of early child syntax: pivot-grammar, the transformational approach and telegraphic speech. We discussed the first two of these in 2.2.2.1, and the last one in 3.6.4, where examples were presented from various languages.

The present state of research can only give a fragmentary picture of the development of the hierarchical organization through which children's sentences progress before reaching the adult sentence stage. When, in the first stage we see: *that flower*, and later: *that a blue flower*, we have a case of the development of hierarchical organization: the noun phrase takes the place of a simple noun (see Brown & Bellugi 1964:158). The development of grammar forms not only depends on their formal complexity (see Brown & Hanlon 1970), but also on the degree of their cognitive difficulty (Slobin 1966a; 1971a; Schlesinger 1971a). For this reason, conditional sentences, and sentences with conjunctions such as *because*, appear relatively late in various languages, around the time of the primary expansion stage (see page 4). The same is true of the use of the passive (page 190).

According to Slobin (1971c:345), at every stage of early syntactic development word order appears to have a certain structure which is not arbitrary. As Slobin (1968b) states in his discussion of a series of studies, the most frequent patterns at the three-word stage are SVO (subject–verb–object) and SOV in German and Russian sources, while SVO dominated in English and Bulgarian material. The other four possibilities are less frequent (for more interesting cases see Brown 1973:156). Gvozdev (1949), however, established SOV as the dominant pattern, which is then replaced by SVO around the age of 1;1 (cited in Slobin 1971c:345; see also 1.2.4 above). Word order of the type *Mutti Buch liest* [mommy book reading] which is also dominant in Park's data (1974:34) from a German speaking child, leads to the interpretation that 'children may expect the order in which communicative elements occur to be an important determinant of their meaning' (Slobin 1968b:22). Wundt (1911:217) and Stern & Stern (1928:222f) had previously analyzed this problem – it is the tendency to place the concrete first, and this depends on the degree of concreteness or abstractness. This is clearly demonstrated in the sign language of deaf mutes, in which the adjective follows the verb, the verb the object, negation that which is negated, and the question word that which is asked. The sentence 'The big man is shooting bears' becomes 'Man big bear is shooting' in sign language. Stern & Stern present examples of *apfe wo?* and *saubä nich taschentuch* [apple where?] and [clean not hanky] Hilde (1;10).

Another tendency, which is also used to explain irregular word order in adult speech, is that of placing emotionally weighted items first (see Leopold 1949a:70). Interestingly enough Stern & Stern observe that children use word order as a means of emphasis much more often than adults, who use stress more often to accent the word in question; compare: 'It's the *knife* I want' with 'I want the *knife*.' Word order can become the natural symbol of value (1928:220). Of course, both tendencies may overlap. Stern & Stern (1928:223f) discuss a series of examples.

After the second year, more complex sentence types and morphological structures are found: question, negative sentences, chains of sentences, conjunction, declension, comparatives (see above page 10). Of particular interest are the cases in which word order varies from the simple declarative sentence, as for example in questions and negatives. The three American children whom Brown and his team studied used auxiliary verbs in yes/no questions, with the correct inversion of the subject – *Will Robin help me?* (approx. 3;0). In the same period, wh-questions (i.e. questions which begin with *where*, *why, what, when*) were formed without the inversion: *Where I should put it?*, *What she will do with it?* (Bellugi 1971:99) Bellugi points out that the child insists on his own word order even after an adult attempts to correct him:

Adult: *Adam, say what I say: Where can he put them?*
Adam: *Where he can put them.* (1971:100)

Bellugi (1971:102ff) establishes a similar independent system for negative sentences with indefinite pronouns. At first, the child forms negative sentences with pronouns which only occur in reaffirmative positive sentences – *some, something, someone: I don't want some supper.* Two steps are necessary for correct negation; at first the child performs only one. This principle can be established for negative questions, too. The child can form inverted positive questions such as *What will you do?* but not negative ones, therefore, *Why you can't sit down?* From these and similar instances, it can be concluded that the child does not simply learn expressions, but rather rules, which he extracts from the adult language and applies in his own way (see Bellugi 1971:115; Brown & Hanlon 1970:49f; Slobin 1971a:183f).

Between 3;0 and 5;0 syntax develops more and more in the direction of adult language, but the individual differences are so great that statements such as Bellugi's 'By four or five, the normal child's syntax is already extremely complex and intricate, and his language bears a strong resemblance to that which he hears around him' (1971:95) only carry very limited weight, since it is not clear which syntactic processes are under control and in which language. Further, attention must be given to the explanatory value of the model used.

Menyuk states, as mentioned above, p. 40, that children at approximately four years of age have already learned the basic generative grammar rules, but emphasizes that syntactic development also continues after the age of 7;0. Apart from the fact that it cannot be proved that children actually have control of rules in the sense of transformational grammar, as can be seen in Kaper's (1968) criticism, there is no overriding unity of opinion as to which criteria are important for judging the productive use of transformations, as on the other hand presented by Ervin-Tripp (1966:78). The features of development already presented by Stern & Stern in 1907, (see 1.2.2 above) can, however, be used as criteria for most children and their developmental stages can be found in most children.

There are very few statements about which sort of syntactic complexity a child does *not* have command of after the age of 5;0.

Ferreiro et al. (1976) found that correct strategies for various relative clauses could be first discovered around ten years of age. They studied how French and English speaking children understood, produced and judged relative clauses for grammatical correctness. Carol Chomsky (1969) tested understanding for four types of linguistic complexity in children between the ages of five and ten years. Constructions of type 1) *John is easy to see* in which the grammatical relationships are not present in the surface structure, were tested by asking 'Is this doll easy to see or hard to see?', about a doll with blindfolded eyes (1969:24). This type of construction was first acquired between 5;6 and 9;0. Five-year-olds still interpreted *doll* as the subject of an active sentence, but all the nine- and ten-year-olds correctly understood the sentence. The latter was also true for constructions of type 2) *John promised Bill to leave*, in which the syntactic structure connected to *promise* varies from the more frequent pattern *John told Bill to leave*. For example, the children were told 'Bozo promises Donald to stand on the book. Make him do it' (1969:32f). Type 3) *John asked the teacher to leave the classroom*, in which either *John* or *the teacher* can be the subject of *leave*, still led to difficulties for ten-year-olds, while children of 5;6 already had command of type 4) *He knew that John was going to win the race.*

As is always the case with tests, the results depend on the method employed. Various critics have pointed out that for the first sentence type, the attention of the children could have been diverted from the interpretation of the sentence by the unusual situation. Kessel (1970, cited by Morsbach & Steel 1976) performed an altered test with similar sentences with kindergarten children aged 5;9 and 6;6, and determined that the majority could interpret the sentences correctly. Morsbach & Steel (1976) repeated Chomsky's test with children from 5;0 to 5;11 and 6;0 to 6;11 and found no significant differences in the results. When the test method was changed, only a minority could not interpret the sentences correctly.

Carol Chomsky's results illustrate the difficulties which children have in developing and using perception strategies. Bever (1970), who handles this in more detail, considers linguistic behavior, as has already been mentioned, as perception behavior. However, he seems to lack a model for co-ordinating individual perception strategies.

Regarding investigations into the acquisition of the passive, which is first mastered between seven and nine years of age, we now look at factors which lead to the conclusion that certain syntactic and semantic operations are more difficult to learn. Turner & Rommetveit (1967) trace these difficulties to the contradiction of syntax and semantics in the passive. If the syntactic structure of a declarative sentence in the active voice – subject–predicate–object – is compared with the semantic structure – agent–action–goal of action (acted upon) – it can be seen that they run parallel, that is, the subject corresponds to the agent, etc. In the passive, however, the structures are opposite to each other, as can be seen in *A is eaten by B*. Here the subject is the goal of the action, and the agent is in the position of the object. In order to understand a passive sentence, a child must be able to differentiate between the grammatical and semantic structure of a sentence in a manner in which more information is analyzed than for an active sentence. Turner & Rommetveit use the factor of semantic reversibility to show that the additional information which must be analyzed to understand a passive sentence can lead to considerable difficulties. A sentence is semantically reversible when it remains meaningful after the positions of action and goal of action are reversed. *The mother kisses the child* is semantically reversible; *The doctor is eating the apple* is not, it is irreversible. Since the action and the goal of action are easily confused in a semantically reversible sentence and the child must therefore learn to differentiate between them, a semantically reversible sentence must be more difficult to learn than an irreversible one, according to Turner & Rommetveit's hypothesis. This leads to the assumption that the passive is more difficult to learn than the active, semantically reversible more difficult than irreversible.

48 children in five age groups between four and nine years were tested for imitation, comprehension and production by the authors, and the two factors were connected in four sentence types: reversible active sentences (RA), reversible passive sentences (RP), irreversible active sentences (IRA) irreversible passive sentences (IRP). Their results support their hypothesis, but they also show that the contrast active–passive is more difficult to learn than that of reversible–irreversible. The difference between IRP and RP is noticeable in comprehension and reproduction tasks with seven to eight-year-olds: the RP sentences are 10 to 25 per cent below IRP. The combination of passive and reversibility, according to this, can be regarded as particularly difficult; IRA and RA did not differ in nearly the same degree. Ninety per cent of the errors made on the production and imitation questions were in connection with semantic reversibility. Approximately one-third of these instances involved an exchange in IR sentences, mostly with the youngest groups. The authors locate the reasons for this in the fact that semantic reversibility is a relative term:

the extent of the reversibility varies in various sentences. Although *Father is reading a newspaper* and *the child is stroking the cat* are both irreversible, the latter is more nearly reversible than the former, since sentences such as *the cat is stroking the child* border on the meaningful.

Turner & Rommetveit's results confirm for the age groups between four and nine the statement of Fraser et al. (1963) that, for three-year-olds, the tasks of imitation, comprehension and production become more difficult, in that order; that is imitation precedes comprehension and this precedes production. A later study by Baldie (1976) with 100 children between three and eight years in Sydney, also confirms this statement. Eighty per cent of the children between 7;6 and 7;11 could produce a passive sentence, while they could all imitate and understand one. Also of interest is the jump in production ability after 7;5. While the answers of the age group 7;0 to 7;5 were 40 per cent correct for RP and ten per cent correct for IRP, they were 70 per cent and 50 per cent correct for the age group 7;6 to 7;11. Baldie connects this statement with the observation that the children are at Piaget's stage of concrete operations and asks:

> Could it be that children around 7;0 or 8;0 acquire the ability to apply an animate/inanimate classification to passive sentences? Having reached the 'operational' stage they can apply this rule and consequently handle relatively more easily the production of the non-reversible form? (1976:343)

As Turner & Rommetveit (1967) point out, the relative lateness of the acquisition of the passive could be influenced by the fact that a child has little or no need to use the passive. Everything which he wants to say can be said in the active. It should be added that children relatively infrequently hear the passive used in the spoken language around them. They also use it sparingly. In his extensive study of spoken language at the elementary school level (see Note 19 to Chapter One), Rickheit (1975:222) states that passive constructions occur extremely rarely. In each of the four age groups (6;0 to 9;11) less than one per cent of the sentences were in the passive. Bever (1970:298f) discusses the acquisition of the passive and a description of various experiments can be found in Menyuk (1971:185–90).

In a preschool child's text construction, paratactic sentence structure, i.e. main clause connected to main clause, predominates, although a child is able to use hypotactic sentence structure some time after 3;0 (see Stern & Stern 1928:208f). The proportion of main clause to subordinate clause in elementary school age children is also not without interest. Rickheit points out:

Elementary school children may use predominantly main clauses, but the relative frequency of subordinate clauses rises continuously from 9.2 per cent at seven years to 14.4 per cent at nine years. It is not surprising that, in respect of the order of precedence, subordinate clauses of the first degree are most common (approx. 95 per cent) and that those of the second degree are infrequent (4.5 per cent) while those of the third degree are very rare (0.2 per cent). (1975:222)[5]

According to a comparison of Rickheit's results and those of Lange & Neuhaus in 1934, the percentage of subordinate clauses used by seven-year-olds and even more so by eight-year-olds, has hardly changed in the last 53 years, but that of the school-age child has (Rickheit 1975:144). The percentage of dependent clauses in the language of seven-year-olds was 2.6 according to Lange & Neuhaus, and 9.18 according to Rickheit.

One question, which has not lost its topicality, concerns the order in which language is learned: does morphology develop first, or syntax? It seems to be generally accepted that syntax is more developed than morphology in two-year-olds (see Leopold 1956/ 57:124; Weir 1962:69). This statement is based on Indo-European languages. As is known, it can often be difficult to differentiate inter-lingually between syntax and morphology. If, for example, one considers the Estonian material (Oksaar 1971:342–52) it can be seen that units which belong to the morphology of the system are part of the syntax in other systems. The Estonian comitative form *isaga* corresponds in English to three free position-bound morphemes: *with the father*. Other Estonian cases such as illative, inessive, allative, adessive and ablative, just to name a few, also correspond to syntactic units. One can, therefore, only indicate which features the child's language system has at a certain time, and demonstrate paths of development of the system by comparing as many synchronic cross sections as possible. Studies in many different languages as possible are necessary here.

Slobin (1968b:28ff) offers a good comparative summary of morphological development. In most of the studies it can be seen that inflexional endings appear rather suddenly, a few months after the appearance of two-word sentences. The rapid development of inflexions is also established by Stern & Stern. They emphasize that inflexion does not appear in clear sequences of various kinds: declination, conjugation, comparative, but rather affects main word categories more or less all at once (1928:248). With Velten's English speaking daughter: 'In swift succession there appear prepositions, demonstratives, auxiliaries, articles, preterite forms, conjunctions, and possessive and personal pronouns' (1943:290). In Estonian, Sven used declination before conjugation, but the time lapse was slight. At the age of 2;6, the use of personal morphemes stabilized and a series of case endings were used.

Gvozdev (1948) reports the following development in his Russian speaking son. All words were unmarked until around 1;10 and then in one month, from 1;11 to 2;0, contrasting morphological elements appeared in various grammatical categories. In the course of a month, unmarked nouns became marked in relation to 1) number, 2) nominative, accusative and genitive, 3) diminutive. A similar process took place with the verbs in relation to 1) imperative, 2) infinitive, 3) past, 4) present (cited by Slobin 1968b:28).

Observations of this sort lead to the following conclusion. It seems that when the principle of suffixing is acquired, e.g. the principle of inflexion and derivation, it is applied to different types at once. However, it is also known that it is much harder for a child to use a rule than to learn it. As Slobin emphasizes: 'When a child does use a given form, it is almost always appropriately used, but it may not always be used in cases where it would be appropriate' (1968b:29).

This would also apply to numerous over-generalizations which occur in the development of the morphological system: *Opa hat gesitzt und gelest* [Granpa sitted and readed] Kirsten 2;9. Stern & Stern, who state that even four- and five-year-olds have difficulty with the many forms of inflexion, explain this by the principle of economy:

> In general, there is a principle of economy, according to which the weakly inflected and regular forms are acquired more easily than the strongly inflected and irregular forms; hence most of the false analogy forms refer to the latter (*dachen, haussen*, instead of *Dächer, Häuser*; *getrinkt, gebindet* instead of *getrunken, gebunden*; *guter, hocher* instead of *besser, höher*) (1928:248f) (translated by K. Turfler) [or *mouses foots*, instead of *mice, feet*; *hurted* and *falled* instead of *hurt* and *fell*; and *gooder* instead of *better*; (translator's note)]

However, the inverse analogical forms can be found, too, even if they are rarer: *umkoppen* instead of *umgekippt*, *kloben* instead of *geklebt*, in analogy to *gehoben* (see Stern & Stern 1928:249). In my own German material, Kirsten (2;9) uses *gereisen* (correct form: *gereist*) at the same time that she uses *gelest* (correct form: *gelesen*) (for more German data see Park 1974:14f; on the effect of analogy in American children see Ervin 1964:177ff).

A more detailed analysis of morphological over-generalization in three Harvard children can be found in Brown (1973:324ff). An interesting discovery is that these over-generalizations were found in all types of inflexions except the progressive form. How can this be explained? Brown discusses a series of explanations – as for example that the child could operate at once with the information '*ing*able or not' for every verb, according to the practice of his mother – but he discards them all and states: 'No explanation has been established. Ideas have been put forward but for none is there any strong evidence.' (1973:328) This caution is necessary. Although, as Ervin-Tripp concludes from various studies, there is no need to doubt that 'children make *inductive generalizations* which go beyond what they hear, accounting for their persistent idiosyncratic grammatical patterns' it is also clear that 'the basis for the child's most important and complex achievement still remains unknown' (1966:81).

Leopold lists repeated observations that, at first, linguistically correct forms are used, then abandoned for over-generalizations, or are used in parallel, such as *did* and *doed*, *broke* and *broken* (Ervin 1964:179) as evidence for a child's own constructive ability, while the correct form could be the result of mechanical repetition.

The system building function of over-generalization can be clearly seen in Sven's Estonian (see Oksaar 1971:349f). Around the third year he had formed his own inflexional system for nouns, and particularly in relation to the partitive, the case for partial objects. In Estonian, the partitive is signalled by six morphemes: *d*, *t*; *a*, *e*, *i*, *u*; according to rules which take vowel harmony into consideration. The child reduced all these possibilities, which occur with approximately the same frequency in the daily vocabulary, to one, *t*, and grouped all lexical items around the two relatively frequent types in Estonian which differ in the genitive. Instead of six classes, the child had two; in the first, the partitive morpheme is attached either to the nominative or the genitive, in the second, to the genitive (the total object is in the nominative or the genitive). The information given in this system functions undisturbed, the necessary differentiations are formally made and the system is considerably simpler and more unified than that of normative grammar. For more details on morphological over-generalizations and on the question of morphological development in Russian, Latvian, French and English children see the articles in Ferguson & Slobin (1973 Part II).

In conclusion, one question should be touched on which is often neglected by researchers into the language of preschool children: the expressive style in sentence sequences. During the period when parataxis dominated in Sven's language, i.e. between 2;0 and 2;11, a simple, clear structure of sequences was noticeable. In communicative acts which were initiated by the child himself, that is when he related something he had just experienced, one characteristic of style was noticeable, that of parallelism with binary word groups, of the type: *Mutter geht in die Stadt zur Arbeit, Sven geht in die Stadt zur Arbeit*[6] [Mother goes into the city to work, Sven goes into the city to work]. Here, there is a clear attempt at symmetry which is often seen in the folk songs of different peoples. Another type, which appeared after this one, was three part. In the first sentence, the whole experience is presented, usually including two agents; both of the following sentences offer more information in parallel form: *Zwei Onkel sind hier. Eins ist im Badezimmer. Eins ist draussen.* [Two uncles are here. One is in the bathroom. One is outside]. Compare: *Wir zwei messen. Eins ist Grossmutter. Eins ist ich.* [We two are measuring. One is grandmother. One is me] (translated literally from the Estonian sentences).[7]

4.4 SUMMARY

In the first section of this chapter, different opinions on when speech begins in children and on the average length of time of the stages of development were discussed. In the 'pre-stages and beginnings of language learning,' which include approximately the first ten months, various communicative vocalizations can already be established in the earliest stages from birth on; non-cry vocalizations can be observed considerably earlier than has been assumed – from the first day.

In discussion of the babbling period, after questions concerning the structure of sound sequences, their communicative status, and the expressive value of intonation, the most important one concerns the functional aspect. Contradictory opinions on the importance of babbling in the child's linguistic development were approached by reviewing various arguments. Among the arguments which regard babbling as a basis for further development of the child's spoken language, the fact should be mentioned that the first words of the child contain sound combinations which occur frequently during the babbling period. Knowledge of the child's linguistic behavior during this period is restricted to production, so that most studies observe the sender perspective. We know very little about the receiver perspective in the first year. It is generally accepted that the child understands the language of the reference person earlier than he speaks. A series of cases were discussed concerning this complex question. Based on empirical evidence, the necessity for creating a transitional stage between the babbling period and the one-word stage was discussed, since the child uses sound combinations consistently in recurring situations during the babbling period.

The 'development of linguistic structures' was introduced by a detailed discussion of the theoretical and empirical problems of one-word sentences. In the present theoretical dilemma Bühler's definition, according to which one-word sentences should be considered as 'not yet' words and 'not yet' sentences, was found helpful. We know that, at this stage, the child communicates successfully with his surroundings, with the help of paralinguistic and kinetic means, among others, and that these global utterances have a situation dependent reference. The question of over-generalization which was frequently discussed later on, was mentioned here, and a series of empirical cases was analyzed, which led to an evaluation of the child's understanding based on intonation and semantic development.

The section on 'phonetics and phonology' dealt in detail with the best known of the four theories of phonetic development – Jakobson's structuralistic panchronic model, based on the principle of maximum contrast and minimum use of energy. Several empirical examples were cited as evidence against this theory; for example, that children probably contrast words rather than sounds. Further, even for sound acquisition, which of course does not take place completely dissociated from words, a complex of guiding factors must be taken into consideration, which involve the effects of the semantic system and communicative-functional factors. Experiments and observations concerning production and perception were discussed. Among the questions still unanswered are: What relationship is there between child phonology and adult phonology? Is there a general sequence in the acquisition of sounds and oppositions?

Next, the development of 'semantics and the lexicon' and various theoretical approaches were discussed. Words seem almost always to be learned with meanings, and here the situational context plays an important part. The development of semantic structures runs from coarse differentiation to ever finer. In the process, which is influenced by the reaction from the surroundings, two contradictory forces are at work – expansion and restriction of meaning. The problem of semantic features was handled in some detail. Numerous examples from natural situations indicate not only different lines of development but also contradict the 'Semantic Feature Hypothesis', according to which the child identifies the meaning of a word by using only one feature, and expands the word to apply to other objects primarily by means of perceptual similarity. A series of observations supports a greater flexibility than that presented in the hypothesis. The fact that important theoretical differences occur is evidence of the complexity of the problem, and directs attention to the methodological difficulties in studying it. Further questions raised here are: How does a child learn oppositions? Do over-generalizations occur in comprehension too? How and when does a child learn semantic congruences?, and further problems in the area of comprehension. In conclusion, the question of vocabulary size and growth was discussed, as well as spontaneous word formation.

In the development of 'syntax and morphology', which like other areas discussed in this chapter should be subject to analysis based on the entirety of verbal and non-verbal communicative behaviour, first two-word sentences, then the importance of word order and its structuring at the three-word stage, and various functional tendencies such as a means of emphasis were discussed. The development of grammatical forms not only depends on their formal complexity, but also on their degree of cognitive difficulty, which leads to the passive, among others, being acquired later in various languages. Questions concerning the acquisition of the passive, which demonstrate a simultaneous connection between syntax and semantics were dealt with in some detail. Difficulties in the acquisition of the passive were traced to contradictory syntactic and semantic operations. The most difficult of these are those cases involving semantic reversibility. Previous to these discussions was an analysis of the acquisition of the more complex sentence types which occur after the second year, such as questions and subordinate clauses. The fact that children at first deviate from adult models here seems to be connected to an inability in children at first to perform more than one operation at a time, as these sentence types demand two. Further questions concerning comprehension and production were touched upon and test results in older children were discussed.

In several Indo-European languages morphological development seems to take place after syntactic, after which development is relatively rapid. As can be seen in numerous over-generalizations, using a rule is harder than learning it. In conclusion, the economy principle was discussed as a guiding principle of development and the expressive style in sentence sequences was mentioned.

The results of paedolinguistic research also depend, as we have

197

seen, on their interdisciplinary emphasis. As a methodological basis for such research, the complementary principles of Roman Jakobson are, I find, a useful guide:

> They can be given the titles *Autonomy* and *Integration*. Every level of language, from its last discrete elements to the totality of conversation, and every level of language production and perception, should be treated with regard to immanent, autonomous laws and, at the same time, with regard to constant interaction of the various levels as well as the integral structure of linguistic code and message, (alias *langue* and *parole*), in its continuing interplay. The necessary bond between the two basic principles cautions the scientist against two traditional mistakes. These are, on the one side, *Isolationalism*, which deliberately ignores the interconnection of the parts and their solidarity with the whole, and on the other, *Heteronomy*, (or, metaphorically, *Colonialism*) which subjects one level to the rules of another, and denies the peculiarity of their structure as well as the autogenesis of their development. (1971:716) (Translated by K. Turfler)

QUESTIONS

4.2 What early signs of language acquisition does the author discuss? What criteria does she use to divide them?
What characterizes the earliest stages? What two sorts of vocalization can be differentiated during this phase?
What significance does babbling have for language acquisition?
4.3 Should one word-utterances be considered as sentences? Why or why not?
4.3.2 Describe Jakobson's theory of phonological development in child language.
What limitations does this theory have? What suggestions have been made to improve this approach?
4.3.3 How does semantics develop in children? What unit is learned first? What are some important factors in this development?
4.3.4 What stages of development do two-word utterances go through?
What functions have been suggested for two-word utterances?
At what age does a child start to use three-word utterances? What influences their structures?
Give some examples of the principle of economy which children employ in acquiring the morphological system.
Using passive sentences as an example, show how the degree of cognitive difficulty, as well as formal complexity, affects the development of syntax.

Notes and References

Chapter 1

1 Oksaar (1975a:719).
2 Its beginnings date from the year 1951; see Osgood & Sebeok (1965:V).
3 Compare Stern (1967:142): 'The psychological law that every mental function has its main phase of development is also valid for language; and this main development covers the period of time from approximately two until four or five years.'
4 Transcription according to Schultze.
5 Compare Leopold (1948a:4).
6 Compare Taine in Bar-Adon & Leopold (1971:26).
7 Compare Leopold in Bar-Adon & Leopold (1971:19).
8 For a critical consideration of this field see Stern & Stern (1928, Chapter XVII).
9 In addition to this see Stern & Stern (1928:5) and Richter (1927:50f).
10 On one-word sentences see 4.3.1.
11 Compare the criticism of Jakobson (1972:18).
12 Compare Slama-Cazacu (1972b:528).
13 For the development of instrumental phonetics see Fudge (1972:290ff).
14 For linguistic pathology in adults and children see Hécaen (1972) and McCarthy (1954:602ff).
15 Stern & Stern (1922:430) claim that their book, published in 1907, has only been slightly considered by linguists and produced almost no active effect.
16 McCarthy (1954:492f).
17 For different new studies in 42 languages besides English see Slobin (1972:111–30). Since 1967 longterm comparative studies of mono-, bi-, tri- and quadri-lingual children have been carried out by Els Oksaar and her team in the 'Seminar für Allgemeine und Vergleichende Sprachwissenschaft' in Hamburg, the first linguistics institute in the Federal Republic of Germany to conduct such studies.
18 The International Association for the Study of Child Language was set up here.
19 For modern German works on school-age children see above all the studies of Pregel (1970) which are based on 2400 verbal and 800 written conversation texts covering the corpus of the Braunschweiger work centre, *Sprache im Schulalter* (Language at the School Age), Pregel & Rickheit (1975) and Rickheit (1975). König (1972) investigates the written language of ten- to twelve-year-old pupils; see also Hanning (1974) and Klann (1975).

Chapter 2

1 See for example Braine (1963), Brown & Bellugi (1964), Brown & Fraser (1964), Menyuk (1964; 19769), Gruber (1967) and Bloom (1970).
2 Compare this to Brown (1973) and the chapter on 'Psychology and Language learning' by Bolinger (1975).

3 Compare the second stage in Stern, see page 10.
4 The copula may also be missing in similar contexts in spoken Estonian.
5 The influence of the Geneva school was very evident in the 21st International Congress of Psychology in Paris 1976, where such topics in the field of developmental psychology as 'Wahrnehmung im Kindsalter' (Perception in School-age Children) 'Sensitive Entwicklungsperioden' (Sensitive Developmental Periods) 'Entwicklung des aggressiven Verhaltens' (Development of Aggressive Behavior) were treated. Piaget's questions were first available in German translations in the Federal Republic of Germany relatively late (after 1972). On Piaget's work, see also G. Furth, *Intelligenz und Erkenntnis* (Intelligence and Recognition), *Die Grundlage der genetischen Erkenntnistheorie Piagets* (The Foundation of Piaget's genetic cognition theory) Frankfurt/M. 1972.
6 Stern had already in 1914 pointed out the one-sidedness of always observing children only from certain social classes, that is 'children from the upper class'. He assumes that the major characteristics of the child's mental development have a universal character. However, concerning the chronological conditions of development and meaning of certain milieu conditions, 'there probably exist among children from the lower class deviations which are even less well-known. Here one still has a broad and important field for future research' (1967:VIIf). Stern & Stern (1928:292f) discuss experimental findings which confirm class-specific influences.
7 Deviations from established lines of development are dismissed as irrelevant: 'There are a number of small, but intriguing differences, which may excite the technical interests of the psycholinguist, but what is remarkable at first glance is the uniformity in rate and pattern development.' (Slobin 1971a:175)
8 For a many-sided view see the first volume of the *Proceedings of the Eleventh International Congress of Linguists* ed. by L. Heilmann, Bologna, 1974. See also Oksaar (1972b).
9 See the arguments by Kaper (1968; 1969), Peizer & Olmsted (1969), Olmsted (1971:19f), Derwing (1973:50–76) and Oksaar (1975a:722f).
10 K. Mollenhauer 'Das Problem einer empirisch-positivistischen Pädagogik'. In *Zur Bedeutung der Empirie für die Pädagogik*. New edition of the supplementary part of Vierteljahresschr.f.Wiss. Pädagogik 5, 1966, 58.
11 For criticism of the so-called correspondence hypothesis which assumes an immediate analogy between the rules of competence grammar and psychic organization see Kegel (1974:159–65) and Baldie (1976:347).
12 For the 'deep-structure concept' compare Oksaar (1976b:15).
13 On text linguistics see among others S. J. Schmidt, *Texttheorie: Probleme einer Linguistik der sprachlichen Kommunikation*. München, 1973 and W. Dressler, *Einführung in die Textlinguistik*. Tübingen, 1972.
14 Cited by Eco (G. 1972:21). The term 'paralinguistics' is not always uniformly used; e.g. in A. A. Hill *Introduction to Linguistic Structures* New York, 1958, 408f, it covers both paralanguage and 'patterned body motion'. Nowadays paralinguistics and kinesics are considered as two independent fields, see Sebeok et al. (1972:153).
15 In our time not only ethologists, psychologists and psychiatrists have been

interested in the kind and importance of non-verbal behavior as a signal, above all gestures and facial expressions, but also sociologists and anthropologists. See Blurton Jones (1972) and Sebeok et al. (1972). A classification of gestures can be found in Wundt (1911:162–200).

16 For further development of speech act theory see Schmidt, Note 13, 111f, 153f.

17 Wegener (1885:22f, 27) differentiates furthermore between the situation of remembering, the situation of consciousness and the cultural situation. For speech situation see Hymes (1967:19).

18 A critical view of the theories of social interaction is found in T. P. Wilson 'Conceptions of interactions and forms of sociological explanation' in *Am. Soc. Review* 35, 1970,697–710. For questions of the theory of roles see U. Gebhardt *Rollenanalyse als kritische Soziologie*. Neuwied, Berlin 1971 and the articles in J. A. Jackson (ed.) *Role* Cambridge, 1972. For Parsons' general theory of action, which differentiates between three types of empirical action systems – the personal, social and cultural – see Parsons & Shils (1951), compare Oksaar (1976b:102ff.108). Problems which could arise are shown in the work of H. Ramge *Spracherwerb und sprachliches Handeln*, Düsseldorf, 1976, in which the author is compelled, among other things by the infant in the third year of life, to divide the concept 'overtaking a role' into 'cognitive acting' and 'symbolic acting' (page 68). Here again, the danger appears of letting not the facts, but the theory speak.

Chapter 3

1 These questions are closely connected with articulatory movements. For the psychology of speech production note the investigations of Bernstein. See Jakobson (1974:208).

2 At present such interdisciplinary projects are organized at the University of Linköping, Sweden, see Tema *Ny väg för forsknig vid universitetet i Linköping* Linköping, 1976.

3 For questions of age limit in language acquisition see under 3.7.

4 See in addition to this 3.3.2.

5 For studies with chimpanzees, carried out by Köhler, see Bühler (1930:10–17). For recent research compare Brown (1973:32–51).

6 Bruner differs from Piaget, among other things, in his emphasis on the cultural and social aspects of developmental processes; he agrees much more with Vygotsky and Luria: '. . . language is acquired as an instrument for regulating joint activity and joint action.' Language acquisition must be considered as 'a transformation of modes of assuming cooperation that are prior to language, prior both phylogenetically and ontogenetically.' (1975:2)

7 The time is, according to Vygotsky (1962) controversial. Whether it should be set at the age of two or at school age – independent of all these uncertain questions remains the undoubted fact that these two lines of development cross.

8 Details about the experiment are difficult to obtain; compare Lawton (1969) who suggests that certain experiments should be repeated.

9 In addition see 3.6.2.

10 On this developmental test series see Furth (1966).
11 Sinclair also points out in *Cognition* 1, 1972, 317f, that Fodor misunderstood Vygotsky and Piaget. Piaget's school does not regard development as an accumulation of isolated new operations.
12 It is not justifiable that many pertinent observations of child language in natural situations are dismissed as anecdotes, whereas individual reactions in a setting which is unnatural for the child, the experiment, are fully accredited.
13 Edward Sapir (1884–1939), Professor at Chicago and Yale and expert on American Indian languages, was one of the first to investigate the interrelations between linguistics and anthropology.
14 In addition see Öhman, *Wortinhalt und Weltbild*. Stockholm, 1951, 163, who demonstrated that one can observe how children who have a common grandmother disagree on their grandmother's name: 'the children are divided from the very beginning into two sides, that is they associate another emotion with *mormor* than with *farmor*. These emotions which cling to names are naturally, if necessarily, reformed and modified by the grandmother's personality. However, the difference is undoubtedly present and is certainly the starting point for an intuitive attitude towards the grandmother.' (Translated by K. Turfler)
15 See F. de Saussure, *Grundfragen der allgemeinen Sprachwissenschaft* 2nd edition, Berlin, 1967, 79f, 'l'arbitraire du signe'.
16 For special factors of play activity see Stern (1967:260–73). Bühler (1930:461) defines 'Spiel' [play] as: 'an activity which is equipped with a desire of function and supported directly by this desire of function or for its own sake . . . whatever else it may provide and whatever other connection it may have.'
17 For a new version of the Illinois Test of Psycholinguistic Abilities (ITPA) 1968, see Dale (1972:270f)
18 J. Drever & W. D. Fröhlich *Wörterbuch der Psychologie* 1969.
19 None of the names is entirely right, for in some cases not only the child, but also the adult, uses the same words and forms of these registers.
20 But from these they may be taken over by the standard language, see in addition to this Oksaar (1977).
21 See V. Rūke-Dravina 'Gibt es Universalien in der Ammensprache?' In *Salzburger Beitäge zur Linguistik* 2, 1976, 3–16.
22 The use of simplified register is not only restricted to child interaction, it is also used, among other contexts, in conversation with foreigners, see Oksaar (1977).
23 Concerning different definitions of 'language' see T. Lewandowski, *Linguistisches Wörterbuch 3*, 2nd edition, Heidelberg, 1976, 695–9.
24 Compare also the discussion on the *origo* of the signal field (1934:102–120) and Messeken (1968:62–9); compare Hörmann (1976:396).
25 The phatic function has its origins in B. Malinowski. In *The Problem of Meaning in Primitive Languages* (1923) he explains: 'The whole situation consists in what happens linguistically. Each utterance is an act serving the direct aim of binding hearer and speaker by a tie of some social sentiment or other' (cited by C. K. Ogden & I. A. Richards *The Meaning of Meaning* New York & London, 9th edition, 1953, 315.

26 On the status of context in semantics see E. Oksaar *Semantische Studien im Sinnbereich der Schnelligkeit* Stockholm, 1958, 7ff.

27 On the other hand Habermas's (1971:101ff) concept of communicative competence, which is based on idealized communication structures, does not have any practical relevance for child language acquisition processes in heterogeneous language communities.

28 These rules are not the same in many language communities.

29 L. V. Scerba *Izbrannye raboty po jazykoznaniju i fonetike I* Leningrad, 1958.

30 Habit is the 'acquired connection of a stimulus S with a response R; acquired latent behavioral tendency. A habit is formed and strengthened through reinforcement, actively destroyed through extinction.' Hörmann (1970:357).

31 Compare to this Piaget's classic work *La formation du symbole chez l'enfant: Imitation, jeu et rêve, image et représentation.* Neuchâtel, 1946.

32 Whereas echo-like repetition is known as echolalia, Stern & Stern consider metalalia as that imitation for which a certain latent period exists between stimulus and reaction. Thus words which the child has often heard and understood may 'appear suddenly at an appropriate opportunity, without having been directly repeated, the stimulus consisting of a summation of effects of natural colloquial speech' (1928:135). (Translated by K. Turfler)

33 Adults' replies are often not complete sentences such as *das ist Kaffee* [that is coffee].

Chapter 4

1 The Swedish *apa* was first learned in relation to a certain stuffed monkey, pronunciation [ápa]. Afterwards all stuffed animals were called [á:pa], [*ahv*], Estonian 'monkey' was first used after 2;6 in other contexts.

2 On semantic features see T. Lewandowski, Note 23, Chapter 3, and Hörmann (1976:87ff). On markedness and unmarkedness see Oksaar (1976b:73f).

3 Author's discussion with Roman Jakobson, Bielefeld 21.5.1975.

4 See note 12 to Chapter 3.

5 Third degree subordinate clauses are subordinate to the second degree, these in their turn are subordinate to first degree clauses, which are directly connected with a main clause (*Und Mutti hat gesagt, sie hätte gar nicht gewusst* (1st degree) [and mother said she didn't know] *wie der Mann rausgekommen wär* (2nd degree) [how the man came out] *der da im Auto war* (3rd degree) [who was in the car]) Rickheit (1975:177).

6 Estonian sentences: *Ema lähe linna tööle. Nenne lähe linna tööle* (2;0). Except for *lähe* instead of *läheb* all grammatical relations are expressed correctly.

7 Estonian sentences: *Üks on vannitoos. Üks on väljas* (2;10). *Onnu + t* instead of *onu* is declined according to Sven's own system. The form *toos* instead of *toas* appears at this point several times. *Üks* [one] is acceptable here according to Estonian norms – *Kahekesi mõõdame. Üks on vanaema. Üks on mina* (2;11). The child's rule for the copula can be described as grammatical congruence between subject and predicate without selection rules: *eins ist ich* [one is I].

Notes and References

General note
Aspects of multi-lingualism were only touched on occasionally in this work, because this important aspect will be fully discussed in a separate publication together with second language acquisition.

Bibliography

Abrahamsen, Adele A. (1977), *Child language. An interdisciplinary guide to theory and research.* Baltimore

Afendras, E. A./Pianarosa, A. (1975), *Le bilinguisme chez l'enfant et l'apprentissage d'une langue seconde: Bibliographie analytique.* Quebec

Aldrich, C. A./Norval, M./Knop, C./Venegas, F. (1946), The crying of newly born babies: IV. Follow-up study after additional nursing care had been provided. In: Journ. Pediat. 28, 665–670

Ament, W. (1899), *Die Entwicklung von Sprechén und Denken beim Kinde.* Leipzig

— (1902), Begriff und Begriffe der Kindersprache. Schiller-Ziehensche Sammlung von Abhandlungen 5, Heft 4

Anastasi, A./D'Angelo, R. (1952), A comparison of Negro and white preschool children in language development and Good-enough draw-a-man IQ. In: Journ. Genet. Psychol. 81, 145–165

Antinucci, F./Parisi, D, (1973), Early language acquisition: A model and some data. In: Ferguson/Slobin (Ed.). 607–619

Arbeitsgruppe Bielefelder Soziologen (Ed.) (1973), *Alltagswissen, Interaktion und gesellschaftliche Wirklichkeit*, 2 Bde. Reinbek

Argyle, M. (1973), *Social interaction.* London

Austin, J. L. (1962), *How to do things with words.* London

Bach, E./Harms, R. J. (Ed.) (1968), *Universals in linguistic theory.* New York

Bain, B. C. (1973), Toward a theory of perception: Participation as a function of body-flexibility. In: Journ. of Gen. Psych. 89, 157–296

— (1974), Toward an integration of Piaget and Vygotsky: Bilingual considerations. Paper 18e Congrès Intern. de Psychologie Appliquée. Montreal

Bakker-Rennes, H./Hoefnagel-Höhle, M. (1974), Situatieverschillen in taalgebruik. Magisterarbeit, Amsterdam Universität

Baldie, B. J. (1976), The acquisition of the passive voice. In: Journ. Child Lang. 3, 331–348

Bar-Adon, A./Leopold, W. F. (Ed.) (1971), *Child language. A book of readings.* Englewood Cliffs

Bates, E. (1976), *Language in context: The acquisition of pragmatics.* New York

Bates, E./Camaioni, L./Volterra, V. (1973), The acquisition of performatives prior to speech. Technical Report 129, Consiglio Nazionale delle Ricerche. Roma

Bates, Elizabeth (1979), *The emergence of symbols, cognition and communication in infancy. Language, thought and culture (Advances in the Study of Cognition).* New York

Bellugi, U. (1971), Simplification in children's language. In: Huxley/Ingram (Ed.), 95–119

Bellugi, U./Brown, R. (Ed.) (1964), *The acquisition of language.* Chicago

Bergius, R. (1971), *Psychologie des Lernens.* Stuttgart

Berko, J. (1958), The child's learning of English morphology. In: Word 14, 150–177

Berko Gleason, J. (1973), Code switching in children's language. In: Moore (Ed.), 159–167

— (1975), Fathers and other strangers: Men's speech to young children. In: Dato (Ed.), 289–297

Berko Gleason, J./Weintraub, S. (1976), The acquisiton of routines in child language. In: Lang.Soc. 5, 129–136

Bernstein, B. (1972), *Studien zur sprachlichen Sozialisation.* Düsseldorf

205

Bibliography

Bever, G. (1970), The cognitive basis for linguistic structures. In: Hayes (Ed.), 279–362

Bielefeld, R. (1972), *Untersuchungen zum Spracherwerb 2—4 jähriger Kinder unter besonderer Berücksichtigung semantischer Aspekte*. Diss. Hamburg

Birdwhistell, R. L. (1952), *Introduction to kinesics*. Louisville

— (1970), *Kinesics and context: Essays in body motion communication*. Philadelphia

Bleuler, E. (1963), *Das autistische Denken*. [2]Berlin. Heidelberg. New York

Bloch, O. (1913), Notes sur le langage d'un enfant. In: Mémoires Soc. Ling. 18, 37–59

— (1921), Les premiers stades du langage de l'enfant. In: Journ. Psychol. pers. path. 18, 693–712

Bloom, L. (1970), *Language development: Form and function in emerging grammars*. Cambridge, Mass

— (1973), *One word at a time*. The Hague

Bloom, Lois/Lahey, Margaret (1978), *Language development and language disorders*. New York

Blount, B. (1970), The prelinguistic system of Luo children. In: Anthropol. Linguistics 12, 326–342

— (1972), Parental speech and language acquisition: some Luo and Samoan examples. In: Anthropol. Linguistics 14, 119–130

Blumer, H. (1968), *Symbolic interactionism*. New Jersey.

Blurton Jones, N. (Ed.) (1972a), *Ethological studies of child behaviour*. London

— (1972b) Categories of child-child interaction. In: Blurton Jones (Ed.), 97–128

Bolinger, D. (1975), *Aspects of language*. New York, London, Sydney

Botts, Marion et al. (1979), *Structure and development in child language: The preschool years*. Cornell University Press

Bowerman, M. (1973), *Early syntactic development*. Cambridge

Braine, M. D. (1963), The ontogeny of English phrase structure: the first phrase. In: Language 39, 1–13

— (1971), The acquisition of language in infant and child. In: Reed (Ed.), 7–95

Brandis, W./Henderson, D. (1970), *Social class, language and communication*. London

Brannigan, Ch. R./Humphries, D. A. (1972), Human non-verbal behaviour, a means of communication. In: Blurton Jones (Ed.), 37–64

Braun-Lamesch, M. (1972), Le rôle de l'imitation dans l'acquisition du language. In: Enfance, 397–417

Brenstiern Pfanhauser, S. (1930), Rozwój mowy dziecka. In: Prace Filo-logiczne 15,273–356

Britton, J. (1970), *Language and learning*. London

Brodbeck, A. J./Irwin, O. C. (1946), The speech behavior of infants without families. In: Child Development 17, 145–156

Broen, P. A. (1972), *The verbal environment of the language learning child*. Monograph of the American speech and hearing Association 17

Bronckart, J.-P./Sinclair, H./Papandropoulou, J. (1976), Sémantique et réalité psycholinguistique. In: Bulletin de Psychologie. La mémoire sémantique. Spécial annuel, 225–231

Brown, R. (1973), *A first language*. Cambridge, Mass

Brown, R./Bellugi, U. (1964), Three processes in the child's acquisition of syntax. In: Harv. Educ. Rev. 34, 133–151

Brown, R./Fraser, C. (1964), The acquisition of syntax. In: Bellugi/Brown (Ed.), 43–79

Brown, R./Hanlon, C. (1970), Derivational complexity and order of acquisition in child speech. In: Hayes (Ed.), 11—53

Bruner, J. S. (1975), The ontogenesis of speech acts. In: Journ. Child Lang. 2, 1–19

Bruner, J. S./Oliver, R. R./Greenfield, P. M. et al. (Ed.) (1966), *Studies in cognitive growth*. New York

Bühler, Ch. (1928), *Kindheit und Jugend. Genese des Bewusstseins*. Leipzig

Bühler, Ch./Hetzer, H./Tudor-Hart, B. (1927), *Soziologische und psychologische Studien über das erste Lebensjahr*. Jena

Bühler, K. (1930), *Die geistige Entwicklung des Kindes*. [6]Jena

— (1934), *Sprachtheorie*. Jena

— (1935), Einleitung. In: Archiv für die gesamte Psychologie 94, 401–412

Bullowa, M. (1974), Non-verbal communication in infancy. Paper. First Congress of the International Association for Semiotic Studies. Milano

Bullowa, M./Fidelholtz, J. L./Kessler, A. R. (1976), Infant vocalization: Communication before speech. In: McCormack/Wurm (Ed.), 67–95

Bullowa, Margaret (ed.) (1979), *Before speech. The beginning of interpersonal communication*. Cambridge

Campbell, B. (1971), The roots of language. In: Morton (Ed.), 10–23

Campbell, Robin/Smith, Philip, T. (eds.) (1978), *Recent advances in the psychology of language. Language development and mother-child interaction*, NATO Conference Series, III Human Factors V. 4a. New York

Campbell, R./Wales, R. (1970), The study of language acquisition. In: Lyons (Ed.), 243–269

Caudill, W. (1972), Tiny dramas: Vocal communication between mother and infant in Japanese and American families. In: Lebra, W. P. (Ed.), *Transcultural research in mental health*. Honolulu

Cazden, C. B. (1970), The neglected situation in child language research and education. In: Journ. of Social Issues 26, 35–60

— (1972). *Child language and education*. New York

Chafe, W. L. (1970), *Meaning and the structure of language*. Chicago. London

Chase, S. (1950), *The tyranny of words*. [7]London

Chipman, Harol H. (1980), *Children's construction of the English pronominal system*. Bern

Chomsky, C. (1969), *The acquisition of syntax in children from 5 to 10*. Cambridge, Mass. London

Chomsky, N. (1959), A review of Skinner's Verbal Behavior. In: Language 35, 26–58

— (1965), *Aspects of the theory of syntax*. Cambridge, Mass.

— (1968), *Language and mind* New York

— (1975), *Reflections on language*. New York

Chukovski, K. (1968), *From two to five*. Berkeley. Russ. Original 1961

Church, J. (1961), *Language and the discovery of reality*. New York

Cicourel, A. V. (1973), *Cognitive sociology. Language and meaning in social interaction*. London

Clark, E. V. (1973), What's in a word? On the child's acquisition of semantics in his first language. In: Moore (Ed.), 65–110

— (1975), Knowledge, context, and strategy in the acquisition of meaning. In: Dato (Ed.), 77–98

Clark, Herbert H./Clark, Eve V. (1977) *Psychology and language. An introduction to psycholinguistics*. New York

Cohen, M. (1925), Sur les langages successifs de l'enfant. In: *Mélanges linguistiques offerts à J. Vendryes*. Paris, 109–127

— (1933), Observations sur les dernières persistances du langage enfantin. In: Journal de Psychologie 30, 390–399

Compayré, G. (1900), *Die Entwicklung der Kinderseele*. Altenburg. French original 1893 and 1896

Condon, W. S. /Sander, L. W. (1974), Neonate movement is synchronized with adult speech: interactional participation and language acquisition. In: Science 183, 99–101

Cook, V. J. (1979) *Young children and language*. London

Correll, W. (1974), *Lernen und Verhalten*. Frankfurt/M

Coseriu, E. (1974), Les universaux linguistiques (et les autres). In: Proceedings of the

Bibliography

Eleventh International Congress of Linguists, edited by L. Heilmann. Bologna, 47–73

Costello, A. J. (1973), The reliability of direct observation. In: Bull. Brit. Psych. Soc. 26, 105–108

Cowe, E. G. (1967), A study of kindergarten activities for language development. Unpubl. doct. Diss. Columbia Univ.

Crystal, D. (1974), Paralinguistics. In: *Current Trends in Linguistics 12*, edited by Th. A. Sebeok. The Hague. Paris, 235–295

Curtiss, S./Fromkin, V./Krashen, S./Rigler, D/Rigler, M. (1974), The linguistic development of Genie. In: Language 50, 528–544

Curtiss, S./Fromkin, V./Rigler, D./Rigler, M./Krashen, S. (1975). An update of the linguistic development of Genie. In: Dato (Ed.), 145 bis 157

Dale, P. S. (1972), *Language development. Structure and function*. Hinsdale, Illinois

Dale, P. S./Ingram, D. (eds.) (1981), *Child language: An international perspective*. University Park Press (1981)

Darwin, C. (1872), *The expression of the emotions in man and animals*. London

Dato, D. P. (Ed.) (1975), *Developmental psycholinguistics: Theory and applications*. Georgetown University Round Table of Languages and Linguistics 1975. Washington D.C.

Davis, E. A. (1937), *The development of linguistic skills in twins, singletons and only children from age five to ten years*. Minneapolis

Day, E. J. (1932), The development of language in twins: I. A comparison of twins and single children. In: Child Development 3, 179–199

Delacroix, H. (1924), *Le langage et la pensée*. Paris

Dennis, M./Whitaker, H. J. (1976), Language acquisition following hemidecortication: Linguistic superiority of the left over the right hemisphere. In: Brain and Language 3, 404–433

Denzin, Norman K. (1977), *Childhood socialization. Studies in the development of language, social behaviour and identity*. San Francisco

Derwing, B. L. (1973), *Transformational grammar as a theory of language acquisition*. Cambridge

Descoeudres, A. (1921), *Le développement de l'enfant de deux à sept ans*. Neuchâtel. Paris

Deutsch, M. (1965), The role of social class in language development and cognition. In: Am. Journ. of Orthopsychiatry 35, 78–88

Deville, G. (1890, 1891), Notes sur le développement du langage. In: Revue de Linguistique et de Philologie Comparée 23, 330–343; 24, 10–42, 128–143, 242–257, 300–320

Dewey, J. (1894), Psychology of infant language. In: *Psych. Review* I, 45–72

Dingwall, W. O. (1975), The species-specifity of speech. In: Dato (Ed.) 17–62

Dore, J. (1975), Holophrases, speech acts and language universals. In: Journ. Child Lang. 2, 21–40

Dore, J./Franklin, M. B./Miller, R. T. /Ramer, A. L. H. (1976), Transitional phenomena in early language acquisition. In: Journ. Child Lang. 3, 13–28

Duncan, S. D., Jr. (1976), Language, paralanguage and body motion in the structure of conversations. In: McCormack/Wurm (Ed.), 239–267

Eco, U. (1968), *La struttura assente*, Milan

Edwards, M. L. (1974), Perception and production in child phonology: the testing of four hypotheses. In: Journ. Child Lang. 1, 205–219

Egger, E. (1879), *Observations et réflexions sur le développement de l'intelligence et du langage chez les enfants*, Paris

Eilers, R. E./Oller, D. K./Ellington, J. (1974), The acquisition of word-meaning for dimensional adjectives: The long and short of it. In: Journ. Child Lang. 1, 195–204

Eimas, P. (1974), Linguistic processing of speech by young infants. In: Schiefelbusch/ Lloyd (Hrsg.) 55–73

Ekman, P./Friesen, W. V. (1969), The repertoire of nonverbal behavior: Categories, origins, usage, and coding. In: Semiotica 1, 49–98

Elwert, S. M. (1960), *Das zweisprachige Individuum. Ein Selbstzeugnis*. Wiesbaden

Ervin, S. M. (1964), Imitation and structural change in children's language. In: Lenneberg (Ed.), 163–189

Ervin-Tripp (1964), An analysis of the interaction of language, topic, and listener. In: Am. Anthropologist 66, Part. 2, 86–102

— (1966), Language development. In: Hoffman, L. and M. (Ed.), *Review of Child Development Research*. Vol. II. New York. 55–105

— (1972), Children's sociolinguistic competence and dialect diversity. In: Gordon, J. (Ed.), *Early childhood education*. Chicago, 123–160

— (1973), Some strategies for the first years. In: Moore (Ed.), 261–286

Ervin-Tripp, Susan/Michel-Kernan, Claudia (eds.) (1979), *Child discourse*, New York

Escalona, S. K. (1973), Basic modes of social interaction: Their emergence and patterning during the first two years of life. In: Merrill-Palmer Quarterly 19, 205–232

Farwell, C. (1973), The language spoken to children. Papers and Reports on Child Language Development 5, 31–62

Ferguson, C. A. (1964), Baby talk in six languages. In: Am. Anthropologist 66, 103–114

— (1976), Learning to pronounce: The earliest stages of phonological development in the child. Paper. Conference on the Early Behavioral Assessment of the Communicative and Cognitive Abilities of the Developmentally Disabled. Orcas Island

— (1977), Baby talk as a simplified register. In: Snow/Ferguson (Ed.), 209–235

Ferguson, C. A./Farwell, C. B. (1975), Words and sounds in early language acquisition. In: Language 51, 419–439

Ferguson, C. A./Garnica, O. (1975), Theories of phonological development. In: Lenneberg/Lenneberg (Ed.), 153–180

Ferguson, C. A./Slobin, D. (Ed.) (1973), *Studies of child language development*. New York. Chicago

Ferreiro, E./Othenin-Girard, H./Chipman, H./Sinclair, H. (1976), How do children handle relative clauses. A study in comparative developmental psycholinguists. In: Archives de Psychologie 45, 229–266

Fillmore, C. (1968), The case for case. In: Bach/Harms (Ed.), 1–88

— (1971), Some problems for case grammar. Working Papers in linguistics 10 (Ohio State Univ.), 245–265

Firth, J. R. (1957), *Papers in linguistics, 1934–1951*. London

Flavell, J. (1974), The development of inferences about others. In: Mischel, T. (Ed.), *Understanding other persons*. Oxford, 66–116

Fletcher, Paul/Garmon, Michel (eds.) (1979), *Language acquisition Studies. In: First language development*, Cambridge, Mass.

Flores d'Arcais, G. B./Levelt, W. I. M. (Ed.) (1971), *Advances in psycholinguistics*. Amsterdam. London

Fodor, J. A. (1972), Some reflections on L. S. Vygotsky's *Thought and Language*. In: Cognition 1, 83–95

Fodor, J. A./Jenkins, J. J./Saporta, S. (Ed.) (1967), Psycholinguistics and communication theory. In: Dance, F. E. X. (Ed.), *Human communication theory*. New York, 160–201

Francescato, G. (1970), *Il linguaggio infantile – strutturazione e apprendimento*. Torino

Fraser, C./Bellugi, U./Brown, R. (1963), Control of grammar in imitation, comprehension and production. In: Journ. verb. Learn. verb. Beh. 2, 121–135

Fraser, C./Roberts, N. (1975), Mother's speech to children of four different ages. In: Journ. of Psycholinguistic Research 4, 9–16

Fudge, E. C. (1972), Phonology and phonetics. In: Sebeok (ed.), 254–312

Furth, H. G. (1966), *Thinking without language*. New York

Gardiner, M. (1975), EEC indicators, of lateralization in human infants. Paper. Symposium on Lateralization 4, Society of Neuroscience. New Brunswick. New Jersey

Bibliography

Garnica, O. (1973), The development of phonemic speech perception. In: Moore (Ed.), 215–222
— (1975), Nonverbal concomitants of language input to children. Paper. Third International Child Language Symposium, London
Garvey C. (1975), Requests and responses in children's speech. In: Journ. Child Lang. 2, 41–63
Garvey, C./Hogan R. (1973), Social speech and social interaction: Egocentrism revisited. In: Child Development 44, 562–568
Gazzaniga, M. S. (1970), *The bisected brain*. New York
Geest, A. J. M. van der (1974), *Evaluation of theories on child grammars*. The Hague
— (1975), *Some aspects of communicative competence and their implications for language acquisition*. Amsterdam
Geschwind, N. (1970), The organization of language and brain. In: Science 170, 940–944
— (1972), Language and the brain. In: Scientific American 226, 76–83
Gheorgov, J. A. (1905), Die ersten Anfänge des sprachlichen Ausdrucks für das Selbstbewußtsein bei Kindern. In: Archiv f. d. ges. Psych. 5, 329–404
— (1908), Ein Beitrag zur grammatischen Entwicklung der Kindersprache. In: Archiv f. d. ges. Psych. 9, 242–432
Ginneken, J. van (1917), *De roman van een kleuter* Nijmegen
— (1924), *De ontdekkingen van den kleuter* Utrecht-Nijmegen
Gipper, H. (1972), *Gibt es ein sprachliches Relativitätsprinzip?* Frankfurt/M.
Gleitman, L. R./Gleitman, H./Shipley, E. F. (1972), The emergence of the child as grammarian. In: Cognition 1, 137–164
Goldfarb, W. (1955): Emotional and intellectual consequences of psychological deprivation in infancy: a re-evaluation. In: Hoch, P. H./Zubinn, J. (Ed.), *Psychopathology of childhood*. New York, 105–119
Grammont, M. (1902), Observations sur le langage des enfants. In: *Mélanges linguistiques offerts à M. Antoine Meillet*, Paris, 61–82
Greenberg, J. H. (1966), Language universals. In: Sebeok (Ed.), 61–112
Grégoire, A. (1937), *L'apprentissage du langage*: Vol. 1. *Les deux premières années.* Paris
— (1947), *L'apprentissage du langage:* Vol. 2. *La troisième année et les années suivantes.* Liège. Paris
Grennfield, Patricia Marks/Smith, Joshua H. (1976), *The structure of communication in early language development*. New York
Grice, H. P. (1975), Logic and conversation. In: Cole, P./Morgan, J. (Ed.), *Syntax and semantics*, Vol. III. New York
Grimm, H. (1973), *Strukturanalytische Untersuchung der Kindersprache*. Bern. Stuttgart. Wien
Gruber, J. S. (1967), Topicalization in child language. In: Found. of Language 3, 37–65
Guillaume, P. (1925), *L'imitation chez l'enfant. Etude psychologique*. Paris
Gumperz, J. J. (1964), Linguistic and social interaction in two communities. In: Gumperz, J. J./Hymes, D. (Ed.), The ethnography of communication. Am. Anthropologist 66, II, 137–153
— (1967), Language and communication. In: The Annals of the Am. Ac. of Pol. and Soc. Science 373, 219–231
Gumperz, J. J./Hymes, D. (Ed.) (1972), *Directions in sociolinguistics The ethnography of communication*. New York, Chicago
Gutzmann, H. (1894), *Des Kindes Sprache und Sprachfehler*. Leipzig
Gvozdev, A. N. (1949), *Formirovaniye u rebenka grammaticheskogo stroya russkogo jazyka*. Moskva. 2 Bände
Habermas, J. (1971), Vorbereitende Bemerkungen zu einer Theorie der kommunikativen Kompetenz. In: Habermas, J./Luhmann, N. (Ed.), *Theorie der Gesellschaft oder Sozialtechnologie*, Frankfurt/M.

Hakes, David T. (1980), *The development of metalinguistic abilities in children (Springer Series in Language and Communication)*. New York

Hall, E. T. (1966), *The hidden dimension*. New York

Halliday, M. A. K. (1975), *Learning how to mean – Explorations in the development of language*, London

Hannig, C. (Ed.) (1974), *Zur Sprache des Kindes im Grundschulalter*, Kronberg

Hayes, J. R. (Ed.) (1970), *Cognition and the development of language*. New York

Hécaen, H. (1972), Studies of language pathology. In: Sebeok (Ed.), 591–645

Hess, R. D./Shipman, V. C. (1965), Early experience and the socialization of cognitive modes in children. In: Child Development 36, 869–886

Hetzer, H./Reindorf, B. (1928), Sprachentwicklung und soziales Milieu. In: Zf. für angew. Psychologie 29, 449–462

Hiebsch, H. (Ed.) (1969), *Ergebnisse der sowjetischen Psychologie*. Stuttgart

Higgenbotham, D. C. (1961), A study of the speech of kindergarten, first and second grade children in audience situations. Doct. Diss. Northwestern Univ. Evanston Ill.

Hoijer, H. (Ed.) (1954), *Language in culture*. Chicago

Holenstein, E. (1975), *Roman Jakobsons phänomenologischer Strukturalismus*. Frankfurt/M.

Holmlund, C. (1974), *Barns talspråk ur socialpedagogisk synvinkel*. Stockholm

Honig, A. S./Caldwell, B. M./Tannenbaum, J. (1970), Patterns of information processing used by and with young children in a nursery school setting. In: Child Development 41, 1045–1065

Hörmann, H. (1970), *Psychologie der Sprache*. [2]Heidelberg

— (1976), *Meinen und Verstehen, Grundzüge einer psychologischen Semantik*. Frankfurt/M.

Howard, R. W. (1946), The language development of a group of triplets. In: Journ. Genet. Psych. 69, 181–188

Hoyer, A./Hoyer, G. (1924), Über die Lallsprache eines Kindes. In: Zf. für angew. Psychologie 24, 363–384

Huttenlocher, J. (1974), The origins of language comprehension. In: Solso, R. L. (Ed.), *Theories in cognitive psychology*. Potomac, Md.

Huxley, R./Ingram, R. (Ed.) (1971), *Language acquisition: Models and methods*. London. New York

Hymes, D. (1962), The ethnography of speaking. In: Gladwin, T./Sturtevant, W. (Ed.), *Anthropology and human behavior*. Washington D.C., 15–53

— (1967), Models of the interaction of language and social setting. In: Journ. of Social Issues 23, 8–28

— (1971), Competence and performance in linguistic theory. In: Huxley/Ingram (Ed.), 3–28

Idelberger, H. A. (1903), Hauptprobleme der kindlichen Sprachentwicklung. In: Zf. f. päd. Psych., Pathol. u. Hyg. 5, 241–297, 425–456

Ingram, D. (1976), *Phonological disability in children*. London

Ingvar, D. H. (1975), The human being as a receiver of information. In: *Man in the communication system of the future*. (Swedish Cabinet Office) Stockholm, 15–23

Irwin, O. C. (1947), Development of speech during infancy: Curve of phonemic frequencies. In: Journ. Exp. Psych. 37, 187–193

— (1948), Infant speech: The effect of family occupational status and of age on use of sound types. In: Journ. Speech Hearing Disorders 13, 31–34

— (1960), Language and communication. In: Mussen (Ed.), 487–516

Jaffe, J./Stern, D. N./Peery, J. C. (1973), 'Conversational' coupling of gaze behavior in prelinguistic human development. In: Journ. of Psycholing. Research 2, 321–329

Jakobson, R. (1972), *Kindersprache, Aphasie und allgemeine Lautgesetze*. 1st edn. Uppsala 1941. [3]Frankfurt/M.

— (1960), Linguistics and poetics. In: Sebeok, T. A. (Ed.), *Style in language*. New York,

Bibliography

350–377
— (1971), The role of phonic elements. In: R. Jakobson. *Selected Writings I, Phonological studies.* ²The Hague, 705–719
— (1974), Die Linguistik und ihr Verhältnis zu anderen Wissenschaften. In: Jakobson, R., *Aufsätze zur Linguistik und Poetik,* edited by W. Raible. München, 150–224
Jenkins, J. J. (1965), Learning theories. In: Osgood/Sebeok (Ed.), 25–35
Jersild, A. T./Markey, F. V. (1935), *Conflicts between pre-school children.* Child Development Monogr. 21
Jespersen, O. (1922), *Language. Its nature, development and origin.* London. ¹¹1959
Johansson, B. A. (1965), *Criteria of school readiness.* Stockholm
Johnson, D. L. (1974), The influences of social class and race on language test performance and spontaneous speech of preschool children. In: Child Development 45, 517–521
Jonas, Doris F./Jonas, A. David (1979), *Das Erste Wort. Wie die Menschen Sprechen Lernten.* Hamburg
Jones, R. M. (1970), *System in child language.* Cardiff
Kainz, F. (1962), *Psychologie der Sprache.* Bd. I. ³Stuttgart
Kaper, W. (1959), *Kindersprachenforschung mit Hilfe des Kindes, Einige Erscheinungen der kindlichen Spracherwerbung erläutert im Lichte des vom Kinde gezeigten Interesses für Sprachliches.* Groningen
— (1968), Kindersprache und 'linguistic competence'. In: Lingua 21, 224–236
— (1969), Productive rules or imitation. In: *Nomen. Leyden Studies in Linguistics and Phonetics.* The Hague. Paris, 51–67
Karlin, I. W. (1947), A psychosomatic theory of stuttering. In: Journ. Speech Disorders 12, 319–322
Karmiloff-Smith, Annette (1979), *A functional approach to child language* (Cambridge Studies in Linguistics 34). Cambridge
Katz, D./Katz, R. (1928), *Gespräche mit Kindern.* Berlin. Heidelberg. New York
Keenan, E. O. (1974), Conversational competence in children. In: Journ. Child Lang. 1, 163–183
— (1975), Evolving discourse – the next steps. In: Papers and Reports on Child Language Development 10, 80–88
Kegel, G. (1974), *Sprache und Sprechen des Kindes.* München. Rowohlt Taschenbuch
Kendon, A. (1970), Movement coordination in social interaction. In: Acta Psychologica 32, 100–125
Klann, G. (1975), *Aspekte und Probleme der linguistischen Analyse schichtenspezifischen Sprachgebrauchs.* Max-Planck-Inst. für Bildungsforschung Studien und Berichte 31, Berlin
König, G. (1972), *Strukturen kindlicher Sprache.* Düsseldorf
Krashen, S. (1973), Lateralization, language learning and the critical period. In: Language Learning 23, 63–74
Kussmaul, A. (1859), *Untersuchungen über das Seelenleben des neugeborenen Menschen.* Leipzig. Heidelberg
Labov, W. (1969), The logic of nonstandard English. In: Georgetown Monographs on Language and Linguistics 22, 1–31
Lakoff, G. (1971), On generative semantics. In: Steinberg, D. D./Jakobovits, L. A. (Ed.), *Semantics.* Cambridge, 232–296
Lamb, S. (1971), The crooked path of progress in cognitive linguistics. In: Monograph Series on Language and Linguistics 24, 99–123. Also in Makkai/Lockwood (Ed.), 12–33
Lawton, D. (1968), *Social Class, Language and Education,* London
Lee, L. C./Kagan, J./Rabson, A. (1963), The influence of preference for analytic categorization upon concept acquisition. In: Child Development 34, 151–155
Lehmann, W. P. (1974), Über konvergierende Theorien der Sprachanalyse. In:

Sprache der Gegenwart 26. Düsseldorf, 306–318

Leischner, A. (1973), Neurolinguistik. In Althaus, H. P./Henne, H./Wiegand, H. E. (Ed.), *Lexikon der Germanistischen Linguistik*. Tübingen, 287–299

Lejska, V. (1972), Einfluss einiger wichtiger Gesellschaftsfaktoren auf die Entwicklung der richtigen Artikulation der Kinder. In: Ohnesorg (Ed.) 144–151

Lenneberg, E. H. (Ed.) (1964a), *New directions in the study of language*. Cambridge, Mass.

— (1964b), A biological perspective of language. In: Lenneberg (Ed.) 65–88

— (1967), *Biological foundations of language*. New York

Lenneberg, E. H./Lenneberg, E. (Ed.) (1975), *Foundations of language development: A multidisciplinary approach*. 2 Vols. New York

Leont'ev, A. A. (1971), *Sprache – Sprechen – Sprechtätigkeit*. Stuttgart. Russ. original 1968

Leont'ev, A. N./Luria, A. R. (1972), Some notes concerning Dr. Fodor's Reflections on L. S. Vygotsky's 'Thought and language'. In: Cognition 1, 311–318

Leopold, W. (1939–49), Speech development of a bilingual child. 4 Bde. Evanston (1939, 1947, 1949a, 1949b)

— (1948a), The study of child language and infant bilingualism. In: Word 4, 1–17

— (1948b), Semantic learning in infant language. In: Word 4, 173–180

— (1952), *Bibliography of child language*. Evanston

— (1956/57), Das Sprechenlernen des Kindes. In: Sprachforum 2, 117–125

— (1959), Kindersprache. In: Phonetica 4, 191–214

Leuninger, H./Miller, M. H./Müller, F. (1972), *Psycholinguistik*. Frankfurt/M.

Lewis, M. M. (1951), *Infant speech*, [2]London

— (1963), *Language, thought and personality in infancy and childhood*. London. Toronto. Wellington. Sydney

Lieberman, P. (1967), *Intonation, perception and language*. Cambridge, Mass.

Lind, J. (Ed.) (1965), *Newborn infant cry*. Uppsala

Lindner, G. (1882), Beobachtungen und Bemerkungen über die Entwicklung der Sprache des Kindes. In: Kosmos 6, 321–342, 430–441

List, G. (1972), *Psycholinguistik. Eine Einführung*. Stuttgart

Löbisch, J. E. (1851), *Entwicklungsgeschichte der Seele des Kindes*, Wien

Lock, Andrew (1978). *Action, gesture and symbol. The emergence of language*. London

— (1980), *The guided reinvention of language*. London

De Long, A. J. (1974), Kinesic signals as utterance boundaries in preschool children. In: Semiotica 2, 43–73

Luria, A. R. (1928), *Reč i intellekt v razvitii rebenka*. Moskva

— (1930), *Reč i intellekt gorodskogo, derevenskogo i bezprisornogo rebenka*. Moskva

— (1959), The directive function of speech. In: Word 14, 341–352

Luria, A. R./Yudovich, F. I., (1959), *Speech and the development of mental processes in the child*, Edited by Joan Simon, London

Lyons, J. (Ed.) (1970), *New horizons in linguistics*. London

Maccoby, E. E./Jacklin, C. N. (1974), *The psychology of sex differences*. Stanford

Macnamara, J. (1972), Cognitive basis of language learning in infants. In: Psychol. Rev. 79, 1–13

Makkai, A./Lockwood, D. G. (Ed.) (1973), *Readings in stratificational linguistics*. Alabama

Malinowski, B. (1935), *Coral gardens and their magic 2*. London

Malson, L./Itard, J./Mannoni, O. (1972), *Die wilden Kinder*. Frankfurt/M.

Mann, Lise (1978), *Pattern, control and contrast in beginning speech. A case study in the development of word forms and word function*. Bloomington, Indiana

Maratsos, M. P. (1973), Nonegocentric communication abilities in preschool children. In: Child Development 44, 697–700

Maruszewski, M. (1975), *Language communication and the brain. A neurophysiological*

Bibliography

study. The Hague, Paris. Polish original 1970

Mayr, E. (1974), Behavior programs and evolutionary strategies. In: American Scientist 62, 650–659

McCaffrey, A. (1975), Three problems in the development of speech perception. In: Word 27, 205–224

McCarthy, D. (1930), *The language development of the preschool child*. Inst. Child Welfare Mon. Ser. 4, Univ. of Minnesota. Minneapolis

— (1954), Language development in children. In: Carmichael, L. (Ed.), *Manual of child psychology*. New York, 492–630

— (1959), *Research in language development: Retrospect and prospect*. Mon. Soc. Res. Child. Dev. 24

McCarthy, J. J./Kirk, S. A. (1961), *Examiner's manual: Illinois test of psycholinguistic abilities*. Champaign, Ill.

McCawley, J. D. (1968), The role of semantics in a grammar. In: Bach/Harms (Ed.), 124–169

McCormack, W. C./Wurm, S. A.(Ed.) (1976), *Language and man. Anthropological Issues*. The Hague. Paris

McNeill, D. (1966), Developmental psycholinguistics, In: Smith, F./Miller, G. A. (Ed.), *The genesis of language. A psycholinguistic approach*. Cambridge, Mass. 15–84

McNeill, D. (1970), *The acquisition of language*. New York. Evanston. London

Mead, G. H. (1935), *Mind, self and society*. Chicago

Menyuk, P. (1964), Alternation of rules in children's grammar. In: Journ. of Verb. Learning and Verb. Beh. 3, 480–488

— (1969), *Sentences children use*. Cambridge, Mass.

— (1971), *The acquisition and development of language*. Englewood Cliffs

Merleau-Ponty, M. (1945), *Phénoménologie de la perception*. Paris

Messelken, H. (1968), *Drei Aspekte der anthropologischen Sprachtheorie*. Ratingen

Meumann, E. (1902), *Die Entstehung der ersten Wortbedeutungen beim Kinde*. Leipzig

Miller, G. A. (1963), *Language and communication*. [2]New York. Toronto. London

Miller, J. F. (1973), Sentence imitation in pre-school children. In: Language and Speech 16, 1–14

Miller, S. A./Shelton, J./Flavell, J. H. (1970), A test of Luria's hypotheses concerning the development of verbal self-regulation. In: Child Development 41, 651–665

Miller, W./Ervin, S. (1964), The development of grammar in children. In: Bellugi/Brown (Ed.), 9–35

Milner, E. (1951), A study of the relationships between reading readiness in grade one school children and patterns of parent-child interaction. In: Child Development 22, 95–112

Mittler, P. (1971), *The study of twins*. London

Moerk, E. (1972), Principles of interaction in language learning. In: Merrill-Palmer Quarterly 18, 229–257

— (1975), *Process of language teaching and language learning in the interaction of mother-child dyads*. Fresno

— (1977), *Pragmatic and semantic aspects of early language development*. Baltimore

Moore, T. E. (Ed.) (1973), *Cognitive development and the acquisition of language*. New York. San Francisco. London

Morsbach, G./Steel, P. M. (1976), 'John is easy to see' re-investigated. In: Journ. Child Lang. 3, 443–447

Morse, P. A. (1974), Infant speech perception: a preliminary model and review of the literature. In: Schiefelbusch/Lloyd (Ed.), 19–53

Morton, J. (Ed.) (1971), *Biological and social factors in psycholinguistics*. London

Moskowitz, A. I. (1973), Acquisition of phonology and syntax: a preliminary study. In: Hintikka, J. et al. (Ed.), *Approaches to natural language*. Dordrecht, 48–84.

Mowrer, O. H. (1960), *Learning theory and the symbolic processes*. New York

Mueller, E. C. (1971), An analysis of children's communications in free play. Doct. Diss. Cornell University

Mueller, M./Lucas, J. (1975), Peer interaction among toddlers. In: Lewis, M./ Rosenblum, L. A. (Ed.), *Friendship and peer relations*. New York, 223–257

Murai, J. (1963), The sounds of infants. In: Studia Phonol. 3, 17–34

Mussen, P. H. (Ed.) (1960), *Handbook of research methods in child development*. New York

Nakazima, S. (1966), A comparative study of the speech developments of Japanese and American English in childhood: The acquisition of speech. In: Studia Phonol. 4, 38–55

Nelson, K. (1973), Structure and strategy in learning to talk. Monogr. Soc. Res. Child Development 38. Nos 1–2

— (1974), Concept, word, and sentence. In: Psychological Review 81, 267–285

Nelson, Keith (ed.) (1978), *Children's language*, vol. 1. New York

Ochs, Elinor/Scheffelin, B. (eds.) (1979), *Developmental pragmatics*. New York

O'Donnel, R. C./Griffin, W. J./Norris, R. C. (1968), Grammatical structures in the speech of children: A transformational analysis. In: Journ. Experim. Education 59, 70–77

Oftedal, M. (1973), Notes on language and sex. In: Norwegian Journal of Linguistics 27, 67–75

Ohnesorg, K. (1948), *Fonetická studie o dětské řeči. Etude phonétique sur le langage de l'enfant*. Praha

— (1955), Kapitola ze srovnávací fonetiky dětské řeči. Sbornik filos. Fak. brněnské univ. IV A, 95–101

— (1959), *Druhá fonetická studie o dětské řeči*. Praha

— (Ed.) (1972), *Colloquium paedolinguisticum*. Proceedings of the First International Symposium of Paedolinguistics held at Brno, 14–16 Oct. 1970. The Hague. Paris

Oksaar, E. (1971), Zum Spracherwerb des Kindes in zweisprachiger Umgebung. In: Folia Linguistica IV, 330–358

— (1972a), Bilingualism. In: Sebeok (Ed.), 476–511

— (1972b), Zentrierung und die Satzperspektive. In: Linguistische Studien I (=Sprache der Gegenwart 19). Düsseldorf, 126–158

— (1972c), Zum Erwerb der estnischen Quantitätsregeln im zweisprachigen Milieu. In: Ohnesorg (Ed.), 93–98

— (1972d), Sprachliche Interferenzen und die kommunikative Kompetenz. In: Pilch, H./Thurow, J. (Ed.), Indo-Celtica (= Commentationes Societatis Linguisticae Europaeae II). München, 126–142

— (1973), Sprache und Denken. Bericht. In: ZGL 1, 317–330

— (1975a), Spracherwerb und Kindersprache. In: Zf. f. Pädagogik 21, 719–743

— (1975b), Psycholinguistics, language and changing social structures. In: Intern. Journ. of Psycholinguistics 3, 41–58

— (1976a), Prinzipielles zur Entwicklung der linguistischen und kommunikativen Kompetenz im Vorschulalter. In: *Akten des 1. Salzburger Kolloquiums über Kindersprache*, edited by G. Drachmann. Tübingen, 383–391

— (1976b), *Berufsbezeichnungen im heutigen Deutsch. Soziosemantische Untersuchungen* (= Sprache der Gegenwart 25). Düsseldorf

— (1977), Zum Prozeß des Sprachwandels: Dimensionen sozialer und linguistischer Variation. In: Sprachwandel und Sprachgeschichtsschreibung (=Sprache der Gegenwart 41). Düsseldorf, 98–117

— (1981), Linguistic and pragmatic awareness of monolingual and multilingual children. In: Dale/Ingram (Ed.), 273–285

Oller, D. K./Wieman, L. A./Doyle, W. J./Ross, C. (1976), Infant babbling and speech. In: Journ. Child Lang. 3, 1–11

Olmsted, D. L. (1971), *Out of the mouth of babes. Earliest stages in language learning*

Bibliography

(=Janua linguarum, series minor 117). The Hague. Paris

Olson, D. (1970), Language and thought: Aspects of a cognitive theory of semantics. In: Psych. Review 77, 257–273

Oltuscewski, W. (1897), Die geistige und sprachliche Entwicklung des Kindes. Berlin. Sonderdruck aus Mediz. päd. Monatsschr. f. d. ges. Sprachheilk. 6

Osgood, C. (1957), A behavioristic analysis of perception and language as cognitive phenomena. In: Bruner, J. S. (Ed.), *Contemporary approaches to cognition*. Cambridge, Mass., 75–125

Osgood, C./Sebeok, T. A. (Ed.) (1965), *Psycholinguistics: A survey of theory and research problems*. Bloomington

Pačesová, J. (1968), *The development of vocabulary in the child*. Brno

Panconcelli-Calzia, G. (1955), Das Motiv vom 'Wilden Knaben'. Zur Sprache verwilderter Kinder. In: Sprachforum 1, 272–277

Parisi, D. (1972), *Il linguaggio come processo cognitivo*. Torino

Park, T. Z. (1974), *A study of German language development*. (Mimeo) Bern

Parsons, T./Shils, E. (1951), *Toward a general theory of action*. Cambridge

Pavlov, J. P. (1953/1956), *Sämtliche Werke, Bd. 1–7*. dt. Berlin

Pavlovitch, M. (1920), *Le langage enfantin: Acquisition du serbe et du français par un enfant serbe*. Paris

Peizer, D. B./Olmsted, D. L. (1969), Modules of grammar acquisition. In: Language 45, 60–96

Penfield, W./Roberts, L. (1959), *Speech and brain mechanism*. Princeton

Pérez, B. (1878), *La psychologie de l'enfant; les trois premières années*, Paris

Phillips, J. (1970), Formal characteristics of speech which mothers address to their young children. Doct. Diss. Johns Hopkins University, Baltimore

Piaget, J. (1968), *Barnets själsliga utveckling*. Lund. French original *Six études de psychologie* 1964

— (1955), *The language and thought of the child*. Cleveland, Ohio. (French original: 1923)

— (1928), *Judgement and reasoning in the child*. New York. (French original: 1924)

— (1972c), The epistemology of interdisciplinary relationship. In: *Interdisciplinarity. Problems of Teaching and Research in Universities*. OECD (CERI). Paris

Pike, K. (1964), Discourse analysis and tagmeme matrices. In: Oceanic Linguistics III, 5–25

— (1967), *Language in relation to a unified theory of the structure of human behavior*. The Hague.

Poyatos, F. (1976), *Man beyond words: Theory and methodology of non-verbal communication*. Oswego

Pozner, J./Saltz, E. (1974), Social class, conditional communication and egocentric speech. In: Developm. Psych. 10, 764–771

Pregel, D. (1970), *Zum Sprachstil des Grundschulkindes* Düsseldorf

Pregel, D./Rickheit, G. (1975), *Kindliche Redetexte*. Düsseldorf

Preyer, W. (1882), *Die Seele des Kindes*. Leipzig. ^{9}1923

Raffler-Engel, W. von (1968), Suprasentential and substitution tests in first language acquisition. In: Folia Linguistica II, 166–175

— (1973), The correlation of gestures and verbalizations in first language acquisition. Paper. IX Intern. Congress of Anthropological and Ethnological Sciences. Chicago

Raffler-Engel, W. von/Lebrun, J. (Ed.) (1976), *Baby talk and infant speech*. Lisse

Ramer, A. L. H. (1976), Syntactic styles in emerging language. In: Journ. Child Lang. 3, 49–62

Rebelsky, F./Starr, R. H./Luria, Z. (1967), Language development: The first four years. In: Brackbill, J. (Ed.), *Infancy and early childhood*. New York, 289–357

Reed, C. E. (Ed.) (1971), *The learning of language*. New York

Rheingold, H. L./Gewirtz, J. L./Ross, H. W. (1959), Social conditioning of vocalizing

in the infant. In: Journ. of Comp. and Physiol. Psychology 52, 68–73
Richter, F. (1927), *Die Entwicklung der psychologischen Kindersprachenforschung bis zum Beginn des 20. Jahrhunderts*. Münster
Rickheit, G. (1975), *Zur Entwicklung der Syntax im Grundschulalter*, Düsseldorf
Rieber, R. W. (1975), The role of language and thought in developmental psycholinguistics. Paper. Third International Child Language Symposium. London
Riegel, K. (1973), Dialectic operations: The final period of cognitive development. In: Human Development 16, 346–370
Ronjat, J. (1913), *Le développement du langage, observé chez un enfant bilingue*. Paris
Rosansky, E. J. (1975), Neurophysiological and cognitive developmental factors and the critical period for the acquisition of language. Paper. Third International Child Language Symposium. London
Rosenthal, M. K. (1973), The study of infant-environment interaction: Some comments on trends and methodologies. In: Journ. Child Ps. Psychiat. 14, 301–317
Ryan, J. (1973), Interpretation and imitation in early language development. In: Hinde, R./Stevenson-Hinde, J. (Ed.), *Constraints of learning*, 427–444
— (1974), Early language development: Towards a communicational analysis. In: Richards, M. (Ed.), *The integration of a child into a social world*. Cambridge
Sachs, J./Brown, R./Salerno, R. (1976), Adults' speech to children. In: v. Raffler-Engel/Lebrun (Ed.), 240–245
Sachs, J./Devin, J. (1976), Young children's use of age-appropriate speech styles in social interaction and role-playing. In: Journ. Child Lang. 3, 81–98
Salus, P. H./Salus, M. W. (1974), Developmental neurophysiology and phonological acquisition. In: Language 50, 151–160
Sapir, E. (1921), *Language*, New York
Savic, Svenka (1980), *How twins learn to talk. A study of the speech development of twins from 1–3*. London
Scherer, K. (1970), *Nonverbale Kommunikation*. IPK-Forschungsbericht 35, Hamburg
Schaerlaekens, A. M. (1973), *The two-word sentence in child language development*. The Hague
Schiefelbusch, R./Lloyd, L. (Ed.) (1974), *Language perspectives – acquisition, retardation and intervention*. Baltimore
Schlee, J. (1973), *Sozialstatus und Sprachverständnis*. Düsseldorf
Schleicher, A. (1861), Einige Beobachtungen an Kindern. In: Beitr. zur vergl. Sprachforschung 2, 497–498
Schlesinger, I. M. (1967), A note on the relationship between psychological and linguistic theories. In: Found. of Language 3, 397–402
— (1971a), Learning grammar: from pivot to realization rule. In: Huxley/Ingram (Ed.), 79–94
— (1971b), Production of utterances and language acquisition. In: Slobin (Ed.), 63–101
— (1972), *Acquisition of grammar: What and how should we investigate*, (Mimeo) Jerusalem
— (1975), Learning mechanisms. In: Lenneberg/Lenneberg (Ed.), 216–222
Schloon, M. (1976), *Soziale Interaktion in Kleinkindgruppen*. Diss. Hamburg
Schmidt, W. H. O. (1973), *Child development: the human, cultural and educational context*. New York
Schultze, F. (1880), *Die Sprache des Kindes*. Leipzig
Searle, J. R. (1970), *Speech acts. An essay in the philosophy of language*. Cambridge.
Sebeok, T. A. (Ed.) (1972), *Current Trends in Linguistics 9*. The Hague. Paris
Sebeok, T. A./Hayes, A. S./Bateson, M. C. (Ed.) (1972), *Approaches to semiotics*. ²The Hague. Paris
Segerstedt, T. T. (1947), *Die Macht des Wortes*. Zürich
— (1966), *The nature of social reality*. Stockholm

217

Bibliography

Seiffert, H. (1970), *Einführung in die Wissenschaftstheorie 1*. [2]München
Seiler, H. (1975), *Das linguistische Universalienproblem in neuer Sicht*. Opladen
Shatz, M./Gelman, R. (1973), The development of communication skills: modification in the speech of young children as a function of listener. Monogr. soc. Res. child Development 38
Shields, M. M. (1975), Cognition and communication in the acquisition of language. Paper. International Child Language Symposium. London
— (1976). Some communicational skills of young children – a study of dialogue in the Nursery School. Paper. The Psychology of Language. International Conference. Stirling
Shinn, M. W. (1905), *The biography of a baby*. Boston. New York
Shipley, E. F./Smith, C. S./Gleitman, L. R. (1969), A study in the acquisition of language: Free responses to commands. In: Language 45, 322–342
Shvachkin, N. K. (1973), The development of phonemic speech perception in early childhood. In: Ferguson/Slobin (Ed.), 91–127. Russ original 1948
Sigismund, B. (1856), *Kind und Welt*. Braunschweig
Sinclair, H. (1967), *Acquisition du langage et développement de la pensée. Sous-systèmes linguistiques et operations concrétes*. Paris
— (1969), Developmental psycholinguistics. In: Elkind, D./Flavell, J. H. (Ed.), *Studies in cognitive development*. New York, 315–366
— (1973), Language acquisition and cognitive development. In: Moore (Ed.), 9–25
— (1975), The role of cognitive structures in language acquisition. In: Lenneberg/ Lenneberg (Ed.), 223–238
Skalička, V. (1948), The need for a linguistics of 'la parole'. In: Recueil Linguistique de Bratislava I, 21–38
Skinner, B. F. (1957), *Verbal behavior*. London
Slama-Cazacu, T. (1961), *Dialogue la copiè*. Bucuresti
— (1962), The oblique cases in the evolution of child language. In: Revue Roumaine de Linguistique 8, 71–90
— (1966), Essay on psycholinguistic methodology and some of its applications. In: Linguistics 24, 51–72
— (1972a), Fifty years of European child language studies, and perspectives in this field. In: Ohnesorg (Ed.), 17–36
— (1972b), The study of child language in Europe. In: Sebeok (Ed.), 512–590
— (1976), The role of social context in language acquisition. In: McCormack/Wurm (Ed.), 127–147
Slobin, D. I. (1966a), The acquisition of Russian as a native language. In: Smith, F./Miller, G. (Ed.), *The genesis of language. A psycholinguistic approach*. Cambridge, Mass., 129–152
— (1966b), Soviet psycholinguistics. In: O'Connor, N. (Ed.), *Present-day Russian psychology: A symposium by seven authors*. Oxford, 109–151
— (1967), *A field manual for cross-cultural study of the acquisition of communicative competence*. Berkeley
— (1968a), Imitation and grammatical development in children. In: Endler, N. S./Boulter, L. R./Osser, H. (Ed.), *Contemporary issues in developmental psychology*. New York, 437–443
— (1968b), Early grammatical development in several languages with special attention to Soviet research, Working Paper 11. Lang.-Beh. Res. Lab. Univ. Calif. Berkeley
— (1971a), Universals of grammatical development in children. In: Flores d'Arcais/ Levelt (Ed.), 174–186
— (Ed.) (1971b), *The ontogenesis of grammar*, New York. London
— (1971c), Grammatical development in Russian-speaking children. In: Bar-Adon/ Leopold (Ed.), 343–348. First published 1965
— (1972), *Leopold's bibliography of child language*. Bloomington. London

— (1973), Cognitive prerequisites for the development of grammar. In: Ferguson/ Slobin (Ed.), 175–208

Slobin, D./Welsh, C. A. (1971), Elicited imitation as a research tool in developmental psycholinguistics. In: Lavatel, C. S. (Ed.), *Language training in early childhood education*. Urbana, 170–185

Smith, C. S. (1970), An experimental approach to children's linguistic competence. In: Hayes (Ed.), 109–135

Smith, M. E. (1926), *An investigation of the development of the sentence and the extent of vocabulary in young children*. Univ. Iowa Stud. Child. Welf., No. 5, Vol. III

Smith, N. V. (1973), *The acquisition of phonology: A case study*. London

Snow, C. E. (1972), Mothers' speech to children learning language In: Child Development 43, 549–565

— (1977), Mothers' speech research: From input to interaction. In: Snow/Ferguson (Ed.), 31–49

Snow, C. E./Ferguson, C. A. (Ed) (1977), *Talking to children. Language input and acquisition*. London. New York. Melbourne

Sperry, R. W./Gazzaniga, M. S. (1967), Language following surgical disconnection of the hemispheres. In: Millikan, C. H./Darley, F. L. (Ed.) *Brain mechanisms underlying speech and language*. New York

Spitz, R. A. (1945), Hospitalism: An inquiry into the genesis of psychiatric conditions in early childhood. In: Psychoanal. Study Child. 1, 53–74

— (1965), *The first year of life*. London

Stampe, D. (1969), The acquisition of phonetic representation. Papers, 5th Regional Meeting, Chicago Linguistics Society, 443–454

Stemmer, N. (1973), *An empiricist's theory of language acquisition*. The Hague

Stern, W. (1967), *Psychologie der frühen Kindheit. Bis zum sechsten Lebensjahr.* ⁹Heidelberg

Stern, C./Stern, W. (1907), Anleitung zur Beobachtung der Sprachentwicklung bei normalen vollsinnigen Kindern. In: Zf. für angewandte Psychologie 2, 313–337

— (1928), *Die Kindersprache. Eine psychologische und sprachtheoretische Unteruchung*. ⁴Leipzig. 3. Aufl. 1922

Strevenson, A. (1893), The speech of children. In: Science 21, 118–120

Sudnow, D. (Ed.) (1972), *Studies in social interaction*. New York

Sully, J. (1896), *Studies of childhood*. New York. London

Taine, H. (1876), Note sur l'acquisition du langage chez les enfants et dans l'espéce humaine. In: Rev. Phil. 1, 3–23

Tanz, Christiana (1980), *Studies in the acquisition of deictic terms*. Cambridge

Templin, M. C. (1957), *Certain language skills in children – their development and interrelationships*. Minneapolis

Terman, L. M./Tyler, L. E. (1960), Psychological sex differences. In: Carmichael, L. (Ed.), *Manual of child psychology*. ²New York, 1064–1114

Thomas, W. I. (1965), *Social behavior and personality. Contributions of W. I. Thomas to theory and social research*. Edited by Edmund H. Volkart. New York.

Thomson, J. R./Chapman, R. S. (1975), Who is 'Daddy'? The status of two-year-old's over-extended words in use and comprehension. In: Papers and Reports on Child Language Development 10, 59–68

Thorndike, E. L. (1914), *Educational psychology II: The psychology of learning*. New York 1914

Tiedemann, D. (1787), *Beobachtungen über die Entwicklung der Seelenfähigkeiten bei Kindern*. 2 edn. edited by C. Ufer. Altenburg 1897

Trager, G. L. (1958), Paralanguage: A first approximation. In: Studies in Linguistics 13, 1–12

Trevarthen, C./Hubleyz, P./Sheeran, L. (1975), Les activités inneés du nourissant. In: La Recherche 6, 56, 447–458

Bibliography

Truby, H. M. (1976), Prenatal and neonatal speech, 'pre-speech', and an infantile-speech lexicon. In: Word 27, 57–101

Turner, E. A./Rommetveit, R. (1967), The acquisition of sentence voice and reversibility. In: Child Development 38, 649–660

Turner, Johanna, (1975) *Cognitive development* (Methuen Essential Psychology Series). London

Velten, H. V. (1943), The growth of phonemic and lexical patterns. In: Language 19, 281–292

Vierordt, K. (1879), Die Sprache des Kindes. In: Deutsche Revue 3, Bd. 2, 29–46

De Villiers, J. G./de Villiers, P. A. (1974), Competence and performance in child language: Are children really competent to judge? In: Journ. Child Lang. 1, 11–22

Villiers, Jill G. de/Villiers, Peter A. de (1978), *Language acquisition*. Cambridge, Mass.

Volkart, E. H. (1965), Einführung. Soziales Verhalten und Definition der Situation. In: Thomas, 13–51

Vorster, J. (1975), Mommy linguist: The case for motherese. In: Lingua 37, 281–312

Vygotsky, L. S. (1962), *Thought and language*. Cambridge, Mass.

Vygotsky, L. S./Luria, A. R. (1930), The function and fate of egocentric speech. In: *Proc. Ninth Int. Congr. of Psychology*. Princeton, 464–465

Wallach, M. A./Kogan, N. (1965), *Modes of thinking in young children*. New York

Wanner, E. (1974), *On remembering, forgetting and understanding sentences*. The Hague. Paris

Waterson, N. (1971), Child phonology: A prosodic view. In: *Journ. of Ling.* 7, 179–211

Watson, J. B. (1924), *Psychology from the standpoint of a behaviorist.* [2]Philadelphia

Watzlawick, P./Beavin, J. H./Jackson, D. D. (1967), *Pragmatics of human communication*. London.

Weeks, T. E. (1971), Speech registers in young children. In: Child Development 42, 1119–1131

Wegener, P. (1885), *Untersuchungen ueber die Grundfragen des Sprachlebens*. Halle

Weir, R. (1962), *Language in the crib*. The Hague

Weisgerber, L. (1962a), *Grundzüge der inhaltbezogenen Grammatik*. Düsseldorf

— (1962b), *Die sprachliche Gestaltung der Welt*. Düsseldorf

Wells, G. (1974), Learning to code experience through language. In: Journ. Child Lang. 1, 243–269

Werner, H./Kaplan, B. (1963), *Symbol formation*. New York

Whorf, B. R. (1956), *Language, thought and reality*. London

Wittgenstein, L. (1967), *Philosophische Untersuchungen*. Frankfurt/M.

Wood, C. L./Goff, W. R./Day, R. S. (1971), Auditory evoked potentials during speech perception. In: Science 173, 1248–1251

Wunderlich, D. (1970), Die Rolle der Pragmatik in der Linguistik. In: Der Deutschunterricht 22, H. 4, 5–41

Wundt, W. (1911), *Völkerpsychologie. Erster Band. Die Sprache. 3.* new edn. Leipzig. 1. edn. 1900

Zazzo, R. (1960), *Les jumeaux, le couple et la personne*. Paris

Zeller, W. (1952), *Konstitution und Entwicklung*. Göttingen

Name Index

Name Index

Subject Index